W9-DIM-067

FLORIDA STATE
UNIVERSITY LIBRARIES

MAR 29 1994

TALLAHASSEE, FLORIDA

THE
COMMON MARKET
TODAY—AND TOMORROW

By

MICHAEL SHANKS
AND
JOHN LAMBERT

FREDERICK A. PRAEGER

Publisher

NEW YORK

HC
241.2
S47
1962

3387.914
$528c

BOOKS THAT MATTER

Published in the United States of America in 1962
by Frederick A. Praeger, Inc., Publisher
64 University Place, New York 3, N.Y.

Second printing, 1963

LIBRARY
FLORIDA STATE UNI. SITY
TALLAHASSEE, FLORIDA

All rights reserved

© Michael Shanks and John Lambert 1962

Library of Congress Catalog Card Number: 62-21228

Contents

Introduction

GREAT BRITAIN stands today on the brink of one of the gravest decisions of her whole history—the decision whether or not to join the European Common Market. This decision will have incalculable consequences, for Britain, for Europe, the United States, the Commonwealth, and indeed the world. A European Community which includes Britain will be a very different organism from one which excludes her. The decision to join will set in train forces which will alter profoundly the face of the world in which we live.

Naturally there has been intense debate in Britain on this issue. Much of it has been characterised by two fallacies. The first fallacy is to assume that the problem concerns only Britain, the Common Market countries and the Commonwealth. The second fallacy is to assume that the European Community is a static organisation. In fact the movement for European integration, of which the Rome Treaty represents only one stage, is a continuing process of which the later stages are not only incomplete but to a large extent as yet indeterminate. This is true, not only of the internal organisation of the Community—for example, whether it will evolve into a genuine federal United States of Europe on the American analogy, and if so how quickly—but also of its external relations: what part, for example, will a new European super-power play in the world? Will it be a partner, or a rival, to the U.S.? Will it be restrictionist and inward-looking, or liberal and outward-looking? Will we see an expansion of the Community idea towards an Atlantic Partnership with the U.S., and if so what are the implications for U.S. policy, for NATO, for the under-developed countries and for the cold war?

These are the vital questions to be asked about the European experiment, which we have tried in this book to answer. They transcend in importance the question of whether Britain should or should not join. But the question of Britain's admission has in the last few months forced consideration of them into the open, and provides an obvious starting point for investigation of Europe's future. For British membership—especially in view of the world-wide ramifications of the Commonwealth, and the close traditional links with the U.S.—is bound to affect profoundly the structure, the objectives and the balance of forces of the European Community.

This book does not try, therefore, to argue directly the case for or against British membership of the Common Market—though it will be plain to anybody who reads it that we believe Britain should join. It tries instead to do three things. We begin with a brief historical sketch of British relations with Europe since the war, analysing the forces which have compelled Britain's leaders—often reluctantly—to try to come to terms with the new Europe. This part of the book I have written from London. The conclusion is that, whatever happens in the current round of talks, sooner or later Britain must find her place in Europe.

The second, and longest, part of the book is written by John Lambert from Luxembourg, in the heart of the European Community. It describes the Community's institutions, how they work, what the future stages of European integration are likely to be, and what their effect has been on the people of the Continent—businessmen, politicians, workers and consumers.

In Part III we return again to London. I try here to answer the questions about the future of a European Community that includes Britain which I have raised above—in particular questions about the relations between such a Community and the outside world.

Like all books on the Common Market, this one has had to be written at great speed, in a situation of rapid and bewildering change. For those parts for which I am responsible I owe a debt of gratitude to Roy Pryce and Max Fisher, who read the text and made many valuable suggestions on it, and to Miss Marion Osman for swift and competent secretarial assistance. For his part, John Lambert has asked me to express his thanks to Signor Emanuele Gazzo for permission to consult the files of Agence Europe in Luxembourg, which enormously facilitated the writing of Part II, and for his invaluable advice on a number of points; and also to his colleagues in the Agence, and to a number of officials of the Communities and other bodies, for replying patiently and expertly to his questions. For any errors in our respective sections, John Lambert and I as authors are of course solely responsible.

M. J. S.

August, 1962.

Part One

A SLOW BOAT TO EUROPE

Fog in Channel : Continent Isolated

THE GREAT ILLUSION

THE BRITISH, it is said, are psychologically incapable of recognising when they are beaten; that is why in the end they always win. Certainly in the dark days after Dunkirk this national myopia enabled us to turn defeat into victory. But in the postwar world it has enormously complicated the task of adjusting ourselves to a new world environment, and accepting the consequences of a diminished national stature. Nowhere has this been more apparent than in our dealings with Europe. After 1945 we could have had the leadership of a united Europe for the asking. By 1961 we had been reduced to begging for membership of a European Economic Community whose members were by no means certain that they wanted us in. The 'Channel fog' which obscured our dealings with Europe between 1945 and 1961 is one of the saddest aspects of British postwar foreign policy. How is it to be explained?

Perhaps the first point to grasp about the six EEC countries is that they constitute an assembly of the defeated. Each one—Germany, France, Italy, Belgium, Holland, Luxembourg—learned in the hardest possible way the limitations of national sovereignty between 1939 and 1945. Each one was invaded, conquered, occupied by foreign troops. In each one—though in varying degrees—the humiliation of foreign conquest was accompanied by economic collapse and the disruption of established patterns of society. Psychologically, therefore, thinkers in all these countries were ready to abandon the trammels of an individual nation-state for something larger, grander and more effective.

Nor was this the only feature which the Six had in common after 1945. Each of them felt, acutely, the shrinkage in the power and security of Europe in the face of the menacing expansion of Russia and the economic predominance of the United States. For centuries the nation-states of Western Europe had dominated the world. For centuries the Germans had stood as a barrier between Western Europe and the East. Now all this was altered. The frontiers of free Europe had been pushed back to the Elbe in the heart of Germany. Confronted by the giant strength of the Soviet Union, the once-great nations of Europe were reduced to sheltering for protection beneath the umbrella of American power.

Moreover, the ruin of Europe had been accomplished, not by outsiders, but by the European states themselves. 1939 was only a repetition, on a greater and more horrible scale, of 1914; and before that there had been the Franco-Prussian war of 1870, and a long record of fratricidal struggle stretching back across the centuries. Therefore, argued the more far-sighted European statesmen after 1945, we must create a political system in Europe which will make it impossible for the European states ever to go to war with each other again.

The same point could be put another way. The menace of Russia made it inevitable that Western Germany must be rebuilt as quickly as possible. But it was Germany who, in 1870, in 1914 and again in 1939, had brought war and ruin to Western Europe. This time Germany's revival must be accomplished in such a way as to make future aggression against her neighbours impossible.

These, I believe, were the fundamental motives behind the movement for unity in war-shattered Europe in the late 1940s. Politically, Europe must be strong enough to withstand the challenge from the East, and to rank as a Great Power in the councils of the world; an end must be made for all time of the wars which had devastated the Continent, each one more horrible than the last. Only by union or federation could this be achieved.

But, while the ultimate aim was—and remains—political union, it was in the economic sphere that the arguments for closer integration were most compelling. Just as the fragmentation of Europe had weakened its political influence in the world, so it had slowed down economic growth. In too many cases the industries of Western Europe found themselves confined to their own national markets, prevented from selling to their neighbours by tariff barriers and other discriminatory devices. Weak industries which would not have been able to withstand competition enjoyed sheltered lives behind State protection. The retreat from free trade during the inter-war years, and the rigid autarky of the Nazi and Fascist regimes, had intensified this stifling economic fragmentation of Europe.

The protagonists of European unity contrasted this patchwork of limited markets with the vast internal markets of the U.S. and the U.S.S.R., which enabled industrialists to reap the full benefits of mass production, specialisation and standardisation, and—at least in America —created a competitive climate in which the least efficient firms went out of business while the more efficient were able to grow to their full stature. Suppose, they said, we were to sweep away all the economic barriers between our six countries, and create a United States of Europe, with a total population equivalent to that of the U.S.A. Would this not be the best and quickest way of starting to raise European living standards towards American levels, and making Europe once again a major force in the world? And would it not also be the best way of demonstrating to the people of Europe that the individual nation-state is a dangerous anachronism, and that federation brings practical benefits?

Such, then, was the motive force behind the drive for European integration which threw up, successively, the European Coal-Steel Community, Euratom and the European Economic Community or Common Market. It is easy now to see the compelling force of these ideas in the postwar European context. But it was less easy for the British to see them in the early postwar period, for Britain emerged from the war in a frame of mind almost totally different from her Continental neighbours.

For one thing, the British had not been defeated or occupied by enemy troops. On the contrary, they had enjoyed their 'finest hour'. The fabric of the nation-state had come through the war not only intact but greatly strengthened. Understandably, British patriotism received a tremendous boost from the successful conduct of the war. The 'old country' had emerged triumphantly from the sloth and lethargy of the thirties, had destroyed her enemies, and resumed her rightful place as one of the Big Three powers of the world—making up in honour and prestige what she perhaps lacked in size and strength compared to Russia or America. Not for nothing had the British sung in their darkest hours, 'There'll always be an England'.

In fact, the euphoria of 1945 was based largely on illusion. The war had really destroyed Britain's status as a Great Power. As with France after 1918, military victory had exhausted her strength, and she remained one of the supreme arbiters of the world by courtesy only. This became quickly evident in the economic sphere. Before 1939 Britain had been the world's greatest creditor nation; after 1945 she was its greatest debtor. This transformation had a profound effect on British power and influence. The debts incurred in paying for the war continued to dog British attempts to achieve international solvency. The attempt to restore sterling convertibility in 1947 was an ignominious failure; Britain's numerous creditors immediately rushed to cash their cheques, which the resources of the British Treasury were unable to meet. Two years later the pound had to be devalued. Supported by dollar aid—first through the 1945 U.S. loan, subsequently through Marshall Aid—Britain steered an unsteady economic course through the postwar years, always having to trim her commitments to her diminished economic capacity. But these successive economic crises hardly affected national psychology.

In any case, the British had strong reasons for wanting to avoid Continental entanglements. Their first preoccupation after 1945 was with internal reforms. The Labour Government was swept into office because British imaginations had been fired during the war with the ideal of a 'new Britain' based on full employment and the Welfare State, a clean break from the stagnant, class-ridden society of the twenties and thirties. The postwar mood of the British people—and to a large extent of the Attlee government—was one of profound introversion.

Externally, in any event, Britain felt no need to look to Europe for friends. Was she not the close ally and associate of her great comrade-in-arms, America? If the British people thought at all of international unity, it was a unity of the English-speaking peoples that they desired and expected. The alliance between Britain and America, an alliance forged in blood and sealed with victory, must remain the cornerstone of British policy; this was common ground to both the great political parties in Britain, despite the grumblings of the Left (and the extreme, nationalist Right). Anything that threatened to separate us from our American allies must be resisted to the death. One of the great illusions harboured by the British after 1945 was that the Americans thought the same way—that they regarded us as equal partners in the cold war. Time was to produce a cruel awakening.

Apart from the Atlantic alliance, our great preoccupation in external relations was with the Commonwealth. Leadership of the Commonwealth was in a sense the symbol of Britain's international power, compensating for our smallness and weakness and justifying our place among the Big Three. It was an international status-symbol of the first importance. But it was a good deal more. In its economic version as the sterling area (a grouping of nations sharing common gold and

dollar reserves which are held by the Bank of England; the area includes all the Commonwealth countries except Canada, plus South
Africa, Eire, Iceland, Burma and certain Middle Eastern states), it
constituted a closely-knit economic bloc, providing Britain with most
of her food and raw materials and an outlet for her industrial exports.
The sterling area was in many ways an ideal economic unit in the
conditions of the early postwar years. Britain provided the capital and
the manufactures, the rest of the sterling area the primary commodities
—food and raw materials—which we lacked. Some of the overseas
sterling countries were large net earners of dollars, which were used for
the benefit of the area as a whole. Since dollar shortage was the free
world's greatest economic problem in the early postwar years, this was
of great importance. The area maintained cohesion by restricting dollar
imports, by exchange controls and a loose (too loose) degree of policy
co-ordination. Britain got her food and materials relatively cheaply
under a system of bulk purchase agreements, while our sterling area
partners had free access to the London capital market. At a time when
the supply of capital was far below the demand for it, and when prices
of primary products on world markets were rising rapidly, this made
good sense. And Britain was able to achieve the expanded exports
which the loss of her pre-war investment income necessitated, by
selling in protected—and therefore easy—sterling area markets. (The
preferential tariffs enjoyed by all Commonwealth countries—including
Canada—were a less important boost to trade at this time. Canada, as
a dollar country, was indeed subject to the same restrictions on trade
with the rest of the Commonwealth as was the U.S.)

Politically, therefore, Britain looked to the U.S. and the Commonwealth; economically, to the sterling area. In each case closer links with
Europe seemed at best an irrelevance, at worst a threat. Despite our
economic weakness, we had in fact made a remarkably swift recovery
after the war, and until the mid-1950s our economic position was much
stronger than that of our neighbours on the Continent. If we were to
throw in our lot with them, what had we to gain? Why should we
seek to share the advantages of the sterling area system, with its inflow
of dollars? Why should we dilute the value of our special access to
Washington? What had the Continentals to offer in return?

I remember in 1953 writing a pamphlet for the Fabian Society on
the sterling area, in which I advocated a more effective system of
planning to strengthen the area's internal cohesion. The Council of
Europe had just published its Strasbourg Plan, suggesting the fusion of

the sterling area and Western Europe into a single economic bloc. This plan greatly impressed me, for it was becoming very clear by this time that the sterling area was overweighted on the commodity-producing side. Britain alone could not supply the investment capital and the manufactures the area needed, nor could she consume enough of the area's commodity output. (The world was at this time moving out of the era of commodity shortage into one of commodity surplus.) The inclusion of Western Europe would right the balance. I discussed this with one of the leading figures in the Labour Party, a man of out-standing intelligence and vision. To my surprise his face became con-torted with anger. 'Those hypocrites at Strasbourg!' he cried. 'All they want to do is lay their hands on *our* dollars!' To my lasting regret I toned down my warm references to the Strasbourg Plan.

To be fair to the Labour Party, its attitude was not entirely com-pounded of 'I'm all right Jack!' Ideological factors also entered into it. None of the Continental countries outside Scandinavia had an effective Socialist government, or looked very like getting one. In France and Italy the leadership of the working-class movement was held by the Communists. The dominant political movement in the Six after 1945 was Catholic in orientation, *laisser-faire* in its economic thinking. Catholic Parties were supreme in Germany and Italy, and powerful elsewhere. The British Labour Party, with its deep-rooted Noncon-formist traditions, was profoundly suspicious of this Catholic resurg-ence in Europe. It was even more suspicious of the economic trend away from planning, State control and *dirigisme* towards economic liberalism and *laisser-faire*. It would have nothing to do with anything which seemed likely to limit Britain's freedom to plan her own economy and develop her own Welfare State, with its emphasis on State ownership and controls.

In fact these fears were largely based on prejudice. The contrast between British and Continental policy was nothing like so pro-nounced as British Socialists thought. All the Six had, and have, sub-stantial sectors of industry under State ownership. All have considerable welfare services. France and the Netherlands have practised economic planning in some form or other ever since 1945, while the French throughout the period of the Fourth Republic operated a very marked form of *dirigisme*. Only in Germany, Belgium and Italy was economic liberalism exalted into a dogma. But the picture of rapacious Latins, socially backward and politically unreliable, seeking to 'horn in' on Britain's privileged position vis-à-vis Washington and the Commonwealth, flattered British pride and British insularity. Consequently, when in 1950 the Six invited Britain to become a founder-member of the European Coal-Steel Community, the first essay in full-scale European integration, the invitation was rejected out of hand, on the grounds that coal and steel were publicly owned in Britain, and that their operation could not be submitted to international control.

This was a tragedy. The idea of integrating the two key industries of Western Europe, as a sort of pilot-plant for a future United Europe, was a stroke of genius. Not only would the abolition of national barriers to trade in these two basic products strengthen the European economies, it would also—by the establishment of supra-national control—make a future war between France and Germany a virtual impossibility. The iron-ore of Lorraine, the coal and steel of the Ruhr would henceforth form the single economic complex which Nature intended it to be. The revival of the Ruhr coal and steel industries— now plainly seen to be inevitable—would take place under supervision by Germany's neighbours, through the institutions of the Community. In such a Community Britain could have exercised a dominant role. Her coal industry is by far the largest in Western Europe, with production not far below that of the Six combined. Her steel industry was at that time the biggest in the area, though it has since been overtaken by Germany. But Britain would also have been welcomed as the makeweight between France and Germany. French nervousness—despite the safeguards of the ECSC Treaty—at entering into too close a partnership with her age-old enemy would have been allayed had her old ally Britain chosen to come in with her. Franco-German rivalry alone would have ensured Britain the leading place in the councils of Europe, had she chosen at any time to exercise it. But, except in the loose groupings of NATO and the OEEC,[1] where each member retained its full sovereignty, and where the Americans were also represented, or at least involved, Britain showed no interest in entering into schemes for European integration.[2]

[1] The Organisation for European Economic Co-operation, set up to co-ordinate European economic development under the aegis of the Marshall Plan. It never acquired supra-national powers, but proved a useful forum for discussions and played an important role in liberalising Europe's trade. The U.S., though closely associated with the work of the OEEC, was not a member. But when it was later replaced by the OECD (Organisation for Economic Co-operation and Development), the U.S. and Canada both became full members of the new body.

[2] For a full account of Britain's relations with Europe from 1945 to 1959, see

EUROPE GOES AHEAD

In 1951 the replacement of the Labour Government by a Conservative one filled the Europeans with hope. In opposition the Tories had been enthusiastic advocates of European unity, and had made great use of the forum presented by the Council of Europe at Strasbourg. The Council, the first institutional expression of the pan-European movement, had come into existence in 1949. One of its architects was Sir Winston Churchill, who in his Zurich speech in 1946 had called for 'a United States of Europe'. Sir Winston in subsequent speeches described Britain as 'geographically and historically part of Europe', and as having 'to play her full part as a member of the European family'. Naturally, his listeners assumed that the Conservative Party when in office would favour British integration in 'the United States of Europe'. This impression was fostered by a galaxy of Conservative Party speakers at Council of Europe meetings at Strasbourg.

This attitude was in marked contrast to the coldness of the Labour Government, which first tried to abort the Council by proposing a Committee of European Ministers as an alternative, and then succeeded in emasculating it by ensuring that the parliamentary body was purely consultative, with no powers to do anything but make recommendations to the Ministers, who were under no obligation to accept them. This ensured that the Council became, what the British subsequently derided it for being, a mere 'talking shop' without any powers. The Council failed in its objective of providing a genuine 'European parliament'. Perhaps this was inevitable, given the fact that the members of the Council were and are primarily national politicians whose main interests and responsibilities are in and to their individual legislatures. In any event, subsequent events pushed it on to the sidelines of the European movement. British M.P.s inevitably tended to gauge the strength of the European movement from the people they met during their visits to the Council at Strasbourg, and mistakenly assumed that the movement lacked real strength because the Council was so obviously operating in a vacuum. They did not realise until too late that this arose only from the restraints imposed on the Council by the

Europe Will Not Wait, by Anthony Nutting (Hollis and Carter). Nutting's account is well-informed and objective, but on the evidence of his own facts he is far too kind in his comments on the behaviour of his Conservative colleagues, and rather too censorious towards their Labour predecessors. He is also very unfair towards Pierre Mendès-France and other 'nationalist' French leaders.

governments concerned—notably the British—and that the hard-headed men who were in fact 'making Europe' were concentrating their efforts elsewhere. Strasbourg did perform some useful work among the foothills of European integration—in developing parliamentary contacts, in cultural work, social security conventions, the European Court of Human Rights, and so on. But essentially it was a sounding board, and little more.

It was a sounding board which the Conservatives used to good effect. In the summer of 1950, Churchill used it to call for the creation of a 'European army under a united command in which we should all bear a worthy and honourable part'. At the same time, in Westminster, the Conservatives attacked the Labour Government for its refusal to join in the talks which led to the establishment of the ECSC. When the Conservatives came to power in the following year, the 'Europeans' expected great things.

They were disappointed. If Attlee and his colleagues had been guilty of myopia towards Europe, for the Churchill administration duplicity is perhaps a more accurate word. Once in office, the Conservatives quickly dropped the idea of joining the ECSC, preferring instead a loose form of association which committed neither side to anything more than consultation. Worse, they went back on the suggestion that Britain would play a part in a European army. In the next few years Sir Winston and his colleagues played a major part in sabotaging the European Defence Community (EDC), which Churchill himself had launched.

The EDC was to be the next stage of European integration after the ECSC. It was to provide a framework in which Western Germany could be re-armed—a point on which the U.S. was pressing—without danger to her neighbours in Western Europe. The EDC was to be accompanied by the creation of a European Political Community (EPC), to do the job the Council of Europe had been prevented from doing.

The problem was to get France to agree (though it was in fact a French Prime Minister, René Pleven, who formally proposed the creation of EDC in October 1950). France wanted Britain in as a guarantor that the EDC would not be dominated by Germany. But in the autumn of 1951 Sir Anthony Eden told the NATO Council that Britain would in no circumstances participate in the EDC. The French then sought, in vain, for British guarantees to maintain the existing number of their forces in Europe, and to operate in association with the institutions of the EPC when it came into being. Having failed to get these guarantees, the French themselves then rejected the EDC in the summer of 1954.

The collapse of EDC had two major consequences. First, it created a dangerous military and political vacuum in Europe which the British reluctantly had to fill. Eden produced the stop-gap solution of Western European Union (WEU), an alliance consisting of the Six plus Britain, without the supra-national powers of the EDC but with political as well as military institutions. Ironically, neither France nor Britain did as well out of WEU as they would have done out of EDC. German rearmament took place with fewer safeguards for her neighbours than the EDC would have provided, and Britain was forced to give the guarantees which she had refused to give to the EDC. Yet WEU was widely hailed as a triumph for British diplomacy; in fact it was no more than a skilful patching-up operation after a totally unnecessary crash.

The collapse of the EDC project was a severe setback to the cause of European integration. Three years had been wasted, and sceptics on both sides of the Channel assumed that the steam had gone out of the 'United States of Europe'. The ECSC High Authority in Luxembourg remained in lonely isolation, attracting little interest and less understanding in Britain. I remember going, in the spring of 1955, with a number of other English journalists, on a visit to the High Authority. I came back fired with enthusiasm, anxious to convey my impressions to my newspaper's readers. The news editor had other ideas. 'The Coal-Steel Community!' he snorted. 'What English business man wants to read about *that*?' I'm afraid he was right. In any case, not a word of my impressions from Luxembourg ever appeared in my paper.

And yet it was at exactly this time that the movement for integration really began to roll. The 'Europeans' had learned the lesson of the failure of the Council of Europe and the EDC, compared to the success of the ECSC. If Europe was to be united, it must be through economic rather than through political means. The ECSC had succeeded because it was carrying out a policy of economic integration which yielded manifest industrial benefits. The time had come to apply what the ECSC was doing in two industries alone to the entire economic structure of the Six member-countries. In June 1955 the foreign ministers of the Six met at Messina in Sicily. Out of this meeting emerged eventually a plan for two new Communities—Euratom and the European Economic Community (EEC) or Common Market. Euratom followed the ECSC pattern in having a limited industrial purview. It was designed to develop atomic energy among the Six on a supra-national basis. The EEC was a much more revolutionary concept, involving nothing less than the complete integration of the economies of the Six, so that they would eventually become in economic terms at least virtually a single nation-state. A full description of what the EEC is and does is given in Part II of this book.

Britain was not represented at the Messina meeting, though she did participate in the earlier discussions of the Spaak Committee which emerged from it. Although invited, she did not think the meeting sufficiently important to justify attendance. The assumption was that the EDC fiasco had disposed of the European movement, and the British press followed the Government's lead in virtually ignoring the meeting. To be fair, the preceding years had seen the birth and death of a number of grandiose projects for European integration besides the EDC, and it is always difficult in these matters to tell swans from geese.

Ignoring the Messina meeting proved, however, to be a monumental miscalculation. Within two years the two new Communities had been approved by the governments of the Six, and the European Common Market had come into existence. The other members, learning their lesson from the EDC failure, leant over backwards to meet the special wishes of France, with the result that the French negotiators were able to drive an extraordinarily good bargain.

With the establishment of the EEC the cause of European integration had taken a giant leap forward. The 'Little Europe' of the Six was now a going concern, and the balance of power on the Continent had been decisively altered. The danger against which British arms and British diplomacy had struggled successfully for centuries—the danger of a super-power on the Continent of Europe—had re-emerged. The union of the Six threatened to divide Western Europe into two groups—the Ins and the Outs; and from this division only the enemies of the West would benefit. The time for a fundamental reappraisal of British policy towards Europe had come.

'IF YOU CAN'T BEAT THEM, JOIN THEM'

At this stage it is worthwhile to go back a bit in time, to try to understand the attitude of the Conservative Government towards Europe.

The Tories did not on the whole share the ideological dislike of Continental policies and politicians which many British Socialists felt (and feel). Moreover, after 1951 the economic pattern in the world at large, and the Commonwealth in particular, began to alter dramatically. The spectre of dollar shortage began to disappear. As the decade wore on, the need for the rest of the world to protect itself by restrictions on dollar imports and by exchange controls became less and less urgent, as the disparity between U.S. economic strength and that of the rest of the world became less and less marked. The importance of the sterling area as a dollar-accumulating, dollar-sharing bloc declined correspondingly.

At the same time the worldwide shortage of commodities gradually gave way to a condition of surplus, which in turn had profound implications for the structure and strength of the sterling area system. A number of things were happening simultaneously in the 1950s, all of which conspired to weaken the tight autarkic links which bound together the sterling area of the early postwar years. The easing of the dollar shortage was one. Second, the Conservative government progressively abolished the long-term bulk contracts under which the Labour government had bought commodities from sterling sources, and the restrictions on imports of these commodities from outside the area. In short, Britain adopted an increasingly liberal policy on commodity imports. Since the prices of most commodities were falling on world markets in relation to industrial goods—a result of the ending of shortages—Britain benefited from this change of policy. Favourable terms of trade helped Britain's balance of payments considerably during the decade.

For the rest of the sterling area, however, the effects were less favourable. Loss of protected markets in London, coupled with increased world production, meant keener competition in world markets for their exports. Consequently they could only maintain the volume of these exports by lowering their prices in real terms; and this meant they had correspondingly less money to spend on imports. At the same time their desire to industrialise, to become more self-sufficient in manufactures, was intensified by the growing weakness of their traditional exports.

The result was a further weakening of the economic cohesion of the sterling area. Overseas sterling countries came to rely less on Britain for their industrial imports. On the one hand they strove to produce more of their own manufactures themselves; new industries tended to be protected from outside competition by quota controls. Second, they tended increasingly to buy from Britain's competitors—the U.S., Japan, or Western Europe—where these countries offered a better bargain. While Britain was liberalising her import policy to the detriment of her sterling area partners, these partners were doing exactly the same thing to the detriment of British exporters. Both parties in fact were discovering the advantages of having a choice of suppliers in a buyer's market.

Third, however, the ability of the overseas sterling area countries to import at all was limited by adverse economic factors—namely, the less buoyant world markets for their main exports, and the big demands on their resources imposed by their own urge to industrialise, which involved massive imports of foreign capital. As a result the sterling area—and indeed the Commonwealth as a whole, for with the ending of dollar shortage Canada became increasingly closely associated with the sterling countries, and her economic conditions came closely to resemble theirs—proved to be a comparatively stagnant market during the fifties. Its rate of economic growth was below that of most of the world, and most of its leading members were beset at one time or another by balance of payments crises which lessened their ability to import.

This weakening of economic cohesion was reinforced by political factors. During the 1950s the Commonwealth ceased to be a predominantly Anglo-Saxon 'club'. Increasingly the balance of power shifted in favour of the newly-freed colonies and former dependent territories of Asia and Africa, though Britain's titular leadership of the Commonwealth was never challenged. The possibility of building the Commonwealth or sterling area into a really effective supra-national politico-economic bloc was never really explored in the early postwar years; supra-national planning and policy co-ordination were never seriously attempted. After 1951 the possibility receded. Not only was the climate of political opinion in London hostile to the concept. More important, ex-colonies like Ghana and Malaya which had previously earned dollars for the whole area and ran substantial payments surpluses were determined on attaining independence to spend what they earned on their own development. These newly-independent countries were inevitably nationalistic in sentiment, and this contributed to the centrifugal tendencies at work in the Commonwealth at this time. (One might add that the task of providing aid to the bigger countries, like India and Pakistan, became increasingly recognised as an obligation of the West as a whole, to which the U.S., Western Europe and Japan contributed as well as Britain.)

The dream of the autarkic, self-contained Commonwealth or sterling area therefore faded rapidly in the 1950s. The system of Commonwealth trade preferences dating from the 1932 Ottawa conference did however provide certain advantages to both parties. British exports to Commonwealth countries, and Commonwealth exports to Britain, both enjoyed certain tariff advantages over their competitors. But these were on the whole comparatively minor, and diminishing, advantages —certainly so far as Britain was concerned; to Commonwealth exporters they were a good deal more important. (Price is usually a more important consideration compared to other factors if you are selling food or raw materials than if you are selling advanced industrial products. Moreover, sales to Britain did not run up against the barrier of import restrictions, as sales to Commonwealth countries frequently did.)

British industrialists therefore increasingly began to switch their sights from the Commonwealth to other markets. In the immediate postwar period about 60 per cent of all British exports went to the Commonwealth, while less than 25 per cent went to Europe. During the 1950s the Commonwealth share steadily declined, while Europe's rose rapidly. By the first quarter of 1962 Europe had replaced the Commonwealth as Britain's biggest single export market, from having been only half as large ten years before.[1] This represents a historic change of pattern for British exports.

Western Europe was also, during this period, acting increasingly as a magnet for Commonwealth commodity exports. The truth enunciated in the Strasbourg Plan—that Europe and the Commonwealth are complementary economic units—began increasingly to be reflected in the patterns of world trade.

British industrialists, disillusioned by the comparative stagnation of Commonwealth markets, welcomed the growth of Europe as an alternative. In the largely unsophisticated markets of the Commonwealth they often found it hard to compete—despite tariff advantages—with the products of lower-cost countries like Japan. In Europe, on the other hand, the high quality and sophistication of British products made them less vulnerable to price competition. But the real reason for the growth of British sales to the Continent was less reassuring. It was the fact that the European countries—and notably the Six—were increasing their

[1] This applies to Western Europe as a whole, not just the Six.

rate of industrial production and adding to their national wealth at a far faster rate than Britain. Between 1953 (the first 'normal' postwar year, when the period of readjustment after the world war and Korea could be said to be complete) and 1960, Britain's rate of industrial production went up by 21 per cent. In the same period Germany's rate of increase was 62 per cent, Italy's 58 per cent, France's 52 per cent, the Netherlands' 39 per cent. Only Belgium and Luxembourg had rates of growth as low as Britain's.

By the mid-fifties the Six seemed to have discovered a rhythm of dynamic growth which Britain could not match. The contrast began to become painfully obvious after 1955, when the boom of 1953–54 petered out in Britain in an atmosphere of inflationary pressure, balance-of-payments difficulties and hostility between Government and unions. For the next three years the British economy virtually stood still, while the Continental countries continued to move forward.

So, as time went on, industrialists in Britain became increasingly aware of the value of the European market, and of the danger of losing it through exclusion from the Common Market. The economic argument for closer integration with Europe became increasingly clear, while the advantages of the rival Commonwealth or sterling area grouping came to seem increasingly nebulous. Why then was the British government so slow to see these advantages?

I think there are a number of reasons. First, as we have seen, the British consistently under-estimated the strength of the urge for unity on the Continent. Consequently they always found themselves playing their cards too late. This was shown over the European army, when we had to concede to the WEU what we had refused to the EDC. It was shown in the belated British discovery in the 1950s of the value of the Council of Europe. At various periods during the fifties Britain tried to bridge the gap between the Six and the rest of Western Europe by strengthening the Council—which included both groups—and subordinating the institutions of the Six to it. But each time the Six rejected the British overtures as being 'too little, too late'—as attempts, in fact, to sabotage the integration of 'little Europe' by imposing a brake on it. Exactly the same sequence of events was to take place over the Common Market.

Second, the British continued to be blinded by the illusion of Great Power status for most of the decade. The moment of truth which came to the Six during the war came to Britain only slowly and partially, and not at all until after 1955.[1] While the Commonwealth progressively lost its economic significance, its mystical importance for the British seemed to grow as it became more vague and nebulous. Increasingly during the 1950s, as British power ebbed, the symbols of power came to be prized above the reality. Like an ageing actress, Britain's statesmen and people sought refuge from the harsh facts in an illusion of grandeur. A dangerous national obsession with prestige began to show itself, an ominous forerunner of decay.

Perhaps I can illustrate this by one incident from my own experience. I vividly remember attending the Labour Party conference in the autumn of 1954, when the Party wrestled in agony with its conscience over the issue of German rearmament. It was an intensely dramatic debate, which split the Party right down the middle. I happened to be sitting in the gallery just between the representatives of the U.S. and the Soviet Union. Both big men, the Russian and the American craned over the balcony, watching intently as the debate went on below. One felt that one was watching a vital battle in the cold war, that these emissaries from the two great camps were visibly contending for the support of a still mighty Britain. Certainly, not only the delegates but the whole British press combined to give the impression that, whichever way it went, this was a debate of fundamental importance.

But of course it was not. To the realities of the cold war it was fundamentally irrelevant. For whatever the British Labour Party said or did, Germany at that stage was going to be rearmed. The British Labour Party was tearing itself to pieces over an illusion of power. The great debate over Britain's H-bomb a few years later was to combine exactly the same ingredients of passion and irrelevance, based on a failure on both sides to see that what Britain did with her puny stock of H-bombs really made practically no difference to the stark realities of world power.

The illusion of world power was fostered by the Churchillian doctrine of the 'interlocking circles'—the theory that Britain was uniquely placed at the heart of three great blocs: the Atlantic alliance with America, the Commonwealth, and Western Europe. This doctrine carried the flattering implication that Britain really was 'at the still centre of the turning world', buttressed and shielded by innumerable friends. To the complacency of Britain's diplomats was added the confidence, until 1955, of her economic leaders. From 1951 to 1955

---

[1] This was however much less true of France than of the others. See below, p. 31.

Conservative economic policy moved forward smoothly and efficiently, correcting the mistakes of the Labour government and translating the doctrines of a modern, liberal Conservatism into practical policies. Until 1955, therefore, a good case could be made out for saying that Britain was doing all right on her own.

1955 really represents the watershed of British relations with Europe. The year of the Messina conference was the year in which Britain seemed to lose her capacity for expansion, in which the economic self-confidence of the Tories ebbed away in the face of intractable problems of cost inflation. By 1956 the Government had at last realised that the Six meant business, and was casting about for some way of preserving Britain's trade links with them. But in the autumn of that year British attention was distracted from Europe by a bigger, more immediate problem—the Suez crisis.

Suez was without doubt Britain's postwar 'moment of truth'. In a blinding lightning-flash her essential weakness was revealed, militarily and politically. The cosy concept of the 'interlocking circles' was cruelly exposed. Faced with a choice between her ally Britain and the goodwill of the Afro-Asian bloc, America unhesitatingly chose the latter. Other than France, there was no support for the Suez operation from the Continent of Europe. Even in the Commonwealth, majority opinion condemned the British action in no uncertain terms. World disapproval would not perhaps have mattered if we could have achieved our ends despite it, as the Russians did at the same time in Hungary. But we could not. Our action produced a run on sterling, as Britain's creditors abroad hurriedly cashed their cheques in fear of a new devaluation. Only a dollar loan could avert bankruptcy. The Americans refused all financial assistance unless we pulled our troops out of Egypt. We pulled out.

This humiliating defeat had a cathartic effect on British public opinion. One section took refuge in an angry xenophobia, burying their heads more fiercely in the sand. But most people felt, however confusedly, that a decisive turning-point had been reached in Britain's relations with the outside world, necessitating fundamental changes of policy. And it was instinctively to Europe rather than the Commonwealth that people turned.

FREE TRADE AREAS, BIG AND LITTLE

For a short time the British Government tried, rather half-heartedly, to dissuade the Six from going ahead with their plans for a Common

Market, on the grounds that European economic integration should be conducted within the framework of OEEC. But at a meeting of the OEEC Council in July 1956 the idea of an all-European free trade area was discussed, and on February 7th, 1957, the British Government published a plan for such a free trade area as a White Paper. The free trade area was first considered as an alternative to a Common Market. Then, when the Six made it clear that their negotiations for a Common Market must take precedence, it was envisaged as a broader framework which would embrace the Six and other European countries, thus minimising the dangers of an economic—and therefore political—split between the Little Europe of the Six and the rest.

The free trade area proposed by Britain would have meant the abolition, over a period of years, of all tariffs and other barriers to trade between the member-countries—at least so far as manufactured goods were concerned. To that extent it resembled the Common Market the Six were setting up. But it differed from it in three fundamental ways.

First, agriculture was specifically excluded. This enabled Britain to avoid the problem of reconciling her policy for agriculture with the very different policies in force on the Continent. In Britain farmers are subsidised out of the Exchequer, and there are few restrictions or tariffs on imports—many of which come from the Commonwealth. The Government subsidy is designed to enable British farmers to make profits while competing on the home market at world prices; the Government in fact pays the difference between what the farmer needs to earn to cover his costs and the price he has to offer to sell his goods against foreign competition. By this means the cost of living is kept down at the taxpayer's expense, and Commonwealth suppliers are assured of a market for their food products in Britain.

On the Continent, on the other hand, agriculture is normally protected by tariffs, so that food prices are kept above world levels. The cost of agricultural protection is paid by the consumer rather than the taxpayer. The British system of farm subsidies would be impracticable on the Continent if only because farmers there are a much bigger proportion of the population, so that the burden on the Exchequer would be proportionally much greater than here. To get round this discrepancy the British proposed quite simply that agriculture should be excluded from the free trade area—though at a late stage, when the negotiations were already doomed, they conceded that some provision would have to be made for it.

28

Second, the free trade area was exclusively an *economic* proposition, without any of the political overtones or objectives of the Common Market. It was designed, as its name implied, primarily to expand trade —not to pave the way for any form of political union or federation.

Third, while members of the Common Market had to equalise their tariffs towards the outside world—so that the area of the Six was surrounded by a common external tariff—this obligation did not apply to members of the free trade area. These countries were free to pursue whatever trade policy they liked towards countries outside the area; their obligations applied only to other members of the free trade area. The advantage of this for Britain was obvious. It meant that Britain could maintain the structure of Commonwealth trade relations— including her trade preferences in Commonwealth markets, and the preferences she gave to the Commonwealth in her home market— unaffected by her relations with the Europeans. This would give her, in a sense, the best of both worlds. It was like taking a new wife without having to divorce, or even stop living with, the old one.

It was on these three crucial differences that the negotiations for a free trade area eventually foundered. The ostensible breaking point was a fairly technical one—namely, French fears that the free trade area would enable cheap foreign imports to find their way into the Common Market via the low-tariff free trade area countries. To take an example, textiles from Hong Kong coming into Britain duty-free would then find their way, disguised as British products, into France —still without having to pay any duty; in this way the common external tariff of the Six would become inoperative. The British argued, unavailingly, that this could be avoided by insisting that goods traded in the area carried certificates of origin. The French insisted that no free trade area was feasible without a common external tariff. Eventually, on November 14th, 1958, the French Government announced out of the blue that the free trade area plan was unworkable, and the protracted negotiations collapsed ignominiously. Britain and the other non-Common Market countries of Europe were left out in the cold.

In retrospect it is easy to see why the free trade area was never a feasible proposition. The argument on certificates of origin was not in fact the decisive factor. The real issue was in a way simpler, in a way more complex. To begin with, both sides approached the negotiations from totally different premises. The British were looking for a purely economic solution, with the minimum of commitments and the minimum of sacrifices. The Six wanted something much more radical. Britain's past record made her suspect to the Europeans. As one of the leading EEC officials put it to me in Brussels at the time: 'Britain must make up her mind whether she is in Europe or not, whether she is prepared to throw in her lot fully with us or not. We can't afford countries just coming along for the ride.'

At the same time, however, the free trade area, despite its drawbacks from the Europeans' point of view, did offer certain advantages. While none of the Six would consider it as a straight alternative to the Common Market, many of them would have liked a two-tier structure, with Britain and the other non-Common Market countries linked with Little Europe through a free trade area. Many German firms, for example, were alarmed at the effect on their export business of a trade war between the Six and the rest of Europe. The Dutch, and to a lesser extent the Belgians, were also anxious about their export trade; the Dutch feared particularly for their agricultural exports to Britain. The Benelux countries were forced to adjust their traditionally low tariffs nearer to the higher French and Italian levels as part of the process of creating the common external tariff. They disliked the protectionist tendencies of the Common Market, and they were fearful of the danger of Franco-German domination. Many people in the Six feared the implications of 'splitting Europe', and there was also a good deal of resentment at the concessions which the French had won as the price of membership—not only for themselves, but also for their African colonies and associates. For all these internal strains among the Six British association could have acted as a useful solvent.

But the British had made their usual mistake of exaggerating their bargaining strength, and so overplaying their hand. The trouble was that, while five of the Six wanted some association with Britain, none of them felt strongly enough about it to stand up to the sixth, France. Faced with a choice between Britain and France, they chose France unhesitatingly. And France's position throughout the negotiations was quite intransigent—though the reasons for this intransigence altered to some extent as the negotiations wore on during 1958.

When she signed the Treaty of Rome in 1957, France was the 'sick man of Europe'. Economically she was even more crisis-prone than Britain. Though her rate of industrial growth was faster, she paid for it by persistent balance-of-payments troubles and a series of devaluations of the franc. Her economy was among the most heavily-protected in Europe, and her industrialists had the reputation of being exception-ally restrictive-minded. Politically, she suffered from chronic instability under a series of weak governments. Abroad, attempts to hang on to her empire had involved her in a host of troubles, culminating in the bitter and costly Algerian war. (Her rigid colonial stance appeared in dramatic contrast to Britain's far-sighted policy of withdrawal and liberation.)[1]

For all these reasons, it was harder for France to open her home market to unrestricted competition than for any other of the Six. Psychologically and politically, too, France was probably the least pre-pared of the Six for integration. The country of Jean Monnet, prime architect of the European movement, was also the country of Charles de Gaulle, at that time an enemy of the Europeans; a strong nationalist and chauvinist streak runs through the French people, and the Fourth Republic was in no position to ignore the wishes of any of the numer-ous vested interests of France.

The French attitude to their partners can perhaps be summarised as follows: 'We want to join with you in building a new Europe, and we know that you cannot do it without us. But because we are weak, we must ask you to pay a high price for our signature to the Treaty. And because we are indispensable, you know as well as we do that you must pay our price.' France's negotiators played their cards with brilliant opportunism, with the result that they won for their country a highly priviliged position in the Common Market. The French approach, essentially, was to see how the clauses of the Treaty of Rome could be twisted to suit France's interest before she signed them. The British, more honest but less intelligent, looked at the clauses to see which of them Britain could reasonably sign as they stood.

When the free trade area talks began, therefore, France had already won all she could hope to from her partners. Her industrialists, having steeled themselves to face German competition, saw no reason why they should face British as well, especially if Britain was not ready to 'pay the price' by signing the Treaty of Rome. Why should France

---

[1] This was to change with the transformation of the French Union into an assembly of independent states on the pattern of the Commonwealth under the Fifth Republic. The process of liberation of France's African possessions is now, as I write, being completed with the negotiation of a peace settlement in Algeria. But the fact remains that in the peaceful abdication of colonial power Britain has a much better overall postwar record than France—or for that matter the Benelux countries.

share her privileged position with Britain? Why should she dilute the benefits won for her African *confrères* by agreeing to let Commonwealth countries share them? In short, France had nothing to gain and quite a lot to lose from the free trade area.

As 1958 wore on, and the Fourth Republic gave way to the Fifth, France's economic objections to the free trade area began to ease, but her political objections hardened. French industry staged an astonishing upsurge during this period, helped by the stability which the Gaullist regime brought with it. To her astonishment, France found that her industries could compete on equal terms with the rest of the Six, and with this discovery came a great increase in self-confidence. But this did not, unhappily, reconcile General de Gaulle and his colleagues to the free trade area. De Gaulle was not a friend to the European movement, but when he came to power he accepted the Treaty of Rome as a French commitment, and soon came to see it as an invaluable political weapon with which to assert France's place in the world against the unloved Anglo-Saxons. This change of attitude was facilitated by the close working relationship achieved with Dr. Adenauer. Determined to maintain the cohesion of 'Little Europe', the German Chancellor made a point of deferring to French leadership wherever possible. The results were momentous. For the first time since 1870, France lost her fear of Germany—and with it, her need for Britain. As leader and spokesman of the Six, France could carry weight in the councils of the West at least equal to that of Britain. The free trade area would not help her to do this; it could only hinder her. Hence de Gaulle applied the French veto, for political rather than economic reasons.

This veto came as a shock to Britain. Public opinion had been quite unprepared for failure. It had indeed only just acclimatised itself to the idea that free trade with Europe would be a good thing. A numbed pause followed. Then Britain proceeded to set up her free trade area together with six other European states who, like her, had been concerned in the abortive negotiations with the Six. The Treaty of Stockholm of July 1959 provided for the establishment of a free trade association (EFTA) between Britain, Sweden, Norway, Denmark, Switzerland, Austria and Portugal—a group which came to be known as the 'Outer Seven', in contrast to the 'Inner Six' of Little Europe. Finland later became an EFTA associate. The three Scandinavian states had followed Britain's lead consistently since 1945. Switzerland could not join the Common Market because of her traditional commitment to neutrality, Austria because the Russians would have regarded it as an infringement of the neutral status imposed on her by the peace treaty. Portugal had never considered membership of the Common Market, and remained something of an odd man out in the new free trade association.

EFTA has not proved one of the happiest inspirations of British postwar diplomacy. If it was intended as a rival to the Six, the contest was unequal from the start. The Seven lacked the geographical and political unity of the Six. Apart from Britain, all were small countries, with a combined population less than a quarter that of the Six. Their rates of growth were on average a good deal less than those of the Six. Moreover, the three Scandinavian states and Switzerland were in any case low-tariff countries, so that the scope for increasing trade by cutting these tariffs even further was limited. Though it worked smoothly enough in a modest way, the EFTA never began to fire the imagination or arouse the enthusiasm of its peoples as the more ambitious Community of the Six did. Nobody could feel a passionate sense of loyalty to 'Efta'. British exporters considered it from the start a poor exchange for the threatened loss of trade in the Common Market. In 1960 and 1961 British exports were still rising faster to the Six than they were to the Seven in absolute terms, though the proportional increase was less—some 32 per cent against a 40 per cent rise to 'Efta'. Moreover, trade between the Six and the Seven not only remained greater than trade among the Seven themselves, but it actually continued to grow at a slightly faster rate. Paradoxically, in fact, the chief achievement of the EFTA was to demonstrate the strength and vitality of the Common Market. When the British Government finally decided to take the plunge and apply for membership of the EEC, 'Efta' was to prove an embarrassing complication, like the Commonwealth but less important—a secondary albatross which the Ancient Mariner had fastened round his own neck in a fit of pique.

BRITAIN MAKES UP HER MIND

1959 was, like 1954, a boom year in Britain, and the effects of the breakdown of the free trade area talks were hardly felt at all outside Whitehall. In the election that autumn relations with Europe were hardly mentioned, except by the 'European' but still tiny Liberal Party. But in 1960 the tide turned decisively. As in 1955, the boom petered out as exports weakened and the pound once more came under pressure. Once again the vision of steady economic expansion had proved a mirage, and once again the painful contrast between a stagnant Britain and a dynamic Continent presented itself. The problem of economic growth began to assume central importance in British official thinking.

Nor was this just an economic problem. For with the collapse of the free trade area and the growing cohesion of the Six, signs of a shift of power in Europe began to multiply. The prospect of Britain dwindling to the status of an offshore island besides a new Continental super-power began to seem alarmingly close. The EFTA cut no ice in the world; the Commonwealth was increasingly losing cohesion, and increasingly unwilling to accept British leadership automatically. Britain's defence programme was running into growing difficulties; British diplomacy suffered a defeat with the collapse of the Paris 'Summit' conference in the summer of 1960. It was in Washington that this shift of power registered itself most clearly and ominously, particularly when Mr. Macmillan visited the U.S. in April 1960 and came under U.S. pressure to 'get into Europe'. Throughout 1959 and 1960 there were growing signs that the U.S. now regarded the Six as the most important ally in the cold war, and that if forced to choose between Britain and the Six she would back the Six. Britain had lost, in other words, her former position of 'special access' to Washington. With the replacement of President Eisenhower in the White House by President Kennedy, this change became more and more apparent.

In part this reflected a shrewd U.S. assessment of the change in the actual balance of power in Europe, in part American infatuation with the idea of a 'United States of Europe'. The Americans had from the first been enthusiastic advocates of the European movement. Arguing from the analogy of their own history, they believed that only union would make Europe strong again. A strong Europe would be able to dispense with American aid, and eventually with American troops. It would not only act as a bulwark against the spread of Soviet Communism, but would help to share the U.S. burden of distributing aid to the under-developed countries of the world. A united Europe could prove the partner for whom the Americans had been looking since the end of the war, and fill the role which Britain had proved too weak to sustain.

The difficulties of uniting the countries of Europe, with their different languages, cultures, traditions and circumstances, were grossly under-estimated on the other side of the Atlantic. In particular, the Americans could never really understand why the British—geographically an indisputable part of Europe—would not throw in their lot with the Continent and give it the leadership it needed. The Commonwealth as an institution was never really understood in the U.S. Consequently after the free trade area talks broke down, and particularly after the 1960 presidential election, Washington began to apply steady pressure on London to bridge the gap with the Six, even though an all-European union could have unpleasant implications for U.S. exports.[1]

Another reason for American eagerness to see Britain 'in Europe' was concern at the increasingly intransigent and nationalist policy towards NATO followed by General de Gaulle, and the increasing pressure exerted by France on her Common Market partners to challenge the supremacy of the Anglo-Saxons in western defence. As one American diplomat put it to me: 'We want you guys in the Common Market to keep tabs on de Gaulle—and what's more, the Beneluxers and some of the others want you in there for the same reason, though they daren't say so openly.' This was in fact undoubtedly the case.

The pressures pushing Britain towards the Six were therefore steadily growing throughout 1960 and the first part of 1961. So far as the British people were concerned, these pressures were primarily economic. Free competition from Europe would give our industry the stimulus to efficiency it lacked. More important, access to the mass market of the Continent would provide our more efficient industries with the opportunities to expand, to reap the full benefits of mass production, which neither the British home market nor the Commonwealth could any longer ensure. If we went into Europe, industry would face the stick of competition and the carrot of expansion. If we stayed out, the tariff walls would eventually go up against us, and there would be no carrot—only a slow decline into insignificance.

This at any rate was the growing feeling in industry—and it was industry more than any other section of the community which impelled Britain towards the Common Market after 1959. Of course, industry's enthusiasm for Europe—which was by no means universally shared—was far from fully rational. In part, it represented an almost mystical belief that the capacity for growth of the Common Market countries would somehow 'rub off' on us by the simple act of joining. In part, it sprang from an overwhelming sense of frustration and despair, and a feeling that the necessary measures to put British industry on its feet would not be taken so long as Britain remained isolated, because the Government lacked the intelligence or the courage to take

[1] This question is dealt with in Part III, pp. 234-239.

them. This was the frame of mind which the *New Statesman* aptly described as 'collapsing into the Common Market'.

These attitudes were widely shared in the Government itself, in Whitehall and Westminster, and in public opinion at large. Britain, it was felt, had somehow lost her national sense of direction, and was floundering about without a sense of purpose. Joining Europe seemed the only obvious way of regaining it. Of course, this belief by no means commanded universal acceptance. Powerful vested interests—in agriculture, in industry, in the trade unions, most of all in the Commonwealth—opposed it. Many people on both sides of the political fence argued equally passionately against it, on grounds of general principle. Many people on the Left hated the idea of entering a bloc dominated by men like General de Gaulle and Dr. Adenauer, and regarded the Common Market as a profoundly reactionary, anti-Socialist institution. Others thought that to enter an entirely European grouping would be to surrender Britain's freedom of foreign policy—that it would lessen the chances of reducing world tension, and would involve a betrayal of Britain's responsibilities not only to the Commonwealth but to the Afro-Asian world as a whole. High-minded though these arguments were, the assumption that Britain had a special, unique mediatory role to play in the world reflected an exaggerated view of the extent of British power in the world of the 1960s.

Other people, particularly on the political Right, strongly disliked the idea of merging British sovereignty in a supra-national organisation. 'Taking orders from foreigners' was a repellent prospect for a true-born Englishman. Once again, nostalgia for past greatness played a big part here. (In fact the political implications of joining the Common Market were consistently played down by the Government once it had decided to join, presumably for fear of arousing chauvinist passions. The project was presented to the British public essentially as an economic exercise, so that the question of sovereignty was never properly debated.)

The biggest problem, of course, was the Commonwealth. The other Commonwealth countries had approved of the British proposal for a free trade area with Europe, since this would involve no breach in the close ties between Britain and them. But the Common Market was a very different proposition. However much the issue might be fudged or disguised, in joining the Common Market Britain would be making a straight choice between Europe and the Commonwealth in favour of the former. Unless special concessions could be negotiated, Commonwealth goods would no longer enjoy tariff preferences in British markets. The common external tariff would apply to them just as it would to all other non-Common Market countries. The economic and political links which had formerly united the Commonwealth would be weakened if not broken. In some cases Commonwealth products would actually be discriminated against in the British market compared to products from Continental countries, or—even worse—products from former French colonies for whom France had negotiated special terms of access to the Common Market. Inevitably this prospect aroused strong passions in the Commonwealth, many of whose members relied heavily on Britain as a market for their goods. And the Commonwealth did not lack champions in Britain herself, at both ends of the political spectrum.

The debate which ensued in Britain was therefore intense, agonised and confused. For a long time the Government hesitated. For one thing, relations with France had deteriorated so far with the free trade area debacle that it was by no means clear that France would not simply blackball any British attempt to join the Common Market. At all costs such a rebuff must be avoided.

In 1960 and the early part of 1961, therefore, a whole series of feelers emanated from London to the Continent, designed to edge Britain closer to the Six and to convince France of her *bona fides*.[1] Some of these overtures were private, some public. The public overtures included offers to share Britain's trade preferences in Commonwealth markets with the Six, proposals for pooling work on aircraft development and space exploration, suggestions that Britain might negotiate a customs union with the Six, and finally offers to join the two smaller European Communities, Euratom (where Britain would be able to contribute a good deal of technical know-how) and the ECSC.

With each new suggestion, Britain was moving nearer to the inevitable final step. Having privately ascertained that a French blackball need not be feared, and after a whirlwind but inconclusive round of

[1] Historians may note as one of the decisive turning points the transfer of Mr. Selwyn Lloyd from the Foreign Office to the Treasury in July 1960. From then on the conduct of negotiations with the Six was taken firmly out of the hands of the Board of Trade—which remained, however, by an unfortunate arrangement responsible for dealings with 'Efta'—and placed under the Treasury and Foreign Office, both of which were and are a good deal more 'European' in their thinking. At the same time the issue of European integration ceased to be treated in Whitehall in primarily commercial terms—as it had been during the free trade area talks—and became recognised for the fundamentally political question which it is.

consultations with the Commonwealth and EFTA, the British Government finally took the plunge. On July 31st, 1961, Mr. Macmillan announced in the House of Commons that Britain was entering into negotiations with the Six to see if she could join the Common Market as a full member. The Prime Minister insisted that no final decision had yet been taken, that Britain would only join if she could obtain satisfactory terms on agriculture, on the Commonwealth and EFTA, and on other matters. At the same time it was plain that Britain's bargaining position was desperately weak, that the Government was determined to get into the Common Market if it conceivably could, and that it would regard failure to get in as a catastrophic defeat for this country.

As these words are being written, the negotiations on Britain's entry in Brussels are nearing their climax, and a decision of some sort seems likely by September 1962, when the Commonwealth prime ministers are to meet. Meanwhile the debate on whether or not Britain should join, and if so on what terms, goes on—not only in this country, but in the Commonwealth and among the Outer Seven, as well as among the Six themselves. This is not the place to go into the details of this debate, or to speculate on the possible terms of agreement. In Part III of this book I shall try to sketch out the probable consequences of Britain's joining the Six, what it will mean to the people not only of this country but elsewhere. I shall suggest long-term solutions for the particular problems which have been mentioned above as obstacles to British entry. I will consider not only how membership of the Common Market will change Britain, but how and where Britain as a member should seek to change the Common Market. I will not consider the implications of a failure of the negotiations, because I believe —and this chapter, I think, explains why—that the tides of history are inexorably pulling Britain into closer association with Europe. If this round of negotiations fails, there will inevitably at some future date be others that will succeed. I hope, however, that this time we have come to the end of the process whereby in her dealings with the Six Britain is doomed to go on offering more and more for less and less, because of her unwillingness to offer the right price at the right time. Jean Monnet once remarked that the British are slow to recognise an idea, quick to recognise a fact. They would not accept association with Europe when it was an idea; now that it is a fact, they are ready, in my opinion, to pay whatever price is necessary to associate with it.

One fact which people in Britain have been slow to recognise is that the European Economic Community is not a fixed entity, but an organism in process of evolution. This is an argument for joining it now, rather than later—because the sooner we join it, the better we can influence its development. But before we can assess not only how *it* will affect *us*, but how *we* can affect *it*, we must first understand what it is and how it works. That is the subject of Part II of this book.

Part Two

THE EUROPEAN COMMUNITY

I

The Institutional Framework

FOR ALL the polemics of which it has formed the subject, there is still no clear image in the British mind of what the Common Market really is. To some it is merely shorthand for 'the Six', the countries who have committed themselves to the economic integration of 'little Europe'; to others it conjures up the mushrooming institutional apparatus in Brussels under the leadership of that slightly mysterious figure, Professor Hallstein; and to others again it is a complex commercial and economic scheme from which Britain chose to stand aloof but which has now proved so successful that she must apply to join.

Taken literally the term would mean a market in which everyone took part without distinction; and this is in a sense exactly what the Common Market countries have set as their goal. The most immediate objective of the Treaty of Rome is the removal of trade barriers so that anyone in the Six countries can trade with anyone else unhindered by restrictions resulting from his nationality.

Such a description, on the other hand, is very far from adequate. The plan which started to be applied in 1958 is far more ambitious. True, even abolishing customs duties may mean far more to a Belgian or a Dutchman, who has only to drive for a few hours to come up against a frontier running for no good reason through the countryside, than to the Englishman, for whom customs formalities are no more than the irritating accompaniment to the physical fact of crossing the Channel: but for the Six it is only the first step. Their final aim, to be achieved progressively in twelve years (or probably even less) is to merge the economies of their six countries into one.

It is a difficult and complex process: the mass of restrictions on foreigners and foreign goods which have grown up over the centuries must be dismantled and removed, the differences between six sets of economic legislation ironed out, and six different national policies brought gradually into line. By the end of it the whole area of the European Economic Community will be as open to the businessman, the trader or the consumer as his own country is at present. For the manufacturer it means a potential market of 160 million people instead of eight or nine or fifty million at the most. For the worker or the professional man it means the chance to work or practise wherever his services are in demand. Not least, it means for the consumer the chance to buy the best and cheapest products throughout the area.

All this is a sweeping change to carry out in little more than one decade, and though the terms of the Treaty of Rome are strictly limited to social and economic matters—customs duties, farm policy, or equal pay—the repercussions of its application cannot fail to penetrate much further. Besides increasing living standards the Common Market will bring changes too in outlooks and in attitudes. Not only the businessmen but those in many other walks of life will be affected by it; and, not least, the role and importance of the national governments will undergo a change in relation to the unit as a whole.

Nor are such far-reaching effects coincidental. They were foreseen when the Treaty was signed—foreseen by the idealists who conceived it, by the diplomats and ministers who negotiated it, as well as by the Communists and nationalists who opposed it; and foreseen too by the countries which refused to join. There are of course the soundest economic reasons—to be measured in terms of greater prosperity and stability—for setting up an integrated Western European economy: in the language of economic theory it means advantages of scale, greater specialisation, lessened vulnerability to cyclical depressions; in down-to-earth practical terms, cheaper goods, higher wages, and stable prices. Yet the fact that the Common Market is primarily an economic undertaking with 'a constant improvement in living and working conditions' set out in the Treaty's preamble as its essential aim, is due as we have seen largely to historical reasons. The men who thought it up may have been idealists, but they were also political realists. After the success of ECSC and the failure of the Defence Community they saw that the foundations of political unity must be laid in the economic sphere, where integration would mean no dramatic surrender of sovereignty but only a gradual and inconspicuous levelling of barriers whilst the six economies became inextricably inter-dependent. Thus the traditional divisions would be sapped by a sense of common material and economic interest, and the economic centre of gravity would move imperceptibly from the national to the Common Market level.

BLUE-PRINT FOR INTEGRATION

It took the Six countries nearly two years to draw up the Treaty of

Rome, which in view of its scope and implications is hardly surprising. After the Messina meeting, mentioned in Part I, at which the general principles were agreed, there followed months of hard bargaining, at Val Duchesse near Brussels, by a committee of diplomats and leading civil servants under the brilliant and untiring chairmanship of the Belgian Foreign Minister Paul-Henri Spaak. Even when the Ministers had taken their decisions, more long months were needed to put them into due legal form.

The result, the Treaty signed at Rome on March 25th, 1957, can best be thought of as a blue-print for economic integration. It defines objectives, indicates methods, and sets up institutions: but translating it into practical measures requires the same continual process of negotiation, of hard-won compromise and concession exchanged for concession, by which it was drawn up. Signing the Rome Treaty changed nothing: it merely touched off the process from which a new structure will gradually emerge, taking shape at the hands of the governments and the institutions with the Treaty serving as a sort of master plan.

The Treaty itself embodies no political or economic doctrine. The theory which underlies it is that the merging of the six economies will make for more rapid and more stable economic progress; and that in the enlarged economy, free and fair competition has to be ensured. Since the Six countries all have to varying extents free enterprise economies, the merging of them yields a free enterprise Community: but the Treaty and its implementation are the work of economists and politicians of every shade of opinion, and nothing in the Treaty is opposed to planning at the national or the supra-national level.

The creation of the Common Market is a carefully balanced process. The Treaty itself reflects a skilful equilibrium of national interests; and the twelve-year transition period is divided into four-year stages, at the end of which due all-round progress must have been achieved before the measures planned for the next stage can begin. Progress in one sector cannot be allowed to outstrip that in others lest one member country gain greater advantages or make bigger sacrifices than another.

THE MACHINERY AND HOW IT WORKS

In the long run the final objectives of the Common Market are what matter most: but the details of how they are to be achieved, and their immediate effects, depend upon a never-ceasing process of compromise, discussion, consultation and conciliation. As a full member Britain too will take part in this process, at every level and at every stage. The way the institutional machinery works, and the balance between the different bodies as revealed in practice in the last four years, are thus of the greatest interest from the British point of view.

To try to understand the Common Market institutions in terms of the British institutional system would be fatally misleading: for what is called the Parliament has no power to legislate; the EEC Commission —which might appear to be the Cabinet—drafts legislation but can take no major decisions; and the decision-making body (the Council of Ministers) is responsible to no one. The machinery can only be understood in relation to the tasks it was created to perform: namely, applying the Treaty as effectively as possible, and, in order to do so, reconciling conflicting national and sectional interests with those of the Community as a whole.

When the Rome Treaty was drafted there was already a model in existence which had successfully passed its trials: the Coal and Steel Community. There, with only two economic sectors involved, the High Authority stood for the 'Community interest' and was given certain 'supranational' powers—above all the right to take executive decisions—whilst the Council of Ministers was conceived of as being primarily a link between the Community and the governments. In the Common Market on the other hand, with the whole national economy involved, the governments would not give up their powers of decision to a supranational body. Hence the compromise: the Commission is the 'guardian of the Treaty', charged with ensuring that it is fully and fairly applied; but the necessary decisions must be taken by the Council of Ministers. An Economic and Social Committee which the Council must consult ensures that the views of the various economic sectors are never neglected, and a parliamentary Assembly guarantees at least a semblance of democratic control. Any dispute about the correct interpretation of the Treaty is subject to appeal before a Court of Justice.

To obtain some clear idea of what the various Common Market institutions do, and what the relationships between them are, let us trace the progress of a measure through the machinery—one of the steady stream of measures by which the sparse, dry legal phrases of the Treaty are translated into practical steps affecting economic conditions in the member countries. Even when simplified the description is a long one, but it will at least reflect how long and complex is the process itself. It may take a year or eighteen months or more, and involve innumerable meetings, countless memoranda, and a mass of first drafts, amendments and reports before a final text emerges which all the member countries must apply.

THE COMMISSION

The process is set in motion by the European Economic Commission in Brussels. Upon these nine men, who swear an oath on taking office to maintain full independence and serve only the interests of the Community, lies the responsibility for ensuring that the Rome Treaty is applied. Most of the present members were national civil servants or diplomats; two of them are former national ministers. Like the members of a Cabinet, each is in charge of one particular field of activity— the internal market, transport, external relations, agriculture . . .—but the Commission is collectively responsible for its actions. It has under it a formidable and ever-growing administrative apparatus, employing altogether some three thousand people from the six countries, several hundred of them at a level corresponding to the Administrative Grade in a national civil service. In some ways, indeed, the Commission seems very little different from a national Civil Service, though one where all official documents appear in four languages. Quite a large proportion of the Commission's staff are in fact former civil servants, as was indeed inevitable if a sufficient number of qualified persons was to be found at once when the Common Market was set up (and here there is a contrast with the ECSC High Authority in Luxembourg, which recruited a far higher proportion of its staff direct, and thus had from the start a more 'European' and dedicated atmosphere). The allegiance of the Commission's staff is to the Community, however, and even those who return later to their national administrations or to industry do so with a wider outlook transcending merely national interests. One major difference from a national civil service lies in the fact that by far the largest part of the work done is on preparing legislation, rather than administering it; and though this may change later, for the moment the Commission's role is pre-eminently a creative one. When the time comes to put a given clause of the Treaty into effect—the one providing for free movement of workers, to take a concrete example—the first step is for the EEC Commission to agree on the general principles involved. Then the Department concerned consults all those whom the measure will affect: the government departments of the Six countries, employers' and workers' organisations and other bodies with a direct interest. In collaboration with the national experts it goes over every aspect of the situation in the member countries and the problems to be solved. Then a first draft is established, taking into account as far as possible national views, but sticking firmly to the way the Commission has decided the Treaty is to be interpreted. Next follows a long process of negotiation with national representatives in an attempt to establish a text on which all member countries agree. At last the Commission makes its own choice on the points that remain at issue, and draws up a formal proposal to the Council, whose task it is to take the decision bringing it into effect.

This process of continual consultation of national experts is a basic feature of the way the Common Market works. What the Commission is trying to do is not to impose a solution on the member countries but to work out measures which they can all accept. The 'Community' interest is not something apart but a compromise between the interests of the members. Moreover it is only the national civil servants who have in most cases the necessary knowledge and experience to help work out what amounts to detailed legislation—and it is they who will have to apply it.

Before the Council of Ministers can take its decision on the *règlement* or set of Regulations which is now before it, it must consult two other bodies: the European Parliament, and the Economic and Social Committee.

THE PHANTOM PARLIAMENT

In 1952 the Common Assembly was set up, consisting of 71 M.P.s from the Six countries, to provide parliamentary control over the affairs of the Coal and Steel Community. In 1958 its numbers were doubled and it became the European Parliamentary Assembly, debating the affairs of all three Communities—the Common Market and Euratom as well as ECSC: and in March 1962 the Assembly officially decided to call itself the European Parliament. In fact however it lacks for the moment most of the essential characteristics of a genuine parliament. Its members are not directly elected, but are delegates from their national Parliaments (which has enabled the Communists and right-wing extremists to be excluded by tacit agreement); they must thus find time for the six or seven sessions a year which the European Parliament holds in Strasbourg, as well as for frequent committee meetings, over and above their work in their national Assemblies. Secondly, the Parliament has no legislative powers: it merely gives its 'Opinion' on the measures which the Common Market Commission has presented to the Council.

The procedure when a *règlement* is submitted by the Council is for it to be examined first by one of the parliamentary Committees. There are thirteen of these in all, covering the various activities of the three Communities. After a first reading and discussion, often with a member of the EEC Commission attending in person to present and explain the text, a *rapporteur* is appointed to draft the report which, once approved by the Committee, will form the object of a full-scale debate by the Parliament in plenary session, ending with a vote on the 'Opinion' for the Council. Although it usually backs the Commission's proposals, the Parliament goes over each measure in great detail, and often suggests amendments or improvements. As far as possible the Commission tends to make the changes which the Parliament has suggested, but neither it nor the Council is obliged to take any action on them. On other occasions, without waiting to be consulted, the Parliament draws up reports and votes resolutions calling on the Commission or the Council to take action.

In fact the European Parliament's influence in and on the Common Market is much greater than might be expected from its largely consultative role, or from its ambiguous position in relation to the other Community institutions. It does in fact have the formal power to make the High Authority or the Commissions resign by passing a vote of censure, but it is most unlikely to do so in present circumstances and would in any case have no say in replacing them; whilst over the Council of Ministers it has no power at all. Right from the earliest days of the Coal and Steel Community, the Assembly was the most outspoken driving force towards European unity. It has always refused to limit itself to the technical problems of the application of the Treaties, and has repeatedly debated and made recommendations on the general political aspects of unification. The three Executives have always been assured of its moral support in their dealings with the Governments.

Despite the differences from a national parliament—above all the fact that there is no division corresponding to that between government and opposition—the proceedings at its sessions in the hemicycle of the *Maison de l'Europe* in Strasbourg are always as serious and sometimes as lively as those in most national Assemblies. From the first the members have voted along party rather than national lines, and three groups exist: the Socialists, the Christian Democrats, and the Liberals and affiliates. In every debate these groups decide their line of action and the Socialist group in particular (and the others to a growing extent) never fails to appoint a spokesman to put forward its views in detail.

It has become the tradition for the members of the Executives to attend the parliamentary sessions and reply to the points raised in the debate. There is also a steady flow of written parliamentary questions about every possible aspect of the Commissions' and the High Authority's activities.

The Parliament is a deceptive institution. Anyone attending its sessions and hearing the detailed technical debates or the impassioned speeches on political integration may tend to over-estimate its importance. Lacking the essential characteristic of a democratic parliament— direct contact with the electors—it remains a phantom assembly; it enacts the role of a parliament, but it has no powers and its members no constituencies. In the Paris and Rome Treaties, provision is made for it to be directly elected, and this would bring it to life at once as one of the most powerful forces in the Common Market: the implications of such a move, and the reasons it has so far been delayed, we shall look at in a later chapter.

A REPRESENTATIVE 'SOUNDING-BOARD'

At the same time as any measure is submitted to the Parliament, it also goes before the Economic and Social Committee. A body which has no real equivalent in Britain, the Committee was set up to ensure that the various economic interests which will be affected by the Common Market should have their say in how it is created. Of the 101 members, who meet several times a year in Brussels, one third come from employers' organisations of various kinds throughout the Six countries, one third from trade union organisations, and the rest are representatives of 'the general interest' and the liberal professions: leading economists, lawyers, atomic experts and so on. The members of the Committee are appointed by the Council of Ministers on the basis of alternative lists submitted by the governments, which themselves consult the organisations to be represented. The Committee was modelled on the Consultative Committee of workers, employers and consumers which had operated successfully in the Coal and Steel Community.

To provide a sounding-board for the Common Market a body was needed where a railway workers' representative from Germany would sit alongside a French industrialist, a Dutch farmer with an Italian economist, to give their views on the effects of the EEC Commission's proposals. When opinions are divided in the Committee—which is often—the divisions are less along national lines than between employers on the one side and workers on the other, with the third group holding the balance and often wary of coming down on one side or the other.

As a result the Committee's major role in its first four years has been as a forum for the views of the various sectors, enabling the Commission to estimate the reactions that its proposals have provoked throughout the member countries. The actual 'Opinions' which the Committee adopts on the measures before it tend to reflect the diversity of the views held by its members, rather than to contain a single clear-cut synthesis. On occasions where it is unanimous, however, as it may well be on technical amendments or proposals, its views inevitably carry considerable weight, and are likely to be taken into account by the EEC Commission. Despite the strictly limited role which the Governments rather cautiously assigned to it, efforts were made during the first four years of the Committee's existence to give it publicity and increase its influence. It seems not unlikely—and highly desirable—that with the development of the Common Market it will grow in importance.

The Committee's working methods resemble very much those of the Parliament. It is divided into a number of 'specialised sections' containing those of its members particularly interested in a given field. After a *règlement* has been presented by the member of the Common Market Commission responsible, it is given a first reading by the relevant specialised section, which then works out first and final drafts of the 'Opinion' which the Committee, after a debate in plenary session, will adopt. As with the Parliament, the work is done in the greatest detail and the whole procedure may take anything up to a year.

DECISION BY COMPROMISE: THE COUNCIL OF MINISTERS

At last the measure whose course we have been following is officially before the Council, accompanied by the detailed comments and suggestions of the Parliament and the Economic and Social Committee. It is up to the Council to take the decision which will bring it into effect. It is here, however, that the toughest stage of all begins. Any proposal from the Commission is bound to contain some elements with which some of the member States do not agree, and before the final decision can be taken an attempt must be made to reach a compromise.

The Council itself is composed of ministers from the Six countries— usually the six Foreign Ministers, although others may join them or take their place when their particular sector, such as agriculture or transport, is under discussion: the debate on the common agricultural policy in December 1961 and January 1962 saw all six Ministers of

Agriculture present, as well as most of the Foreign Ministers and several Ministers of Economic Affairs—more than a dozen ministers in all.

Before the proposal comes before the ministers, a further attempt is made to iron out the differences. Under the auspices of the Council, which has its own Secretariat in Brussels, groups of national experts again go through the Commission's text, making what concessions they can on the points at issue. Then the Permanent Representatives of the Six States, national diplomats who meet regularly in Brussels to prepare the work of the Council, themselves engage in a last careful examination of the difficulties. Once this sifting process is complete the only problems which are put to the ministers are those where a major decision, which only the minister himself has the authority to make, is required to grant the concessions needed for agreement.

The importance of the Council grows steadily as the process of creating the Common Market gets into full swing. Meetings are now held at least once a month, and last several days: the agenda grows in length and variety and may range from detailed decisions on tariff quotas to crucial debates on the Commission's proposals concerning one or other of the common policies. The most spectacular so far, the session on the common agricultural policy and the move to the second stage of the Common Market, lasted on and off for three weeks, with a total of over 150 hours of sittings.

Inevitably the fact of working so closely together over a period of time gives the ministers a genuine appreciation of each other's problems and outlook. There is never any question of measures being steam-rollered through against the opposition of a member State: always a compromise is sought. The Council works closely with the Common Market Commission, whose members take part in the Council meetings, and which may be called in to make changes in its proposals to accommodate the compromises on which the ministers are agreed. The Treaty incidentally lays down that even where a majority decision is possible, the Council cannot make amendments in the Commission's proposals without the Commission's agreement, except by unanimous vote.

Once the règlement has been adopted by the Council, it acquires force of law throughout the Community as soon as the texts in the four official languages are published. The next move then lies with the Commission. In most cases the règlements give only a general outline of how the Treaty is to be applied, and the Commission proceeds to draw up detailed directives for their implementation: these too have to be approved by the Council. Once they have come into effect it is up to the Commission to ensure that they are applied by the member States. Should it discover an infringement of the Treaty or of the Council's decisions, there are a series of steps which it can take: first a letter to the State concerned asking for an explanation; then a 'motivated opinion' calling on it to put an end to the infringement; and if that fails to have any effect, then recourse to legal action before the Court of Justice of the European Communities.

HIGH COURT OF APPEAL, AND INTERPRETER OF THE TREATY

The Court of Justice, like the Assembly, was one of the original institutions of the Coal and Steel Community, and had its jurisdiction extended in 1958 to include all three Communities. It is probably the least known of the Institutions, mainly because most of the numerous cases it has dealt with over the past ten years have concerned complex aspects of the coal and steel market: the operation of a fund for equalisation of scrap prices, the breaking-up of coal marketing cartels, or publicity for transport rates and conditions.

The Court is perhaps best thought of as a supreme court of appeal for the whole European Community. Individuals, firms, the Institutions of the Communities and the member Governments can all bring cases before it, and all are bound by its decisions. The Court is the final authority on the interpretation of the Treaties.

Housed in a specially constructed modern building in a quiet side-street in Luxembourg, it has all the procedural solemnity which befits its vast responsibilities. The Court is composed of seven judges (two Italians and one from each other member country) and two 'advocates-general' (one French and one German). The procedure it follows is normal practice in Continental courts, but naturally differs markedly from what is known in Britain. Let us assume that the Common Market is bringing a case against a member State for infringing the Treaty (which was indeed the form taken by the first major Common Market case in 1961). First the two parties present their cases in writing, exchange written arguments, and supply documentary evidence: then there is a public hearing at which both sides plead their cases. Some time later there is a further hearing at which one of the Advocates-General gives his own impartial estimate of the merits of the case and his considered views as to what judgement the Court should pass. This is, however, merely an expert interpretation of the facts of the case and the relevant clauses of the Treaty: it is not binding on the Court, which when it gives its ruling, at a later session, not infrequently departs from what the Advocate-General has suggested.

The very fact that there is no appeal against its judgements, added to the fact that it is sole judge of what the Treaty really means, makes the Court potentially an extremely powerful institution. It is too early to say what role it will play in shaping the Common Market, but if the first ten years of the Coal and Steel Community are anything to go by it will be an important one. Every ruling it makes finds its justification in the text of one of the Treaties, which all leave scope for interpretation. From the start the Court refused to limit itself to narrow interpretations of the Paris Treaty, setting up the ECSC, but took into account a wide range of factors, economic as well as legal, in assessing whether the actions or decisions on which it had to pass judgement served the aims of the Community as set out in the first few articles of the Treaty. To an even greater extent than the Paris Treaty the Treaties of Rome are 'outline' treaties which are given substance by the decisions of the Council and the Commissions, and there are numerous points at which the Court is likely to be called upon sooner or later to determine how the Treaty should be interpreted. The first few Common Market cases have mostly concerned infringements by member countries of the measures reducing obstacles to trade, but already there are indications of the shape of things to come. A Dutch Court has appealed to the Court of Justice of the Communities for a ruling on the interpretation of the articles of the Treaty relating to rules of competition—anti-cartel and monopoly rules—and many cases can be expected in this field once the Regulations which came into force in 1962 start to be applied.

Meanwhile the running of the Coal and Steel Community continues to involve a steady flow of cases, many of them brought by individual firms which quarrel with a High Authority decision—others, as we shall see, by member States which dispute the High Authority's interpretation of the Treaty.

* * *

That then is how the Common Market works—the machinery which is being used to set it up and will run it when it is complete. There are other institutions, such as the Social Fund or the European Investment Bank, but the five bodies we have mentioned—one drafting legislation, one taking decisions, two of a consultative nature and the Court to settle disputes—provide the essential institutional framework.

The framework for the other two Communities (ECSC and Euratom) differs very little. They share with the Common Market the European Parliament and the Court, and Euratom also comes within the scope of the Economic and Social Committee, though it has in addition a more specialised Scientific and Technical Committee and an Advisory Committee on Nuclear Research. The Coal and Steel Community differs from the other two, as we have seen, mainly in the fact that its Executive, the High Authority, has greater powers in relation to the Council of Ministers. It also has its own source of income—a levy of up to 2 per cent on the annual turnover of the coal and steel firms of the Six—whereas the Brussels Communities are dependent upon contributions from the member States. On many matters it can take decisions which are directly binding on firms or even on member States. Nevertheless the experience of recent years has shown that it is virtually powerless (as at the time of the coal crisis in 1958) to enforce a solution with which some of the member Governments disagree.

With this outline before us of the workings of the Common Market institutions in Brussels, Strasbourg and Luxembourg, we can go on to see what the Rome Treaty involves, and what stage has been reached in applying it.

2

From Customs Union to Common Market

WE HAVE seen what is the ultimate aim of the Common Market: to merge the economies of the member States into one, by breaking down the barriers between them and working out common policies. We have outlined the elaborate and carefully balanced system of institutions set up to carry out this aim. Now we can look more closely at what it in fact involves: what are the stages, what are the final goals in the various fields, and what progress has been made towards them.

For the sake of clarity I shall distinguish three stages, though in fact they are closely inter-linked and largely simultaneous. The first stage is the customs union, where all goods can move freely throughout the area; the second is the common market strictly so-called, when all discrimination based on nationality is removed; and the third stage, that of genuine economic union, involves the application of common policies in those sectors where the role of the State in the economy makes them necessary.

DOWN WITH THE CUSTOMS POSTS

Back in 1948 when European unity was still a vague and glowing ideal, a friend of mine was amongst the groups of German students who stormed the frontier to set fire to customs posts. Fifteen years later, the Common Market is well on the way to achieving that most symbolic of all steps to unity, the removal of the customs barriers.

For a customs union—the first step towards the Common Market—means two quite simple things: that goods of all kinds move freely from one member country to another, unhindered by customs or quotas or other restrictions of any kind; and that goods from the rest of the world are subject to an identical level of duty wherever they enter the area.

Under the Rome Treaty the Six countries were to remove the duties on trade between them by 10 per cent stages over a 12-year transitional period. In May 1960, however, the rate of reductions was speeded up. By January 1st, 1962, the cuts made amounted to 40 per cent of the duties in force on January 1st, 1957, and a further 'accelerated' cut of 10 per cent which came into effect on July 1st meant that in three and a half years the customs duties on industrial goods were reduced by half. (For agricultural products, other than those coming under the common farm policy, the two 'accelerated' cuts were both of 5 not 10 per cent, with the second one applying only to a restricted list, so that the total reduction now amounts to 35 per cent.) If things go according to plan, and the economic situation remains satisfactory, then on January 1st, 1967, there will be no customs duties left on trade between the member countries (including the new members) of the Common Market.

Quantitative restrictions on trade were also removed ahead of schedule. On January 1st, 1959, existing import quotas were made available for imports from all member countries without discrimination and increased by 20 per cent; and limited quotas were granted where previously imports had been altogether banned. On December 31st, 1961, a mere three years from the first increases, all quantitative restrictions on trade within the Common Market were removed (for industrial goods though not for agricultural products). At the same time as customs duties and quotas other restrictions with equivalent effects are also being lifted; and where there are revenue duties (intended not to protect home industry but to yield revenue) they must either be removed or replaced by other forms of taxation.

Removing the duties on trade between the Six has its natural corollary in the application of a Common Tariff to goods imported from the outside world. If member countries continued to apply their different national tariffs, there would be an incentive to traders to bring their imports into all parts of the Community via the countries with the lowest duties—in most cases Germany or Benelux—thus causing a 'deflection' of trade.

Establishing the Common External Tariff was a vast and complicated operation. For certain goods of crucial importance to one or other member country (and one or two per cent on a duty may mean survival or extinction to a marginal industry) a level had already been negotiated and written into the annexes to the Treaty. For most of the rest it was the arithmetical average of the four existing customs tariffs (the three Benelux countries already had a single tariff) which the Six adopted, and this meant some eighteen months of continual work for customs experts combining the thousands of different headings in the national tariffs into a single list. Lastly there remained the hard core of some seventy products, known as 'List G', for which the common duty had to be negotiated. These were the products over which national interests were in collision, and in very many cases the experts failed to agree and the matter went to the highest level. For over a year there was hardly a meeting of the Council at which the Ministers did not have the Tariff on their agenda, until eventually in mid-1961 agreement was reached on all items except oil and petroleum products, which are still unsettled. A random example shows the kind of difficulties involved: deciding the level of duty on aircraft parts involved the Ministers in a prolonged debate on the future of the Community's own aircraft industry. The Common External Tariff was one of the first questions to cause matters on which the experts reached deadlock to go to the Ministers for decision.

In its importance to the Common Market, however, the Tariff has repaid the labour that the Six put into it. Its role in cementing their awareness of the Common Market as a unit has been inestimable. Hardly was the Tariff ready (in February 1960, long before the negotiations on List G were over) than it had to be presented to the rest of the world in GATT.[1] It had to serve as a basis for two major sets of negotiations, in which under the terms of Article 111 of the Treaty the EEC Commission negotiated on behalf of the whole Community, and the Six had thus no option but to operate as a unit.

First came the 're-binding' operations: the Six had to prove to their trading partners that the total effect of their new single tariff was no more restrictive than that of the four separate tariffs which they had previously 'bound' (i.e. committed themselves not to raise without negotiations) under the General Agreement. Although the high French and Italian duties would be coming down as they were gradually aligned on the Common Tariff, the German and Benelux duties on many products were due to be raised to bring them into line, and countries traditionally exporting to this area inevitably protested.

[1] The General Agreement on Tariffs and Trade, signed after the war by all the major non-Communist trading countries, is the 'charter' of international trade— the 'rules of the game'. It is built upon the 'Most Favoured Nation' clause by which any tariff concessions made to another country must be extended to all the Contracting Parties. The exception under which the creation of the Common Market is possible allows a group of countries to create a customs union amongst themselves provided they have precise plans, with a time-limit, for reducing *and finally removing* customs duties amongst themselves. The Contracting Parties to the GATT meet regularly and it provides a forum for the discussion of world-wide trade problems.

When this first round was over—though not to everyone's satisfaction—the Six went into the negotiation for all-round tariff cuts proposed by the then American Secretary of State, Mr. Douglas Dillon. In exchange for equivalent concessions, they offered to make a twenty per cent cut in the level of the Common External Tariff before it was ever applied. How these negotiations progressed we shall see in the following chapter. From the point of view of the rest of the world, the gradual application of the Common External Tariff inevitably causes the Six to be thought of as a single trading unit. Correspondingly, the negotiations on the tariff and the reactions (often hostile) which it provoked strengthened their sense of unity and provided the first step, as we shall see below, towards a common commercial policy.

'ACCELERATION'

The Treaty of Rome lays down a detailed time-table for the implementation of the Common Market, and the decision to start making cuts in duties at a faster rate than the Treaty required provided the clearest possible proof of both the success and vitality of the Common Market, and also of its flexibility. First mooted in the summer of 1959, when it was becoming clear that the first cuts in duties made at the start of the year would have none of the dire consequences which had been foretold, the 'acceleration' received the general support of industry throughout the Community. The EEC Commission emphasised that the Six should take advantage of the boom conditions to press ahead as fast as possible with the customs union. At the same time, lest the balance of the Treaty be disturbed, it was agreed to speed up work on applying all the aspects of the Treaty and especially on preparing the common farm policy. The second 'acceleration' was decided on in May 1960 after only technical difficulties, and the half-way mark on the removal of customs barriers was reached two and a half years ahead of schedule.

WORKERS ON THE MOVE?

Unrestricted movement of goods means a steady growth in trade amongst the member countries, and bigger markets and increased competition for the industrialists: but if all other barriers remain intact, it does nothing to bring about a merger of the separate economies. To achieve a common market the movements of the other factors of production—labour, services and capital—must be freed as well.

If a Clydeside mechanic decides to take a job in Slough, there are no frontiers or restrictions to hinder him; a manufacturer in Lille has no difficulty in taking on a charge-hand from Marseilles: and it is just such freedom of movement and decision that the Common Market is to bring about from one end of the member countries to the other. Employers will be able to advertise their vacancies, and workers take jobs and settle with their families, irrespective of national frontiers.

Despite alarmist talk of floods of foreign workers—and the bogey of 'cheap Italian labour' is not the sole preserve of English left-wing Jeremiahs—free movement of labour has had little immediate effect inside the Common Market. For one thing, there has always been a steady flow of workers from the centres of unemployment to the industrial areas where manpower was short: tens of thousands of Italians were working in the mines and on the building sites of Belgium, Germany and Luxembourg long before the Treaty of Rome was thought of or signed. Indeed, the first steps the EEC Commission took were to ensure that these migrant workers could obtain in any member country the full social security benefits to which the contributions they had paid in any part of the Community entitled them.

The over-riding principle of the Regulations on free movement, which came into effect in 1961, is, it is true, the right of workers to take jobs wherever they wish within the Common Market. But their most important practical effect is to give the thousands of migrant workers in the Community full equality of status with the nationals of the countries where they work. They will be able to settle freely and bring their families to join them; and, most important of all, the ever present threat of a cancelled work permit when conditions on the labour market slacken will now be removed. Foreign workers will cease to be a useful commodity, to be exploited when labour is short and sent back whence they came when they are no longer needed: they will cease, from the point of view of labour legislation, to be 'foreign' workers at all.

Machinery is to be set up to bring the employment bureaux of the member countries into close liaison, but for the first fortnight after a job becomes vacant national workers will retain priority (except where a foreign worker is asked for by name). Similarly, workers from inside the Common Market have priority for a limited period over workers from non-member countries.

Important though the principles of free movement and of equal rights undoubtedly are, two developments have combined to lessen their effects. The first is the not-too-distant prospect of a labour shortage in the Common Market as a whole. Throughout 1961 and early 1962 both Germany and the Netherlands, with the acutest labour shortages, had three or more jobs vacant for every person registered as unemployed: but what they need are skilled or semi-skilled workers, and Italy herself—with the only remaining reserves of manpower in the Common Market—has begun since the middle of 1961 to face a similar problem in the industrialised areas of the North: she is liable to need her own workers as fast as she can train them.[1] As a result 'occupational mobility'—the ability to tackle a more highly skilled job —has become an essential complement to mere geographical mobility. The EEC Commission has recognised this from the start, and in 1961 it worked with the German authorities on a 'crash training programme' in Italy for thousands of workers to fill vacant posts in Germany. In 1962 it went further and drew up far-reaching plans for a common vocational training policy, to be operated at Community level, co-ordinating the work of the member countries in an attempt to meet the requirements of the Community as a whole.

Whilst these long-term plans are being drawn up to train the workers of the member countries, increasing numbers of Greek, Spanish and even Turkish citizens are being called upon to meet the German labour shortage in particular, and from the member countries' point of view at least one of the most valuable elements of the Community's association with Greece (see below, p. 131), and probably with other less developed countries, will be the assurance of a steady flow of manpower.

Secondly, a longer-term development which cannot be overlooked is the undoubted decline in the importance of movement of workers as compared with movements of capital. It is becoming more profitable to take the job to the worker than to expect the worker to come to the job. Modern industries using electric power and easily transportable materials are no longer tied to the old centres of coal and steel production; and many firms are realising the advantages in terms of morale and stability of setting up their plants in Southern Italy instead of expecting the Sicilian or the Neapolitan to transplant himself to distant, cold and often inhospitable parts of Northern Europe.

NO BARRIERS FOR BUSINESS

It is not only the workers who are to be guaranteed freedom of movement in the Community: by the end of the transitional period—that

[1] Firms in the industrial North of Italy have even begun advertising for skilled and semi-skilled Italian workmen . . . in Germany.

is, by 1970 at the latest—professional men will be allowed to practise, and firms to establish themselves, anywhere within the area of the Common Market.

Unrestricted 'right of establishment' for firms (combined with free movement of capital) will constitute a guarantee that no viable chance of economic development goes by default because restrictions stop another Community firm from stepping in to exploit it. To take an example—and one which has raised much controversy—much good agricultural land in parts of France at present lies unfarmed: under free right of establishment German farm labourers working in France, and at a later stage German farmers too, can move in and start farming it.

Under 'free supply of services' the barriers on the activities of professional men and artisans are to be gradually removed: a draughtsman from Liège will be free to work for a French firm in Mulhouse, a Hamburg architect to set up his offices in Naples, or a Dutch contracting firm to tender for a public works scheme in the South of France.

From the Commission's first studies to the final decision by the Council in October 1961 it took over two and a half years to work out the 'general programmes' for implementing the Treaty in these fields —thus providing incidentally an excellent example of how slow and thoroughly the Common Market mills can grind. Marshalling the data took nine months, haggling with the national experts over the original texts another five; the Assembly and the Economic and Social Committee took a full year to give their views, and it needed from April to October 1961 for the EEC Commission's experts to thrash out the compromises which enabled the Ministers to take their decision.

As it finally emerged the plan has four stages, with restrictions being lifted first where this will raise least problems: thus, for example, restrictions on establishment or the supply of services in textiles, the leather industry, chemicals, metal-working, under-writing, and farming on land abandoned for more than two years must be abolished by the end of 1963; restrictions in insurance, the food industry and (as far as equivalence of diplomas allows) accounting and auditing by the end of 1965; restrictions in the theatrical profession, transport and personal services by the end of 1967, and all other restrictions by the end of the transitional period.

A necessary complement to these measures is an active attempt to ensure mutual recognition of diplomas and professional qualification between the member States—and this in turn will lead to co-ordination of teaching and training programmes.

Following the passage of the 'general programmes' the Commission has begun to produce the long series of detailed 'directives' which will ensure the implementation of the principles of free establishment and free supply of services in the various fields. Their effect is hardly likely to be sudden or spectacular, but in the long run their impact in breaking down barriers of discrimination and prejudice between member countries will be considerable. Free movement of workers, of services, of goods and materials—one last factor of production, and perhaps the most crucial, remains: capital. Inside Britain (or France, or Germany) anyone with capital can invest or use it how and where he thinks it will be most profitable. By the end of the transitional period similar freedom will exist throughout the Common Market; and even more important, firms will be free to seek the capital they need wherever there are funds available.

Freeing capital movements can pose delicate problems because of their possible effects upon the strength of national currencies, and for once no time-table is laid down in the Treaty. The first four years have been at least the easiest steps taken in the desired direction. The first step was a set of directives, issued in May 1960 and indicating minimum levels of compulsory liberalisation. As a result the Six now grant automatically any application to allow capital movements for direct investment, for medium- or short-term financing of trade, or for the purchase of shares with a stock-exchange quotation; they also allow unrestricted movements of funds for personal requirements. Then there is a conditional commitment (which can be withdrawn after consultation with other member countries) to allow capital transfers for purely financial transactions, and for medium- and long-term transactions for securities not quoted on a stock-exchange. The residual group, on which controls are maintained, comprises short-term capital movements, and these are unlikely to be freed until there is some harmonisation of national monetary policies, lest the way be left open for sudden flows of 'hot money' from one country to another with unfortunate effects on the balance of payments situation.

Others of the multiple restrictions in this field are soon due for the axe. Work started in September 1961 on steps to ensure that any citizen of the Community can hold shares in the capital of firms in other member States. Another aim is to free capital movements linked with invisible transactions (payments for services, etc.). In 1961 the Dutch authorities opened their capital market to loan issues by firms from other Common Market countries (or by the Community institutions) and in January 1962 the Commission appealed to other member countries to do likewise.

Like many other aspects of the Common Market, freeing of capital movements is unspectacular, but in its effects it promises to be one of the most important. Capital is in any case the most mobile of the factors of production, and with unrestricted movement it should rapidly begin to flow irrespective of national boundaries. Combined with free right of establishment this will encourage entrepreneurs and investors to think of the Community as a single economy, and to seek the most promising opportunities within the area taken as a whole. Hardly less important, gaps between interest rates on the various money markets will then tend to disappear, thus making a major contribution to the common monetary policy with which the freeing of capital movements must as we shall see be closely linked.

'CONTRE LES CARTELS'

One inevitable—and intended—effect of the Common Market is to encourage the emergence of bigger and more efficient firms. The removal of economic barriers is bound to be followed (and has indeed been followed to a quite striking extent) by mergers and concentrations, trading and specialisation agreements, and the establishment of joint subsidiaries. On the one hand the manufacturers want to be as well equipped as possible, in scale and range of output, to benefit from the new and bigger market—and the easiest way to do so is often to link up with or absorb their direct competitors in the same field. On the other hand they want to protect themselves against increasing competition—and again agreements of one kind or another provide the best answer to their problem.

It is precisely here however that the danger lies. By getting together they may reap all the advantages of the bigger market, preventing the consumer from benefiting as the Treaty means him to. As early as 1959 the head of the EEC Commission's 'Competition' Department stated 'international agreements exist which are intended to frustrate the effects of the first tariff cuts'. Secondly, there is the risk that a single big firm—perhaps resulting from the merger of firms in two member countries—may achieve a dominant position on a sector of the market and exploit it at the expense of the consumer.

The answer to this threat—the way to stop the Community be

coming, as critics from the left have sometimes suggested, the 'common market of the capitalists' (but not of the workers or the consumers)—lies in anti-cartel legislation. Since the cartels and agreements to be combatted are likely to be concluded across national frontiers, it has to be legislation applicable at the Community level. The authors of the Treaty, who had written into the preamble that one of its aims was to 'ensure free competition', set out in Articles 85–88 to provide the necessary means. The principles they laid down, like those in the ECSC Treaty, were directly inspired by American anti-trust legislation. Article 85 bans agreements or concerted practices which 'prevent, restrict or distort competition' and Article 86 any action by firms to take unfair advantage of a 'dominant position'.

Working out the detailed form and the instruments of its anti-cartel legislation proved one of the hardest nuts the Common Market has yet had to crack. Strictly speaking, the Treaty required the member States to ensure the application of Articles 85 and 86 until the Community measures had been drafted. In fact, however, three member countries (Italy, Belgium, and Luxembourg) possessed no anti-trust or monopoly legislation at all, whilst French and German legislation presented an extreme contrast, with the German requiring the registration of all agreements, and the French laying the onus of discovery and proof on the authorities. In working out the rules for the Community a compromise between them had to be found: in general, the German view that all agreements must be registered has been accepted, though with exceptions, and with a major concession to the French view in a provision for full-scale investigations. The regulations for the implementation of Articles 85 and 86 of the Treaty were approved by the Council of Ministers in December 1961, a year behind the schedule laid down in the Treaty, and came into effect in January 1962. The system as it has emerged works like this. From the time the Regulations came into effect, any agreement between firms, association of firms, or concerted trade practices, *which are liable to affect trade between member States*, and which result, intentionally or not, in the restriction or distortion of competition are automatically null and void. Article 85 refers in particular to price-fixing; limiting of output, of marketing, of technical development or of investment; market- or supply-sharing; discrimination between clients; and the tying of contracts to the acceptance of other transactions: it is thus pretty comprehensive. The EEC Commission is however empowered to grant exemption from the ban —a 'negative attestation'—to agreements or practices which (Art. 85—

iii) contribute to improving total output or distribution, or promoting technical or economic progress, and which ensure the consumers a fair share of the benefits which result without imposing on the firms involved any restrictions not strictly necessary for the purpose or giving them the chance to prevent competition for a major part of the output involved.

With certain exceptions, all agreements, associations or concerted practices concluded after the Regulations came into force have to be notified to the Commission, which may then either grant them the desired 'negative attestation', or alternatively take a decision requiring the firms to put an end to them as infringements of the Treaty. The kinds of agreement for which the obligation to notify the Commission does not apply are specifically indicated in the regulations, viz.: those between firms in one member State only which do not affect either imports or exports; those between two firms only (even in different countries) which merely limit re-sale conditions of one partner, or the activities of a licence-holder; and those between any number of firms which cover only standardisation of products or technical research the fruits of which are available to all participants.

As for agreements, associations or concerted practices already existing when the Regulations came into effect, they have to be notified to the Commission by November 1962, unless of course they come under the exceptions mentioned above: the firms concerned are now given the chance to bring them into line with the new requirements before notifying the Commission.

The Regulations now in force, although mainly devoted to cartel (Art. 85), also cover the application of Article 86 on monopolies. They quite simply state that the Commission may take and enforce decisions putting an end to infractions of Article 86, which is aimed at 'one or more firms abusing a dominant position in the common market or in a substantial part of it' to impose unfair prices or other conditions of sale or to limit competition in any of the other ways defined in connection with cartels.

The Commission is endowed with wide powers to enforce the Regulations. On its own initiative or at the request of any interested party it may investigate, in collaboration with the national authorities, the affairs of firms or associations. Also, should market conditions and price fluctuations in any particular sector give it reason to suspect the existence of a cartel it can carry out a full investigation—a major concession, this, to French practice. It can impose small fines for false information and fines of up to a million dollars or a tenth of the annual turnover of the firms involved for wilful infringements of Articles 85 or 86.

It is too early yet to estimate what the force of the anti-cartel and monopoly Regulations will be. Much will clearly depend on the severity of the criteria by which the EEC Commission applies them. The Commission does not have to give its prior authorisation, as does the ECSC High Authority, for mergers or concentrations such as are bound to occur in increasing numbers as firms adapt themselves to the increased scale of the common market, and the effectiveness of the Regulations in ensuring that the benefits of the Common Market are passed on to the consumer may well depend on the interpretation the Commission gives to the terms of Article 86 on 'dominant positions' in the market.

DUMPING, STATE AID AND STATE MONOPOLIES

Looking at the economies which were to be merged to form the Common Market the authors of the Rome Treaty discovered quite a number of factors which would put the businessmen of the member countries on an unequal footing—and duly worked out how to achieve a fair equality of conditions.

One of the dangers foreseen was the old trading bogey known as dumping—by which producers facing a glut on their home market export the goods on their hands at less than cost price, thus undercutting producers in another country. As customs barriers fall, dumping theoretically becomes easier. An ingenious formula was therefore devised, known as the 'boomerang clause', and came into effect in 1959: under it a producer may send back to the exporting country, free from duties of any kind, goods being dumped on his market—thus presumably beating the culprit at his own game. Ingenious though it is, the formula has so far been little used: where dumping has occurred, a note or recommendation from the EEC Commission, backed by the threat of action before the Court of Justice, has sufficed to bring about a satisfactory settlement.

Far more important is the question of 'State aid'. All governments provide assistance of one kind or another from their own resources for some sectors of the national economy—thus giving them what becomes, inside the Common Market, an unfair advantage. Under the terms of the Treaty (Arts. 92–4) such aid has to be gradually withdrawn, although a number of valid exceptions are permitted (aid to develop backward areas, aid to parts of West Germany hit by the division of the country, aid to projects which are of common European interest, and aid granted to individual consumers for social rather than economic reasons).

The Commission's work on the investigation of State aid, in close collaboration with groups of national experts, got into its stride in the early months of 1962 and as a result of agreements reached, or of recommendations from the Commission, the following cases of aid were either adjusted so as not to contravene the Treaty or else were brought to an end: in Germany a system for equalising out the costs of the synthetic and natural rubber industries; in France, aid to investment goods industries; in Italy tax advantages for home-produced cars, indirect financial aid to the agricultural machinery industry, and aid to the ship-building industry (the aid being withdrawn in the case of orders from Common Market countries). Ship-building is one of the industries most heavily dependent on aid: the situation in France has also been under review, and in April 1962 the Commission asked the Federal German government to drop plans for helping its ship-building industry.

Thirdly, there is the case of 'State monopolies'. In France and Italy especially, the State has the sole right to manufacture and sell certain commodities—cigarettes and tobacco, for instance, or salt—which are sometimes a considerable source of revenue. For conditions to be equal, other manufacturers clearly had to be granted access to these markets. The Treaty therefore lays down that the national monopolies must be adjusted so as not to put them at a disadvantage. By the beginning of 1962 steps had been taken to adjust the Italian tobacco, cigarette-paper and quinine monopolies, and already Dutch and Belgian cigarettes are appearing in the tobacconists' kiosks alongside State-produced 'Nazionali'. In April 1962 the Commission sent recommendations to Italy about its monopoly on matches, and to France about monopolies on matches, tobacco, potash and imported oil.

So far the Commission has taken no stand on whether it is sufficient to take steps to ensure other EEC producers access to the markets or whether in the long run the monopolies will have to be abolished altogether.

HARMONISATION OF LEGISLATION

Complex though it is, even the staunchest advocates of the Rome Treaty have never pretended that it is exhaustive: only time and experience could reveal some of the less obvious (though not necessarily less important) cases of legislative or administrative discrimination against citizens of other member States. Consequently the Treaty (Arts. 100–102) gives the Commission a free hand to deal with 'the ones that got away'. During the first four years work was started on a mixed bag of subjects. One of the most important concerns patents and trade marks: in close collaboration with national experts the Commission is working out European patents legislation which would not replace national legislation but would enable inventors or manufacturers to obtain a patent which would be valid for the whole of the Common Market.

Rules on colouring-matter and additives in food are another case where free trade makes it essential to do away with differences between national legislation. Again, the Commission is seeking to dove-tail national campaigns against tobacco mildew and measures to prevent the spreading of plant or animal diseases (an important consideration for trade in agricultural produce).

In each case it is the Commission which has taken the initiative in consulting the States, and it has where necessary drawn up directives aimed at getting them to co-ordinate their action. It is not generally realised to what an extent the Common Market involves not merely the lowering of customs barriers, or major decisions on this or that common policy, but also an immense amount of quiet valuable work on removing the pointless and out-dated differences and restrictions which have grown up over the years around the frontiers which are now due to come down.

It is the gradual removal of restrictions and discrimination of all kinds that will eventually merge the economies of the member countries into a common market. The process has only just begun, and even when it is complete its effects will not be spectacular—indeed they may go almost unnoticed: but once legislative and administrative barriers are gone, the psychological and emotional barriers to understanding which they foster will not long survive them.

3

Common Policies

(i) COMMERCIAL AND ECONOMIC POLICY

THE PROCESS of removing barriers and ending discrimination, essential though it is to the creation of the Common Market, is little more than a preparatory phase: it leaves untouched many large and vitally important sectors of national economic life—both economic policy in a general sense, and certain particularly important sectors, such as agriculture or transport, where the modern State takes a direct hand in the economic process. Clearly, if the member countries are to be successfully merged into a single economy—and it must be clearly recognised that this is the final aim—then at the very least the national policies in the various component parts must not conflict. In some cases, the Treaty requires no more than adequate co-ordination of national policies: in others it specifically calls for the replacement of separate national policies by a single policy embracing the whole of the Common Market. Moreover, even in sectors to which the Treaty makes little or no specific reference, the growing inter-dependence of the national economies resulting from freer movement of goods and of factors of production has already begun to make the governments aware of the need to co-ordinate their policies; and this realisation will be brought home to them to an ever-increasing extent.

The harmonisation of national policies—and *a fortiori* the adoption of a common 'Community policy'—is a much more complex and far-reaching step than the removal of discrimination. It impinges more sharply and directly on national autonomy and on vested interests of all kinds. That is why the first four-year stage of the transitional period was devoted essentially to clearing the ground by getting the removal of barriers and discrimination under way. The second stage, which began for the Six member countries in January 1962, has already begun to see common or co-ordinated policies worked out and in some cases the first steps taken in applying them.[1] In commercial policy the ground-work had been started during the first stage; in agriculture the

[1] The early months of 1962, when these chapters were being written, saw

first major decisions had to be taken as a condition of the move to the second stage, and started coming into effect on July 1st, 1962; in other sectors—transport, energy, or monetary policy—there is still a long way to go, and the basic decisions on the shape of the policy have often still to be taken. Yet in all these fields, and others too, the end of the transitional period (1970 or probably even sooner) should see either a single policy for the Community or at least the closest collaboration between the member governments in the policies they apply.

It is evident that the fields of policy dealt with below, although at present treated separately by the Community authorities who have to follow the outline of the Treaty, cannot be kept in water-tight compartments: they inter-act and are inter-dependent, as will emerge to a growing extent. To take only one example, regional planning, the activities of the Investment Bank and the Social Fund, farm structure policy, and vocational training policy are all aspects of one problem: that of the smooth transfer of manpower from farming to industry. Although there is little sign of it as yet, such links can hardly fail to increase the importance of the Common Market Commission, as the only body in a position to ensure co-ordination both between national policies (though without necessarily supplanting them) and between Community policies in the various sectors.

A COMMON COMMERCIAL POLICY

It has often been stressed by the Six that outsiders should not make the mistake of thinking of the Common Market *merely* as a commercial arrangement. It is understandable, however, that this is the aspect which should have attracted the most attention, for it is the field where the need for a merger of national policies into joint Community action is the most urgent and the most clearly evident. A common commercial policy is the logical consequence of a common external tariff, which makes the Community a single unit as far as its trading relations with the rest of the world are concerned.

almost daily developments in all the fields dealt with below: the account given here, based on the situation and probable developments towards the middle of May, will already have been out-dated in many respects—with the outlines of Community policy emerging more clearly—by the time this book appears. I have therefore attempted above all to indicate the lines along which agreement seems likely.

The Treaty (Arts. 110–116) provides for progressive co-ordination of national policies during the transitional period and after that the application in relations with the outside world of a common policy based on uniform principles covering tariff changes, trade and tariff agreements, export policy, and 'defensive trade policy' (including reactions to dumping from abroad).

Although the Treaty lays down no time-limits, pressure of events has left the Six with little option but to begin at once to work out a common policy. We saw above how difficult it proved for them to negotiate some of the crucial duties in the Common External Tariff. Once fixed, although it will be several years before national duties are finally aligned upon it, that Tariff became in a very real sense the basic instrument of the Community's commercial policy.

In the first place, the granting of tariff quotas (quantities of a given product which may be imported either into a particular member country or into the Common Market as a whole, duty-free or at a reduced rate of duty) is now a matter for joint decision. For a certain number of products it is the EEC Commission which has the power to grant tariff quotas, for a specific period, if member States can show that their processing industries are suffering from a shortage. In its decisions taken so far, the Commission has examined each case on its merits, and has not hesitated to refuse quotas, or to grant considerably smaller ones than were applied for, basing its ruling on the interests of the Community as a whole: on a number of occasions, when the member State applying claimed that adequate supplies were not available in the Community, the Commission organised meetings between consumer industries in the country concerned and producers in other member countries with a view to stimulating the flow of intra-Community trade. For other goods, for which member States traditionally depend upon supplies from third countries (and thus could be adversely affected by having to apply a stiff duty under the Tariff), the Commission makes annual proposals on the quotas to be granted for the year, but it is the Council of Ministers which takes the decision, by a qualified majority.[1] In addition the EEC Commission has the power, which it has used in some cases, of permitting member States to delay the alignment of their national customs duties on the Common Tariff. Early in 1962 the first hesitant steps towards a common export policy were taken, when the EEC Commission recommended to member governments to

[1] See Chapter 7 below for an explanation of the significance of 'qualified majority' voting.

restrict the export of one or two products in short supply in the Community as a whole.

A second major aspect of a common commercial policy is the requirement that negotiations with non-member countries about the level of the Tariff should be carried out by the Community as a whole. It is the EEC Commission which is charged with conducting the negotiations (Art. 111) under the terms of a mandate from the Council of Ministers, and with the advice of a Special Committee set up by the Council. As we saw in the previous chapter, the Six have already negotiated about the level of the Tariff with their partners in GATT. One of their first major acts of concerted policy was to offer an across-the-board cut of 20 per cent in the Tariff (with a limited number of exceptions) before it was ever applied, if other major trading countries, and in particular the United Kingdom and the United States, would reciprocate. The GATT Tariff Conference which went on throughout most of 1961 and well into 1962 provided them with an excellent grounding in the difficulties of achieving, on every point to be negotiated, a common position which all the member countries could accept. Time after time points which cropped up in Geneva in the negotiations with one or other country had to be referred back to the Ministers in Brussels; on one occasion it was rumoured that a possible package deal had fallen through because the Belgian Minister felt unable to accept a further half-a-per-cent cut in the Common Tariff on component parts for cars.

The results achieved in the negotiations were less than had been hoped, and varied greatly from country to country. The main agreement negotiated was with the United States, and involved reductions in the American tariff and the future Common Tariff of the Community affecting a flow of trade worth some $1,600 million. This was clearly a major act of common policy, which did much to bring the importance of the Community as a trading unit home to non-member countries.

By the end of the transitional period all tariff or trade agreements of any kind with non-member countries will have to be negotiated for the Common Market as a whole—and by the EEC Commission. For the moment, the first steps have been taken to harmonise the separate agreements which the member countries remain free to conclude. In July 1960 it was agreed that all new agreements with non-member countries should henceforth contain a 'Community clause' under which they could be revised as and when Common Market developments made it necessary. In May 1961 the Six went a step further and accepted a procedure for prior consultation with their Common Market partners and the EEC Commission before concluding any trade agreement: it was also decided that no new separate agreements out-running the transitional period should be signed by member countries.

Since trade and aid are now recognised to be the two sides of one coin, it is reasonable to include under the heading of commercial policy the whole of the Six's policy towards the under-developed world (other than their associated African States). It was in March 1960 that the Finance Ministers of the Six set up an *ad hoc* group to look into the possibility of co-ordinating their policy in the field of aid. When the Development Aid Group was set up (a sort of club of the major industrialised countries, intended as a forum for the discussion of policy on aid to the under-developed countries) those of the Six who were members met first to co-ordinate their approach. In May 1960 the *ad hoc* Committee was turned into a permanent body which provides a framework for regular consultation between high officials on general development-aid policy. In addition the Six now exchange information on specific technical assistance projects as a first step towards co-ordination.

A particularly complex aspect of commercial policy, but a crucial one for trade with the less-developed countries in particular, is that of export credit guarantees, credit insurance, and direct financial credit for trade. Its importance derives from the fact that the less developed countries increasingly seek to pay for their imports over long periods, and that differing national policies as regards the credits which exporters must therefore obtain could give traders in one or other country a marked advantage over their competitors. There already exists an international agreement, known as the Berne Union, laying down rules for credits up to five years. The Six agreed in May 1962, by a formal Council decision, to compulsory prior consultation in all cases where they intend to give direct or indirect State guarantees, partial or total, for credits to exporters covering periods longer than five years. As far as the granting of direct financial advances to the traders by the government or other public authorities is concerned (again for over five years), there is for the moment only an agreement to exchange information, as is also the case for national policy in the field of export credit insurance. A certain amount of progress has however been made towards bringing the various national systems into line, and work is being actively continued.

One field in which the Six are under strong pressure to concert their attitudes and their policy is that of trade relations with Latin America. On the one hand the Latin-American countries are a traditional and rapidly expanding market for European exports, mainly of manufactures and investment goods: on the other, more important still, they are major exporters of commodities, and above all of coffee, to the Community. They have seen their export trade threatened by the preferences granted by the Six to their associated States in Africa, or else, in other cases, by the possible effects of the common farm policy. In July 1960 Brazil, which had been one of the most outspoken critics of Community policy at successive GATT sessions, took the lead in asking the Six for a statement of their policy on such matters as long-term contracts and the stabilisation of world commodity prices. A similar note to the Six from Argentina followed, and in May 1962 a representative of the Organisation of American States arrived in Brussels to explain the concern of the 14 coffee-exporting countries of the area. It was not until early in 1962, however, that the Council of Ministers began considering relations with Latin America as a specific problem, and there is at present no indication of what attitude the Community will officially take: it seems bound to depend on their new association with the African States, on the settlement reached for the Commonwealth countries in the event of British entry, and on future tariff talks with the United States.

A LIBERAL COMMUNITY?

Even with its Six founder members alone the Community is the world's biggest importer of commodities. Its commercial policy will inevitably be of major importance for the whole free world economy, and it is therefore natural to ask whether that policy has shown signs of developing along sufficiently liberal lines.

As far as the actual level of the Common External Tariff is concerned most of the criticism which it provoked came as we have seen from countries which were to be faced with higher duties in their traditional markets (Benelux or Germany) as a result of alignments on the tariff: the Six however firmly defended the view that the overall level of the Common Tariff represented no increase in total protection. Since then the offer of a 20 per cent cut in the level of the Tariff (although in the end it did not amount to so much) was a practical and significant indication of the Community's liberal intentions. But the fact that for a number of important products the reduction offered (and eventually granted) was considerably less than 20 per cent reflects the problem which the Community faces over its commercial policy. The statements and actions of the EEC Commission leave no shadow of doubt that it would like the Community's policy to be a liberal one, contributing to the expansion of world trade: but many of the vital duties in the CET already represent the result of tough bargaining (completed only in 1961) and the countries concerned are loth to accept further concessions.

The effects on the Community's external trade of the common agricultural policy cannot as yet be clearly discerned: they will depend essentially on the price levels which are set, and also on whether and at what rate it leads to increased self-sufficiency in foodstuffs. As we shall see below the existence of the Community, and the reactions of other countries, may provide the necessary stimulus for the conclusion of commodity agreements at the world level.

This may also prove true for tropical products. In the meantime the proposals for major reductions in the Common External Tariff on some tropical products as part of the new agreement on the Association with the African States (see below, pp. 126–130) are a distinctly liberal move. It may be added that a reduction in internal taxation on tropical products in some member countries would also be a major move in a liberal direction.

It is difficult to make any clear-cut judgment on the Community's emergent commercial policy. During its first years it has proved far less protectionist than its critics had feared, and probably rather more liberal than even the optimists had hoped. The entry of Britain, Norway and Denmark would mean such a radical change in its position that it seems pointless to make forecasts, save that the influence of these countries is bound to be in favour of a more liberal Community policy.

MONETARY AND GENERAL ECONOMIC POLICY: CO-ORDINATION AS A FIRST STEP

Governmental economic policy in all its complex aspects—budgetary policy (taxation and expenditure), monetary policy (interest rates, exchange rates), investment, etc.—constitutes an interlocking and interacting whole. The authors of the Rome Treaty did not go so far as to suggest that the member States should adopt a common economic policy, or even harmonise their economic policies as such. All that is required, under the section-heading 'economic policy', is a sufficient degree of co-ordination to ensure the maintenance of an overall balance of payments equilibrium. There is also an admonishment to the member States to 'consider their business cycle policy as a matter of common interest', and one reference to 'the co-ordination of monetary policies'.

It is little enough to build on, but after four years of continuous consultation and preliminary study of the implications of the growth of integration, it is beginning to be possible to discern the pattern of future co-ordination between the member countries in the various fields of economic policy, if not perhaps the speed at which such co-ordination will develop or the extent to which it will eventually be carried.

The incentive has come in part from the activities of the EEC Commission, which has realised from the start that monetary and budgetary policy will be crucial for the final development of the Common Market, and in part from the logic of developing integration: the removal of restrictions on trade and on capital movements means growing inter-dependence between the economies and that in turn makes co-ordination of policies a growing necessity.

Since July 1959 the Finance Ministers of the member countries have met regularly once every three months in the different national capitals of the Community. These meetings (not strictly within the framework of the EEC Council) have provided the opportunity for a continuous exchange of views on every economic and financial aspect of the Common Market. The discussions are frank and wide-ranging, and representatives of the Commission are present and express their views. Apart from the general economic situation, or the problems of one or other member country, the Ministers have talked at various times about monetary co-operation, aid to under-developed countries, harmonisation of taxation policy and methods, freeing of capital movements, and many other problems. Such meetings, and the similar ones at lower levels of the hierarchy organised by the EEC Commission, have created a tradition of consultation and co-operation which has paved the way for the acceptance of the first practical measures adopted, at the instigation of the Commission, in the various fields.

FROM ECONOMIC DIAGNOSIS TO ECONOMIC THERAPY

'Each member State shall practise the economic policy necessary to ensure the balance of its overall balance of payments and to maintain confidence in its currency, whilst taking care to ensure a high level of employment and price stability'. So runs Article 104. 'Business cycle policy'—which covers all aspects of economic policy aimed at maintaining an optimum level of activity, in an expanding economy, with full employment and a healthy balance of payments (or, to take the negative view, at preventing a recession)—is the field where the EEC Commission has done the most to prepare the way for co-ordination of national policies. Any real degree of co-ordination remains however only a target for the future: the general climate of expansion during the first four years of the Common Market has prevented any major problems from occurring where national policies might have clashed;[1] and on the other hand the need for co-ordination which will result from the lowering of barriers to the movement of goods and of the factors of production is only just beginning to make itself felt.

Meanwhile the Commission has from the very start set out to provide the necessary basis for co-ordinated action, by studying constantly and in the fullest detail the economic situation in the member States and in the Community as a whole. Its various studies provide in published form a complete picture of the economic situation at any given time, the recent trends and foreseeable future developments—such as was not previously available, in some cases at least, in the member countries. There are monthly 'graphs and brief notes' on the behaviour of the various economic factors (trade figures, employment, output, prices, etc.), full quarterly reports summing up trends and prospects, and a detailed annual survey. In its quarterly reports in particular the Commission makes constructive suggestions about the policies which the member governments should adopt in the best interests of the Community as a whole; when Germany was facing a continual balance of payments surplus, for instance, the Commission persistently called on her to take steps to increase her imports and also to expand the flow of capital to under-developed countries.

In May 1960 the Commission set up a Business Cycle Committee, of top-level economic experts from the member countries, to advise it on economic trends, and the recommendations to member countries are based on the advice of this Committee. Early in 1962, with a view to improving its economic forecasting, it concluded an agreement with the national governments and economic institutes for regular direct

---

[1] In the E.C.S.C., however, such problems have arisen in a very acute form in the energy field. The High Authority has had only a very limited success in tackling them.

investigations, according to a uniform formula, into businessmen's expectations of future economic trends.

All this, however, comes under what Mr. Kapteyn, a Dutch Socialist M.P., in a report to the European Parliamentary Assembly in February 1962, called 'economic diagnosis'. On that occasion, as on others before and since, the Parliament adopted a resolution calling for the 'diagnosis' to be followed by economic 'therapy'—some positive action to co-ordinate national policies. It has been increasingly realised of late that the removal of trade barriers not only increases the repercussions of one country's economic situation and policy upon its neighbours, but at the same time removes some of the major instruments—quotas, protective tariffs, etc.—by which the economic situation was previously controlled. As a result the Commission and the Business Cycle Committee began in 1961 a detailed examination of the instruments of economic policy available in the different member countries (whilst the Monetary Committee as we shall see did the same for monetary policy). M. Robert Marjolin, the member of the EEC Commission responsible for economic policy questions, has repeatedly insisted on the need to be ready to undertake co-ordinated action should the boom conditions which the Community has so far known show signs of ending. Clearly co-ordination would be far more important in the event of economic difficulties, and harder to achieve unless worked out in advance.

One positive step which will be carried out for the first time in 1962 is the drawing up by all the member States of national 'economic budgets'. This was an idea put forward by the Business Cycle Committee and approved by national experts when put to them by the Commission. Economic budgets constitute a detailed quantitative estimate of the development of the economy in the following year, drawn up under the same headings and in the same form as the national accounts. The system was hitherto practised only in the Netherlands and in France: in the autumn of 1962 all the member countries will work out such budgets and present them to the Commission, which will then use them as a basis for elaborating a single 'economic budget' for the Community as a whole. This will remain confidential, but will be used by the Business Cycle Committee and the Monetary Committee when consulted by the Commission.

MONETARY POLICY

In the monetary field, too, increasingly free trade, and above all the freeing of capital movements, will make the co-ordination of national policies more and more necessary. National policies on bank credit, interest rates, and of course exchange rates will inter-act to an increasing extent. As was mentioned above, capital movements between member States cannot be entirely freed until there is sufficient co-ordination of monetary policies to prevent movements of hot money: changes in national exchange rates—revaluation up or down in terms of the dollar —can prove vital if the overall balance of payments equilibrium is to be maintained; and in the long run, as the European Parliament recognised in a resolution adopted in May 1962, 'A common monetary policy is an essential condition for achieving the economic and political unity of Europe'.

Such progress as has so far been made towards co-ordination of monetary policies is largely due to the work of the Monetary Committee, an advisory body set up (Art. 105) in 1958 'to promote the co-ordination of the policies of the member States in the monetary field in so far as is necessary for the smooth running of the Common Market'. Composed of two representatives of each member State (in most cases one is a high-ranking Treasury official, the other from the Central Bank) and two representatives of the EEC Commission, it has become as was intended a forum for full and frank consultation, and as such has begun to play a role of considerable importance.

Meeting once a month, the Committee examines on each occasion the monetary and financial situation in one of the member States: a representative of the country due for its 'check-up' makes a full report on the situation and on the policy being followed, and a member from another country then follows up with a counter-report pin-pointing problems or matters which seem open to criticism. The discussion which follows is frank and can even be outspoken, and particular aspects of a member country's policy may be freely criticised. In view of Article 107, which requires member States to treat their exchange rate policy as a matter of common interest, particular attention is paid to keeping the gap between official and market exchange rates within reasonable limits.

The Monetary Committee is also the scene of wide-ranging discussions on the general monetary and financial situation and its implications for policy. Amongst the problems which have been thoroughly thrashed out is the question of the monetary implications of Britain's joining the Community: whether and how devaluation of the pound might be avoided (either before or after the accession), and even the heretical question of whether in view of the dangerous implications of a sterling devaluation it might not on the contrary be desirable to revalue the lira and the French franc upwards instead.

The recommendations which the Committee makes to the Commission and to the Council on the basis of its discussions carry considerable weight, particularly as they remain strictly confidential. Moreover, the Chairman of the Committee attends the meetings of the Finance Ministers, to whom he presents the Committee's views and preoccupations. On the other hand the influence of the Committee must not be over-estimated: it remains in the last resort only a valuable forum for consultation. To quote its own Fourth Annual Report (April 1962):

> 'The work of the Monetary Committee has enabled those responsible for the monetary policy of the member States to become better acquainted with the economic and financial structures of the partner countries, to achieve a better understanding of the policy followed in the neighbouring countries, and above all a feeling of collective responsibility for the objectives of the Community.'

Nevertheless, the tradition of consultation was not deeply enough rooted in May 1961 to prevent the German Government carrying out its revaluation of the D-Mark without informing in advance either the Commission or the Monetary Committee, or even its partners, so that the Dutch Cabinet was obliged to follow suit with a snap decision and itself had no time for proper consultation with its Benelux partners. True, the decision was along the lines the Monetary Committee had agreed would be suitable, and which the Commission had recommended: but consultation about the level or timing of the action was completely lacking.

The Monetary Committee has also been concerned with the role of the Community in relation to wider monetary problems, especially that of the position of the dollar. In 1961 it carried out a study of the problems of international liquidity, estimating the value of the various more or less academic schemes then under discussion in monetary quarters. The starting point for the study was a general acceptance of the Community's monetary responsibilities, especially in view of the strength of its currencies in relation to the weakened dollar and pound. The Committee also made a detailed examination of possible concerted action by the Six in the framework of the International Monetary Fund, and it is worth noting that of the grants made through the IMF to assist sterling at the end of 1961 the Common Market countries contributed $1,050 million (as against $650 million from the United States)—40 per cent of the total, whereas their original quotas totalled only 10 per cent of IMF funds.

Also in 1961, at the request of the EEC Commission, the Committee undertook a full enquiry into the instruments of monetary policy available to the authorities in the member States to influence economic trends and in particular to meet a possible eventual recession. The conclusion was reached that the differences from one country to another in the range of steps available had been considerably narrowed since 1958, several countries having added new possibilities to their armoury, but that the situation could and should be further harmonised.

Such a study was intended by the Commission to provide the necessary groundwork for co-ordination of national policies, which means essentially that the authorities should take into account what effects any measure they are adopting will have on other member countries, and further that they should see what positive steps they can take to improve the situation in the Community as a whole. There is no question for the moment of expecting the member countries to use, or even to have available, exactly the same range of measures of monetary policy: the differences between banking structures, and between relations with the outside world, make this impossible, at least for the time being. The aim is only that, as the removal of obstacles to the flow of goods and capital makes monetary policy relatively more important as a means of guiding the economy, all the member countries should have an adequate range of instruments available and should use them in a co-ordinated way.

'MUTUAL AID'

This seems an appropriate point to examine the detailed provision that is made in the Treaty (Arts. 108, 109) for the case where a member country runs into balance of payments difficulties. Whilst none of the present member countries has so far had to invoke its aid, it could provide the framework for helping Britain to overcome any possible payments difficulties on or after her entry to the Common Market.

The system works as follows. When a member State meets serious balance of payments difficulties, the Commission examines its situation and makes recommendations to it on the policy it should adopt: such recommendations being of course the fruit of discussions with the country concerned in the Monetary Committee. If the action the member State then takes should prove inadequate, there is a second stage. After formally consulting the Monetary Committee, the Commission can recommend to the Council of Ministers to grant the State the benefit of 'mutual aid', the necessary decision being taken by a qualified majority. The scope available for mutual aid is considerable: it may take the form of concerted action by the member States in or through an international organisation (this would correspond almost exactly to the action by which the pound was bolstered through the IMF in 1961); steps to avoid deflection of trade whilst the country in question is authorised to maintain or even re-impose import restrictions on trade with non-member countries; or the granting of credit facilities by the other member States. During the transitional period the mutual aid can also take the form of special customs reductions to encourage the exports of the country in difficulties.

As a last resort, if the mutual aid proves inadequate (or in the event of the Council's refusing to grant it) the Commission may authorise the member State to apply specifically defined escape clauses—though the Council may revoke or change these by a qualified majority. In a case of emergency (not defined in precise terms) a member State may off its own bat take the steps it feels essential to meet a balance of payments crisis, provided it informs the Commission and the other member States. The Council, on the advice of the Commission and the Monetary Committee, may later require it to revoke or alter such emergency measures. In view of the machinery for continual consultation and the wide scope offered for the other member countries to rally round, it seems however unlikely that a member State would be obliged to take unilateral action which the Council might later disapprove.

TOWARDS A COMMON CURRENCY

As in other fields co-ordination of national policies is seen as being the first step towards the adoption of a common policy, which in the monetary field will be essential when the last barriers between the economies are removed.[1] In 1961 Jean Monnet's Action Committee for the United States of Europe, whose proposals tend to foreshadow future developments in the process of integration, put forward a plan for the creation, as a first step towards a common policy and a common currency, of a European Reserve Union. Modelled on the United

[1] For a fuller discussion of this problem see Chapter 2 of Part III below.

States Federal Reserve Board, it would consist of credits made available from the central banks, and thus provide an organic link between the six currencies, and a backing for each of them. It would follow an autonomous policy, and serve essentially to bring about the closest collaboration between the central banks, which would nevertheless keep full independence in their national policies. The scheme was welcomed by the EEC Commission, but its realisation must clearly wait upon a greater degree of confidence than as yet exists in the strength of the various currencies: the pressure of integration is not yet great enough to bring the other countries to agree to the idea of backing to the hilt, say, the Belgian franc (or indeed, perhaps for other reasons, the French franc). At all events monetary developments are bound now to wait upon the entry of sterling as a Community currency.

HARMONISATION OF TAXATION

Taxation clearly lies at the very heart of national economic policy, and the degree to which it is used as an instrument of redistribution of income must reflect the whole politico-economic outlook of the government in power. It is thus unlikely that budgetary policies within the Common Market can be easily or rapidly harmonised. It is also clear however that certain differences in the structure of national systems of taxation can have a powerful effect on the competitive position of firms and individuals in member States: a firm subject to heavy taxation will be at an obvious disadvantage compared with a competitor in another member State where the government draws its income predominantly from other sources. Most of the immediate references to taxation in the Treaty (Arts. 95-9) are directed to ensuring that goods imported from other member countries are not subject to internal taxation exceeding that levied on national output of those goods; similarly, export rebates must not be allowed to exceed the level of the internal taxation they are meant to compensate. The Commission is also charged in general terms with examining how the legislation of member States regarding tax on business turnover, and also excise duties and other forms of indirect taxation, can be harmonised.

The major problem in this field is that raised by the tax on business turnover. This plays a major role in the tax systems of most Continental countries: it means in effect taxing the process of production rather than imposing a lump-sum tax (purchase tax) on the finished product. The systems employed, however, vary from one country to another. Germany levies a 'waterfall' tax—so much at each stage of processing

—whereas other member countries have either a straightforward 'tax on the value added' or a single tax levied at the last stage of processing. The immediate problem was to find a uniform way of calculating the total amount of tax levied on any product, as a basis for determining what 'drawback' (compensatory refund) on exports would be fair to competitors. The Commission has yet to make precise proposals on this. The more fundamental problem is to reach agreement on a uniform system to be applied throughout the Common Market—and the implications of this for national budgetary policy have made it difficult. Groups of national experts working on the problem have elaborated three alternative schemes, between which the Commission will choose in making precise proposals to the Council during 1962.

The EEC Commission has interpreted the Treaty widely, and as early as 1959 began to study the whole field of fiscal policy. It set up a Fiscal and Financial Committee of national experts to look into the questions raised by the creation of the Common Market. Two general questions were singled out: to what extent differences in national policy or practice hinder or prevent the creation of a common market, and what influence such policies (the whole structure of taxation and government spending) have on the competitive position of firms. This clearly strikes at the heart of the matter: can member States which have accepted a common trade policy and the free movement of goods and capital continue in the long run to apply their own separate fiscal policies?

Detailed work on the problems involved was not begun until the autumn of 1961. The first specific question looked at was the actual ratio of direct to indirect taxation in the member States (do Italian firms, for instance, which receive export 'drawback' on a high level of indirect taxation, have an 'unfair' advantage?). Secondly, work which is intended to lead eventually to proposals for harmonisation of national systems has been begun on several aspects of direct taxation, in particular the possibility of achieving a uniform total effect of taxation on firms; the chances of reducing differences in the level of taxation on dividends; and the effects of the requirement in some countries that shares be made out to a holder by name and thus traceable for taxation. Study is also going on on taxes on capital transfers (an obstacle to free movement of capital) and legislation concerning depreciation allowances. All this is a small beginning in a vast field, and the degree or rapidity of harmonisation likely to be achieved in the future is hard to foretell.

Lastly, the EEC Commission and national experts have been working since 1959 to achieve comparability of national budgets, by bringing national practices into line as regards accounting techniques, timing (it is hoped soon to synchronise the national financial years so that they all run from January to January) and the classification of expenditure and revenue. Making national budgets more comparable will both serve to reveal more clearly the differences between national policies and serve as an essential basis for any later co-ordination of budgetary policy.

As yet, therefore, the Community has no common monetary policy, and no common economic policy. Even co-ordination of national policies is only in its earliest stages. Nor are such policies due to form the subject of debates in the Council or formal decisions. On the other hand some at least of the necessary spade-work has been done, and a tradition of consultation has been established. Both the EEC Commission and the European Parliament have been looking into the future, and at its June 1962 session the Parliament was scheduled to hold a full-scale debate on the co-ordination of monetary and budgetary policies on the basis of a report setting out the EEC Commission's views and plans. At the same time the realisation of the need for co-ordination is being brought home to the Governments, and the coming years may well see dramatic progress on many fronts.

(ii) The Common Agricultural Policy

It was never questioned by the member States that the Common Market should cover agriculture as well as manufactured goods. Farming is of basic importance to the economies of all the Six countries—in some of them it employs 20 per cent or more of the active population as against under 5 per cent in the United Kingdom—and it was unthinkable to remove trade barriers for industrial goods and leave the agricultural markets isolated. On the other hand there was no question of merely lowering or removing trade barriers on farm produce, since all the member countries have managed markets more or less heavily protected. Nor was mere co-ordination of national policies a possibility. Only a thorough-going common policy, worked out and applied for the Community as a whole, could have any chance of balancing the conflicting interests of the member countries: Germany a massive importer of farm produce, with a very large number of vulnerable small farmers (especially in the South East where traditional markets in East Germany have been lost) and a high level of protection against outside competition; France with more efficient farmers, lower prices, and farm surpluses for export, though still a high-cost producer of secondary foodstuffs such as pigs and poultry; and Holland, specialised in the dairying and livestock side of agriculture, importing large quantities of grain and exporting dairy products, pigmeat and poultry. Italy's position, as an exporter of fruit and vegetables, is a special one, and the essential problem was to reconcile the interests of France, Germany and Holland. Nor were there any illusions about the difficulties of merging farm economies with different levels of prices and of productivity and differing systems of protection. It was clear from the start that agricultural policy would be a test case for the Common Market: but if the Six could agree upon a common policy, then it would become the keystone of the whole Common Market edifice.

The negotiators of the Treaty of Rome, wisely refraining from tackling the details of such a thorny problem, merely laid down that there should be a common policy (Art. 38). They defined its aims (Art. 39)—increased productivity, a fair standard of living for the farming population (to be achieved by raising both farm wages and farmers' incomes), and guaranteed supplies to the consumer at reasonable prices—and outlined the methods to be used to achieve them: joint management of markets, at the Community level, by a system appropriate to the position for each product. Nothing could be simpler, or more acceptable—or less suggestive of the vast problems involved.

To get from the unimpassioned phrases of the Treaty to the intricate measures to come into effect for the first time in the summer of 1962 involved a marathon process of study, consultation and negotiation, under the able and untiring direction of the member of the EEC Commission responsible, Dr. Mansholt, a former Dutch Minister. First, in the summer of 1958, there was a full-scale Conference at Stresa, at which the governments put forward their views on what the common policy should involve and the agricultural situation in each member State was examined. Then followed a two-year period during which the EEC Commission, after a full study of the situation and consultation with all the farmers' organisations and other interested bodies, drew up a set of general principles on which the merger of the six farm economies, and the Community's policy after the end of the transitional period, should be based. These principles were approved on July 14th, 1960, by an EEC Council meeting of the Ministers of Agriculture of the member countries, who had been holding regular unofficial sessions under the chairmanship of Dr. Mansholt to thrash out major problems as they arose.

What these basic principles amount to is this:[1] the Community will take over from the member States responsibility for guaranteeing a reasonable level of income for efficient farmers; the measures by which the member countries protect their agriculture will be gradually replaced by a Community system of protection; there will be free trade between the member countries in all agricultural products; cheap food for consumers will be an over-riding aim; and trade links with third countries will be maintained.

On the basis of these principles the Commission worked out its practical proposals—the structure of market organisation to replace the national systems, and specific plans for a first group of products—and the rest of 1960 and the whole of 1961 saw these laboriously ground through the Common Market's consultative and legislative mill. In addition to the detailed and highly critical examination by the Economic and Social Committee and the Parliamentary Assembly, each separate draft had to undergo a vetting by a Special Agricultural Committee set up to advise the Council of Ministers. As the end of the first four-year stage of the Common Market transition period drew near, not a single decision had been taken: it had become clear that the foundations of the common policy had to be treated as a single whole, and that the twelve separate pieces of 'legislation' which the Commission had prepared must be approved in one vast 'package deal'. This was what the Foreign Ministers and Ministers of Agriculture had before them when they met in the week before Christmas 1961: and on their success in reaching agreement hung the decision to move on to the second stage of the Common Market (and also the negotiations on British entry, the agricultural side of which could not be begun until the Six had a common policy).

The Ministers were unable to get through the immense amount of negotiation involved before the end of the year: with major national interests at stake, nothing could be let through by default, no concession be granted below its rightful price. It was not until the early hours

[1] It was formally stated by the Lord Privy Seal in the course of the Brussels negotiations that the British government fully accepts these principles.

of Sunday, January 14th, 1962, that the basic decisions on the common agricultural policy were taken. Due to be implemented over a period of seven and a half years, starting on July 1st, 1962, they will mean a major transformation in the whole managed trading system for farm produce both between the member countries and between the Community and the rest of the world: and they will bring major changes in the structure of the farm economy itself.

THE FARM POLICY MACHINERY

The Regulations approved in January and due to start coming into effect on July 1st, 1962,[1] are only a first step towards the common policy. They cover only a certain number of products—grains, pigmeat, eggs and poultry, fruit and vegetables, and wine: similar proposals for beef and mutton, rice, and dairy products were presented to the Council in May 1962, and others on sugar are due to follow later in the year. Moreover, the most vital decisions of all, determining what will eventually be the price level for grain throughout the Community, have been put off, with no attempt to be made to reduce the gaps between national price levels until the 1963 harvest. A programme of structural policy for the farm economy has yet to be drawn up; and so have rules of competition for the agricultural sector.

Nevertheless, the January decisions are the basic element around which the rest of the policy will be built, and since they will also apply to British agriculture (the Government has made clear that it accepts their broad outline, subject to minor changes to be negotiated) it is worth examining in some detail the machinery they set up. The principles underlying it are, to recapitulate; free movement of produce, Community responsibility for the farmers (and also, gradually, for the disposal of surpluses), and unified management of markets.

Grain is by far the most important single farm commodity, and it also determines to some extent the situation for other products (pigmeat, eggs, poultry) through the effect of forage grain prices. It requires the most complete system of market management—and the most complicated. This centres around three prices: a target price, a threshold or 'weir' price, and an 'intervention' or support price. The key to the whole system is the target price, to be set annually before the autumn sowing. It applies to wholesale transactions at the market centre of the

[1] It seems at the time of writing that that date may in fact only be observed for the grain regulations, sheer pressure of work preventing the details of the schemes for other products from being ready in time.

area of lowest output, i.e., where prices tend to be highest. For the moment each country has a different target price, and although upper and lower limits have been set—the German prices as the 'ceiling' and the French as the 'floor'—no move will be made to start narrowing the gap until 1963. The aim is gradually to bring national target prices closer until at the end of the transitional period there is a single target price for the Community.

The intervention price is that at which the national authorities (during the transitional period) and later a European Grain Office will buy grain to support the market: it will be set between 5 and 10 per cent below the target price. Between the two levels prices will be freely determined by the play of supply and demand and the influence of transport costs. Farmers will be assured of a market at the support price, but this will of course go down each year, in the high-price countries, as the move towards a single target price continues, thus encouraging farmers to produce more efficiently. (Member countries will however be allowed to set 'derived' support prices, during the transitional period, to help producers in distant areas.)

The third of the trio is the 'threshold' price. This forms the basis of the levy system which will take the place of present measures of protection, and is intended, basically, to ensure that farmers do not have to face competition from third countries (or from other member countries during the transitional period) at less than the target price. The threshold price will be equivalent to the target price less freight costs between the point of entry into the country and the marketing area. In the case of imports from other member countries the levies (which will remain until the end of the transitional period, when target prices have been aligned) will cover the difference between the grain price in the exporting area and the national threshold price (less a fixed sum to ensure other EEC countries a margin of preference over exporters in third countries). The levy on imports from non-member countries will consist of the difference between the threshold price (which by the end of the transitional period will be the same for the whole of the Common Market) and the *lowest* price on the world market for delivery free at the external frontier of the Community.

Besides the levies, there will be a second line of defence in an escape clause leaving it open to the governments to suspend import quotas if their farmers are threatened by a flood of imported grain. Such a step would have to be notified to the EEC Commission which, in consultation with other member countries, will decide whether it is justified f it decides it is not, the member State may appeal to the Council, which must give its approval within ten days: otherwise the Commission's ruling stands.

The other side of the scheme is the provision for export rebates—also to be calculated in relation to the threshold price—by which the member Governments, and later the Community authorities, will be able to help farmers to dispose of their surpluses on the world market. During the transitional period member countries can make similar grants to help their farmers sell their high-priced produce on the markets of other member countries.

The system for pigmeat (pork and bacon) and for eggs and poultry is derived from that for cereals, since the main 'raw material' for all of them is fodder grain. The levies are complex ones with a variable element taking into account coarse grain prices and a fixed element allowing for differences in production costs between member countries. The levy on imports from third countries will be determined at the end of the transitional period on the basis of the same variable element plus a percentage of the import price (eventually to be 7 per cent). In addition there is a 'lock-gate price' (a minimum import price) intended to prevent dumping: if import prices fall below this 'lock-gate' price they can be raised again by a corresponding increase in the levy.

For dairy products, for which the Regulations have still to be approved by the Council, the Commission's proposals run along similar lines: the general tendency of the scheme will be to guarantee dairy farmers a certain price level for their milk, but at the same time to keep the price of butter as low as possible—as is essential if it is to remain competitive with margarine.

From the above description of the planned market organisation it will be seen that the target prices will be in the long run all important: they will determine the incentive both to increased efficiency in the present high-cost countries, and to increased output in the more efficient producing countries, and also through the levy system the scale of the Community's imports of farm products. Not surprisingly, the level of the target prices for each year will be set by the Council of Ministers.

FINANCING THE FARM POLICY

The financing of the agricultural policy is a major operation. It is intended that it shall be based on a Common Guidance and Guarantee Fund, which will contribute to three forms of expenditure: the export rebates at the external frontier; intervention at support prices on the internal markets; and measures for improving the structure of the farming economy. During 1962–3 however, the Fund will bear only one-third of the total cost of these activities, its contribution rising by one-third in each of the two following years. During the first three years—after which a full review of financing and expenditure is planned—the member States will contribute to the Fund according to two systems: most of their contributions will be in the same ratio as their share in the Community's general budget (Art. 200), but 10 per cent of the Fund's receipts in the second year and 20 per cent in the third will be paid in proportion to the value of their nett imports from third countries. Lest this means that the importing countries bear an unfair share of the burden, ceilings have been set for each country: Germany may not provide more than 31 per cent, Italy 28 per cent, France 17·5 per cent, the Netherlands 13 per cent, and Belgium-Luxembourg 10·5 per cent.

FRUIT AND VEGETABLES

For fruit and vegetables, and also for wine, the Community system is far simpler. For fruit and vegetables customs duties, quota restrictions and minimum prices will be gradually removed between July 1st, 1962 and the end of 1966. At the same time uniform quality standards will be progressively introduced, and the freeing of trade will operate more rapidly for the better qualities. Clearly the creation of a common market will mainly be of benefit to Italy, and producers in the North of Europe will be able to have recourse to the escape clause procedure save in the case of 'extras', the top-grade produce, if wholesale prices fall below a given level (set at 82 per cent of the average for the three preceding years).

For wine the first step in the common policy is that the two major wine-producing countries will grant quotas (150,000 hectalitres a year) for imports of quality wine from other member countries, including of course each other; Germany too is to grant a large import quota. The corollary of this is a programme for ensuring uniform standards: the establishment of a register of vineyards, and of common rules or standards. The Commission is to establish an annual estimate of requirements and supplies.

STRUCTURAL POLICY

Before looking at the repercussions of the farm policy, it is worth pausing over the third use to which the Guidance and Guarantee Fund will be devoted: improving farming structures. The money will be granted largely to improve marketing systems. In addition, to enable farmers to make the necessary adaptations to changed market conditions, there will be a separate Fund for Improvement in Farm Structures, which will give aid for reconversion to other forms of production, modernisation, mechanisation, and similar improvements. Its grants will also go to improving the infra-structure of a whole area (for instance by the provision of large-scale equipment, silos, etc.). These measures are designed to provide for the long-term trends which are bound to occur, and which the Common Market with its emphasis on increased productivity will hasten. When the Common Market was set up there were in the Six countries some 6,800,000 farms of more than one hectare (4·6 acres) and 3,300,000 of them had an area of 5 hectares (some 23 acres) or less, as against an average in France of around seventy acres.

The creation of the Common Market in these circumstances means two things. The kind of family farm which exists in such large numbers will have to be made considerably more efficient if it is to survive. It is to this end that the Community will have its Structural Improvement Fund, and that the Commission is drawing up what looks like being a far-reaching policy to co-ordinate national policies in this field. On the other hand, with increased efficiency, large numbers of people are going to have to move off the land. Dr. Mansholt himself was reported as saying on one occasion that if the Common Market's agricultural economy became really efficient some eight million people would have to move from farming to industry. Whilst this clearly represents an important source of manpower to meet the growing shortage in Community industry, it poses immense problems of co-ordination: the rate at which the transfer can be achieved will depend on the development of adequate regional development policies, vocational training facilities, and reconversion schemes in which national and Community authorities will have to co-operate. These are problems which have largely been solved in the United Kingdom but are just beginning to loom large in the Community.

THE COMMUNITY'S FARM POLICY AND THE REST OF THE WORLD

The long-term effects of the common farm policy will be of vital importance for the Community's trading relations with the rest of the world. In several sectors the Community of Six is already more or less self-sufficient—eggs, pig-meat, dairy products—although clearly the entry of Britain would radically change the situation: for others, however, it is still a major importer, and a vital market for the exporting countries. The trend in European agriculture in recent years has generally been towards increasing efficiency—thanks mainly to mechanisation and the increasing use of fertilizers—and the gaps which still exist between levels of productivity in Germany on the one hand and Denmark or Holland on the other show how much progress could still be made. Moreover, as we have seen, higher productivity is an avowed aim of the common policy: and although this may be primarily intended to raise living standards, lower prices and release manpower it cannot fail also to result in increased production, which eventually may outstrip the rise in demand.

Although the immediate effects of the farm policy cannot really be judged until the target prices have been set, they will clearly be somewhere between the French and German price levels, and it is reasonable to predict that the resultant rise in French output (in the case of grain) will more than outweigh a hypothetical fall in German or Italian production, both owing to improved efficiency and to the fact that a change to other forms of production is not easily obtained.

The need to maintain trade flows may be written into the Treaty, and explicitly recognised in the basic principles of the common policy: nor is the fall in Community imports likely to be spectacular. Nevertheless, rising output in member countries and increasing intra-Community trade, combined with the levy system, are capable, to say the least, of limiting the growth of the Common Market's need for imports of foodstuffs. At the GATT Ministerial Conference in the autumn of 1961 Dr. Mansholt expressed the view that the Community's common policy should provide the stimulus for the conclusion of world-wide commodity agreements. The Community has committed itself to talks with the United States, in three years' time about the effects on trade of the common agricultural policy. In the negotiations for British accession, the problem of 'comparable outlets' for the temperate-zone foodstuffs of the Commonwealth seems at the time of writing to be the toughest problem of all, with the Six refusing commitments about their imports. It can thus be seen to what an extent the common farm policy poses a world problem: it is one which, as will be suggested in Part III, must be solved by the enlarged Community and the United States in partnership.

(iii) A Common Transport Policy

The common farm policy may have been the Common Market's biggest hurdle so far, but there are two others ahead which look hardly less formidable, namely transport (for which a common policy is required by Articles 74 and 75 of the Rome Treaty) and energy, a field where the governments have been obliged to recognise the need for a common policy although it does not figure in the Treaties. In neither case is the policy likely to be drawn up in such dramatic circumstances as it was for agriculture, although the Executives, realising the importance of time-limits in obliging the Ministers to reach a compromise, are proposing the adoption for both transport and energy of time-tables with specific dates for taking particular decisions. Nevertheless, the problems are every bit as complex, and the number of conflicting interests to be reconciled probably even greater. In both fields the work on a common policy is in the early stages, and for energy at least the new member countries should be in time to play their part in shaping it.

Transport is of course a basic element in any economy, figuring to a large extent in the costs of all goods and of many services. In 1956 the transport sector accounted for a fifth of the Six countries' combined gross national product, and employed 16 per cent of all the workers in the industrial sector. Thus a uniform system of fair and undistorted competition in the transport sector is an indispensable condition for a successful merger of the separate economies in a common market. Equally, the development of the Common Market area as an economic unit depends upon the provision of a unified and adequate transport network.

It is therefore possible to distinguish three things which have to be achieved in the transport sector: the removal of discrimination; the application of a common policy throughout the Community; and the development of an adequate transport network.

ELIMINATING DISCRIMINATION

Some aspects of the way the transport sector is at present run could well hinder the creation of a fair and balanced common market, and the Treaty therefore makes express provision (Arts. 79–81) for the various existing forms of discrimination to be weeded out. The first and most obvious step was to ban discrimination by a haulier according to the country of origin or destination of the goods transported, or the nationality of the customer. Regulations to this effect passed the EEC Council in June 1960 and began to be applied on July 1st, 1961: all such discrimination is due to disappear by the end of 1965: for ECSC products it had already been banned.

Secondly the Treaty specifically requires the abolition of all 'support tariffs'—special rates and conditions granted, mainly by the railways, in favour of a particular industry or region. Such rates tend to be used as part of regional policy, and since the ban came into effect, automatically, at the beginning of the second stage of the transition period in January 1962 the Commission has authorised the maintenance of certain economically justified support rates—in particular Italian special rates to favour the development of the South. The Treaty itself contains a clause (Art. 82) permitting Germany to make special provision for areas hit by the division of the country.

By the end of the second stage, in 1965, action has also to be taken about common rules for international transport. By far the most important problem in this connection is that of direct through rates, i.e. uniform scales of reduction for distance on international hauls. It is a problem the Coal and Steel Community has already faced and solved, although with a compromise. Forced to reject the ideal of a single straight reduction for through hauls, the national experts and the High Authority eventually adopted a solution best illustrated by an example: on a 500 km haul the ordinary French rate applies for the 250 km to the frontier, and for the second part not the French rate for 250–500 nor the German rate for 0–250 (as was formerly the case), but the German rate for 250–500 km. Another major problem due to be solved in the course of 1962 is that of vehicle dimensions and capacities, where differing national regulations can have a marked effect on competition by enabling one haulier to carry bigger loads than another. Lastly quota restrictions on the national transport markets and restrictions on the right of establishment for hauliers will be abolished by the end of 1965.

REVOLUTIONARY IDEAS FOR A COMMON POLICY

All such steps are, however, only of secondary importance as compared with the application of a common policy for 'achieving in the transport sector the objectives of the Treaty' (Art. 79). It is obvious from the complex structure of the transport economy, and the many other aspects of national policy to which transport has tended to be subordinated, how difficult and revolutionary an undertaking this may prove to be. Thus, for example, the railways in all the member States are nationalised, and also enjoy a natural monopoly (the plain facts of geography prevent one national railway system competing with another): but they also compete with road and water transport, where here is the opposite of monopoly—a plethora of small firms, engaging in keen if not cut-throat competition and able to operate throughout the Common Market area. Moreover, the policy of the railways is subject to many other considerations (apart from the social service obligation which is recognised as important in the Treaty): they are made to serve the ends of regional or agricultural policy (by special rates), social policy (by reduced fares for certain groups: the French railways in 1953 carried 15 billion passengers at normal rates and 10 billion more at special rates), and even defence policy (neglect of some lines, and development of others). Many of these considerations also dictate the development of the national road and inland waterway networks.

The changes that will be required to bring about a single, uniform free-competition policy both between the various forms of transport and between the member States are indeed little short of revolutionary. The EEC Commission itself has admitted that the adaptation of national policies must be a very gradual one; and the Treaty itself lays down no time-limits, although the end of the second stage, in 1965, after which EEC Council decisions on transport can be taken by a qualified majority vote, may prove a decisive point.

The EEC Commission launched its first ideas, framed merely as a Memorandum to the Council and the governments, in April 1961, and a year later the examination and discussion of them was still continuing. Every conceivable organisation and interest group in the Common Market has expressed its views on the complex set of principles which the Commission has set forth as a suggested basis for the common policy. These can be summed up in five points. First, users must be free to choose between different means of transport, and all forms of transport should be free (within limits to be defined) to charge what they please: thus, no *dirigisme* but a free market. Secondly, all forms of transport should receive equal treatment from the State as regards taxation, social service charges and State aid (the implications for the railways are clear). Thirdly, all forms of transport must pay their way (again of major significance for the railways, which do not do so except in Holland). Fourthly, the costs of maintaining and developing the transport infrastructure should be evenly shared out as an element in costs and borne by the users (a new idea for road and water transport). Lastly, it is suggested that there should be co-ordination of investments, in order to promote a rational development of the transport capacities of the Community as a whole and prevent excess capacity leading to uneconomic cut-throat competition.

To implement these principles, which all turn on guaranteeing a system of fair and healthy competition, the Commission proposes the establishment for all forms of transport of 'forked tariffs'—published upper and lower limits within which hauliers would be free to charge whatever rate they choose. The lower limits would be set so as to prevent cut-throat competition, and the upper limits to prevent the exploitation of monopoly positions. Such a system would also solve the problem of whether firms should be obliged to publish their transport rates, which has been and remains a major bone of contention in the Coal and Steel Community. The Commission adds, as a general principle, that there should be parallel progress in opening up national transport markets to hauliers from other member countries and in the application of common market organisation.

For the present, little has been decided. Early in 1962 the member States agreed to a procedure for compulsory consultation before applying any new measures of transport policy: and at the end of May the Commission presented to the Council of Ministers a 'plan of action' setting out a time-table for steps to elaborate and to implement its proposals.

Several other problems concerning the transport sector still remain to be solved. One is the question of whether the cartel regulations should also apply to transport or whether special rules should be worked out: the Commission has come out in favour of the first solution, but the point may yet be taken before the Court. A second is the status of pipelines, and whether they should come under transport policy (as being competitive with other forms of transporting oil or petroleum products) or under energy policy: again the Commission seems to favour the first solution.

A third question, which the Treaty (Art. 84) left it to the Council to decide by a unanimous vote, is whether the Treaty in general, and the common transport policy in particular, shall apply also to air and sea transport. The Commission favours their being put on the same footing as the other forms of transport, with which they are to some extent (and in the case of air transport, to a growing extent) competitive. British (and Norwegian) accession to the Community would greatly increase the significance of this question, which has only just begun to be studied in Brussels.

LINKING UP THE MOTOR-WAYS

The road, rail and canal networks of the Common Market area, developed over the centuries to serve the separate national interests of the member States, and to serve ends often rather political than economic, bear striking witness to the way one country can be cut off from another. Autobahns stop short suddenly within a few miles of a frontier, two canals both navigable to big barges are separated by a bottle-neck left intentionally to prevent through traffic; and international railway lines are electrified with entirely different systems in adjoining countries. To provide the Common Market with an infrastructure that will allow it to develop as a single economic unit, the EEC Commission and the national experts have drawn up a plan which the Council of Ministers approved and which will be carried out by the member States (with aid where necessary from the European Investment Bank), for creating a network which takes no account of national frontiers. Existing rail links between important industrial areas will be improved or electrified; and other links not previously possible are being opened up (as with the canalisation of the Moselle, to link the Ruhr with Alsace-Lorraine, the impetus for which came from the Coal and Steel Community). No time-limits have been set, but work has already begun on many of the projects, and the end of the transitional period in or around 1970 should see the Common Market with a transport network suited to its needs (and perhaps with the Channel Tunnel forming an integrated part of it).

(iv) REGIONAL POLICY AND THE EUROPEAN INVESTMENT BANK

Making a single economic unit out of several adjoining ones is bound to affect the relative importance of the various regions in the countries involved. There are three obvious cases. First, the area distant from the political and economic centre of a country, and therefore neglected, but which now assumes an important central position in the bigger unit: this is the case, for example, of Alsace, and the Eiffel plateau in the part of Germany bordering on Belgium and Luxembourg. Then there are areas which are geographically one, but which a national frontier has prevented from developing as an economic whole: an obvious case here is the area comprising the North-East corner of France, heavily industrialised and with a manpower shortage, and the adjoining Belgian province of West Flanders, economically stagnant, with a manpower surplus.

Thirdly, there occurs the most serious case of the peripheral and consequently under-developed areas: Southern Italy above all, but also parts of France and of Northern Holland. With the creation of a single unit these areas become potentially even further removed from the industrial and economic centre of gravity. The danger has been recognised that the central industrial axis of the Community, extending from the coal and steel triangle of the Ruhr and Nord—Pas de Calais in the North, down the Rhine and Rhone valleys, and into Northern Italy, will attract more capital and tend to develop more rapidly than the outlying areas of the Community. (A comparison is often drawn with Italy, where unification in the nineteenth century, far from promoting the development of the South, meant that resources which might otherwise have gone into its development were attracted to the already more industrialised areas of the North).

All three cases pose problems or open up possibilities which concern the Community as a whole.[1] As national frontiers cease to be a barrier to the movement of workers, the establishment of firms, and the flow of capital, the need for a positive and coherent policy for long-divided areas astride the frontiers will become acute. With every year that passes changing trade flows and increasing inter-action between the economies will increase the appeal to investors of the capital-intensive areas with a highly-developed network of services (finance, communications, contacts) as against the less-developed areas (except of course in so far as manpower shortages drive firms to the outlying areas, as I suggested in the previous chapter).

The role of the Community in this field is not to replace the national and regional authorities, but rather to encourage and to co-ordinate their activities. In December 1961 a first step was taken: the Commission held a Conference in Brussels of all those concerned with regional policy in the member countries, whose close collaboration will become more and more necessary in the future. On its own initiative

[1] The accession of new members would bring the Community new problems similar to its present ones: Norway's backward North to match Italy's underdeveloped South to take only one example. The 'regional problems' which might arise for Britain are dealt with in Chapter 1 of Part III below.

the Commission has drawn up a detailed study of socio-economic areas in the Community (although it unfortunately failed to have the courage of its convictions and treat as single units areas divided by national frontiers). It has also looked at three test cases: the problems of creating a 'pole of industrialisation' in Southern Italy; co-operation between Italy and France in developing the tourist industry in Corsica and Sardinia; and co-operation between Lorraine (which has industry and a water shortage) and the adjoining Belgian province of Luxembourg (with a water surplus and manpower looking for jobs). For the rest Community action is as yet at an embryonic stage, with one striking exception: the European Investment Bank.

THE CAUTIOUS BANK

The Investment Bank is, or at least could become, one of the most striking features of the Community machinery. The general task assigned to it by the Treaty is to contribute to the smooth and balanced development of the Community. It is run by a Management Committee of twelve and a Board of Directors of three appointed by the member States and responsible to the Finance Ministers of those States, who act as its Board of Governors. Its initial capital is $1,000 million (a quarter of it paid up) contributed by the member States. It is not at all intended however to be merely a means of channelling financial aid from the States. It is intended once established to procure its own funds on the capital markets, thus serving rather as a means of re-directing to some extent the flow of private capital. It is therefore run on orthodox financial lines: its loans are granted at interest rates little lower than those on the markets, and intended to cover its running costs and provide for a reserve fund. They must in addition be guaranteed by member States or some other reliable source. In most cases they are intended mainly as 'pump-priming'—to help out where sufficient funds cannot be obtained from other sources: thus the $66.2 million worth of loans granted in 1961 covered on the average 20 per cent of the cost of the projects they helped to finance, and which altogether involved investments totalling $325 million.

All these various considerations and requirements limit the Bank's activity. In addition, however, it has come under very heavy fire from all sides during these first few years of its existence for leaning over-much in the direction of caution and financial orthodoxy. Certainly it has been a long time getting into its stride: the $160 million worth of loans granted up to the end of 1961 were a mere drop in the bucket compared for instance with the $44 *billion* of fixed investment in EEC in 1961 alone. 1961 did in fact see a certain increase in its activity: it granted more loans than in previous years, and also had recourse for the first time to the capital markets, borrowing a total of nearly $50 million in Holland, Switzerland and Italy. Its original capital of $1 billion, serving to back loans up to $2½ billion, is of course only a starting-point. If it is to carry out to any significant extent the role originally intended for it, of providing substantial funds for the development of the Community, it must clearly borrow on a far larger scale.

Here the ECSC High Authority has shown the way. It has established its reputation as a sound risk—though it too had to proceed cautiously in the early years—and has borrowed substantial sums in the United States, Switzerland and the Community to use for ends not unlike those of the Bank. There seems therefore to be no reason why the Bank should not greatly extend its borrowing to meet the need for development capital.

Criticism has in fact been aimed not only at the scale of the Bank's activities but also at the range of projects it has chosen to assist. Its loans must in fact go to one of three kinds of project. First, it has the task of helping the less-developed areas of the Community, and it is here that it will be able to play a major part in stimulating regional policy. In 1961 the EEC Commission, which gives the Bank its views on all projects submitted, gave first priority to activities under this heading in establishing the criteria it would apply.

— The second kind of undertaking which the Bank can help to finance, and which looks like taking on growing importance, covers the modernisation or reconversion of firms or the creation of new plants, made necessary by the progressive development of the Common Market. On the one hand individual businesses can call on it for aid to adapt themselves to meet keener competition; on the other governments or regional authorities can seek its backing in creating new forms of activity in areas where the decline of industries no longer competitive is causing unemployment. Here its activity is complemented by that of the Social Fund.

Thirdly, the Bank is charged with financing major undertakings of interest to several member States which could not be fully financed from resources within the State. A good example of this is its grant to a hydro-electric power project on the Luxembourg-German frontier which will supply power to three countries. Most of the projects financed under this heading seem likely to be in the field of transport infrastructure: loans have been granted for improving various stretches of railway, and one is envisaged for the Paris-Brussels motorway. The Channel tunnel inevitably springs to mind as a likely future candidate for funds from the Bank.

The loans granted in the course of 1961 give some hint of the wide scope there is for the Bank's activity in all the fields mentioned: they ranged from railway electrification in Italy ($21 million) and Germany ($25 million) to experiments in farming in the marshes at the mouth of the Rhone ($1 million), and from the development of the rural electric power network in Brittany ($5 million) to the creation of a sweet factory in Sicily ($400,000).

Lastly, the role of the Bank is being enlarged in two new directions. The Council of Ministers of the EEC has instructed it to provide the $60 million loan which the Community has promised Greece in the two years after the new Association (see below, p. 131) comes into effect. Secondly, there is a considerable likelihood that a special section of the Bank will be created to provide the financial aid which the Community will give the African countries under their new Association (see p. 129).

(v) SOCIAL POLICY AND THE SOCIAL FUND

In Article 117 of the Treaty the member States set down in black and white their commitment to 'promote the improvement of the living and working conditions of labour, enabling them to be equalised upwards'. The Commission is specifically instructed to promote close collaboration between the member States in the major fields of social policy (Art. 118).

In fact the Commission's activities under this general mandate were fairly limited during the first four years of the Common Market—provoking considerable criticism from the trade unions, who called for round-table meetings on the various aspects of social policy. 1962 did however see the beginnings of activity in one or two sectors. In particular, the Commission drew up and presented to the Council far-reaching proposals on vocational training which provide for a closely co-ordinated common policy. In the field of industrial medicine a start was made with the establishment of a single Community list of occupational diseases intended to serve eventually as a basis for eliminating discrepancies between national policies. In others of the fields mentioned by the Treaty, however—such as collective bargaining, working conditions or labour legislation—the Commission has done little. In this it lags behind the High Authority, which has been active in co-operating with workers and employers in a number of fields in the coal and steel industries, and has also financed and promoted research into accident prevention and occupational diseases.

One field where the Common Market has brought a positive contribution to improved working conditions is that covered by Article 119: equal pay for equal work. The recognition of this principle in the Treaty was a victory for France—the only member country where it was already fully applicable—the argument with which the French delegates got their way being that if it were not applied in the rest of the Community French employers would be at a disadvantage. It was also a logical aim in view of the requirement for 'upward equalisation'. It was laid down in the Treaty that the principle should be put into effect by the end of the first stage, and the French required proof that the other member States were at least taking practical steps to apply it before agreeing to the move to the second stage at the end of 1961.

One other activity of the EEC Commission may be mentioned here, although it does not strictly come under the heading of social policy: that is a series of enquiries into wages in major industries throughout the Community. If the experience of the Coal and Steel Community is repeated, these may well provide invaluable ammunition for the unions in countries and industries where wage levels are revealed to be disproportionately low in relation to the rest of the Community.

We have so far neglected however the major instrument of Community social policy, the European Social Fund. We have already seen that the creation of the Common Market is expected to bring about structural changes in the national economies, with the closing-down or reconversion of inefficient firms being amongst the most obvious. Advantageous though this may be to the Community as a whole, it is clearly not so welcome for the workers in the industries concerned, and the aim and object of the Social Fund is precisely to ensure that their interests are protected by helping to finance their re-training or re-settlement or allowances in lieu of wages whilst firms are carrying out reconversion projects.

The action of the Fund is not direct: it is empowered to refund to member governments or public authorities fifty per cent of money

spent on such schemes Moreover, its grants are retro-active and cannot ⎫
be made until the workers concerned have been re-employed or re- ⎬
settled. On the other hand the reconversion project must have been ⎭
presented by the member State and received the prior approval of the
EEC Commission before it was executed. Thus the Fund can in no way
take the initiative: it is intended to stimulate the national authorities to
take action, and to look more favourably on reconversion projects;
and provided the necessary conditions are met its grants are automatic
and unlimited.

This retro-active aspect of the Fund has been severely criticised,
especially by the Community trade union organisations, who have
called for a change in the Fund's statute to enable it to finance directly
reconversion or re-settlement schemes.

The scale of the Fund's activities, even under the present system,
looks like being considerable. The retro-active grants made for 1958
and 1959, when the effects of the Common Market had scarcely begun
to be felt, totalled some £3,500,000 and for 1960 and 1961 it would
appear to have risen steeply; the total for 1961 was thought likely to be
at least £7 million. As tariff cuts reach 50 per cent and more, and the
possibilities of increased competition in the Common Market come to
be fully exploited, the number of firms wishing to take advantage of
aid from the Fund for re-training their workers, or retaining them
whilst they carry out extensive reconversion (possibly with aid from
the Investment Bank), will certainly grow. If its possibilities are exploited to the full, and if national and local authorities are prepared to
co-operate, the Fund seems capable of providing an effective instrument
for protecting the interests of the workers in the Common Market.

4

Energy: Three Communities, One Problem

(i) EURATOM

THE EUROPEAN Atomic Energy Community—known by the usefully international mnemonic 'Euratom'—was set up simultaneously with the Common Market by a separate Treaty signed in Rome in March 1957. It has a separate five-member Commission, but shares all the other Community institutions with EEC, and also has its headquarters in Brussels. As with the Common Market, the motives behind its creation were in part economic, but in part also political.

Europe at that time was still in the throes of its post-war fuel and power shortage, and it was considered that atomic power on a large scale would be urgently needed to meet steadily growing energy requirements and thus ensure the economic expansion of the Common Market. A separate Community was chosen as being the most efficient instrument for rapid action in this new and highly technical sector. Yet hardly was the ink dry on the signatures than a radical change came over the European energy situation: oil began to make rapid headway on the market, natural gas resources were developed, and the coal-mining industry faced a crisis of over-production. The feeling of urgency about the mission of Euratom evaporated, and the emphasis switched from the development of commercial nuclear energy to research. Only in 1961, with the prospect of nuclear energy becoming competitive by 1970 or earlier, was a big scheme launched for sharing the cost of nuclear power development projects.

The second reason for setting up Euratom was the desire to reduce the lead, in the field of peaceful nuclear development, which the United States, the U.S.S.R. and Britain had acquired. The gap was a vast one, even between the United Kingdom and the Continental countries: at the time Euratom was created France was just bringing her first reactor into operation—the only one on the Continent, and Britain already had 180 MW of installed power. (The gap in the field of power reactors remains big—at the end of 1962 the figures for installed nuclear capacity will be: U.K. 935 MW, Euratom 73 MW, representing the French Marcoule reactor and one small German reactor. On the other hand the French peaceful research effort will actually have overhauled the British, in figures for expenditure at least, and that of the Community as a whole exceeds the U.K. effort). The development of nuclear energy is extremely costly, and the European countries could not afford the luxury of separate nuclear industries, possibly even competing for research workers and resources. Moreover, the field to be developed is a vast one, and co-ordination of national efforts could ensure that there was no duplication of effort but rather that the work of the member countries fitted into an interlocking and complementary whole. The role of Euratom was therefore to be one of initiation and co-ordination. There was never any suggestion that it should take over, even less control, the national programmes. Its task was, and is, to ensure their harmonious development. At the same time, having an overall view, it can take the initiative in filling in the gaps, concentrating its own activities in fields not covered by the member States.

The action of Euratom has to be seen against the background of the nuclear situation in the Community. France alone had developed a nuclear industry of her own: far behind her trailed Germany (who was only allowed to start any activities in the nuclear field in 1955) and Italy, with Belgium and the Netherlands almost non-starters (Luxembourg has no nuclear activity and plays no active part in Euratom). This has inevitably shaped attitudes to the Community. France, particularly under de Gaulle, has continued to develop her own nuclear industry; she has given full support to some Euratom projects but has tended to look on the Community as little more than a useful annex to her own programme, and certainly not as a joint undertaking. France has often criticised what she has called the 'dispersion' of Euratom activities on numerous schemes of no direct interest to her. Where she has worked with Euratom, however, her collaboration has been wholehearted. At the other end of the scale German industry, anxious to develop a nuclear industry of its own, tended to be less interested in the Commission's plans for developing new types of reactor than in importing proven American types. The Common External Tariff on reactors and reactor parts was at first suspended but has now begun to be applied. There is full free trade inside the Community in all nuclear material. Fissionable material (uranium, etc.) is incidentally the property of the Community (save for that which the member States devote to military purposes) and a Supply Agency exists to share out supplies should there be a shortage.

The development of atomic reactors offers immensely wide scope, and it is too early yet to know which will prove to be the most effective kinds: any of the types at present being experimented with might, in the evolutionary imagery of the nuclear scientists, give rise to a promising line in subsequent generations. It was therefore natural that the Euratom Commission should prefer to promote research in the Community on new and as yet unproven types, rather than duplicate the work done in Britain or the United States. The three pillars of Euratom's activity, then, are three families of reactors, although it is interested also in many other kinds, and deals too with a wide range of other aspects of the peaceful use of nuclear energy, from biology to marine propulsion.

The methods which Euratom employs reflect the dual role of co-ordination and initiation referred to above. On the one hand it has its own Common Research Centre; on the other, it has developed a complex network of contracts and agreements under which it finances research carried out by scientific institutes, universities and above all by the nascent nuclear industries in the member countries.

THE THREE FAMILIES OF REACTORS

We have seen that the Euratom Commission wanted to develop reactors about which little was known. In the field of natural uranium reactors, the kind using a graphite moderator had already been developed in Britain and France, but natural uranium reactors with a heavy-water moderator were a relatively new field, arousing great interest and being actively pursued only in Canada—with whom Euratom signed a co-operation agreement. The line of reactors the Commission chose to work on has been given the general heading ORGEL. It is on these reactors that much of the work in the Common Research Centre, and also a large number of contracts with industry, are concentrated. The construction of ESSOR, a trial reactor of the Orgel type, has been entrusted to private industry. It is to be built by 1966, opening the way to the construction of an Orgel power reactor by 1968. This would then be producing by the 1970s the plutonium which the 'plutonivorous' or plutonium-burning reactors likely to be coming into use by then will need.

The second type of reactor which has interested the Commission is the 'fast breeder reactor' (of the kind already in operation at Dounreay since 1959, in the U.S. since 1954 and in the U.S.S.R. since 1958, but still offering much scope for experiment). Here the French are well advanced with a reactor poetically known as RAPSODIE (at Cadarache), whilst research on similar lines is going on at Karlsruhe in Germany. The advantage of a fast reactor, and the reason for Community interest in it, is that it seems to offer a reasonable chance of low-cost energy. The second Euratom research programme provides for the development either of a single reactor, in co-operation with both France and Germany, or should the research now going on take different turns, then of two separate reactors. It is planned to build trial reactors by 1967 and one or two power reactors by 1968. It seems that there are enough differences between the Community schemes and Britain's ZEBRA reactor to leave scope for complementary research.

The third reactor family which Euratom has hopes of fostering is that of high-temperature gas reactors. Here the Community is already co-operating with the United Kingdom on the DRAGON project, for which it bears a third of the cost: even without British accession to Euratom the Commission has plans for Euratom to associate itself more closely with DRAGON in the future. Inside the Community Euratom is also taking a direct share in the development of a second project going by the peculiar name (to British ears) of BBC-Krupp.

In addition to these three major branches, on which it is planned to spend sums of the order of $80 million (fast reactors), $62 million (Orgel) and $40 million (gas) over the next five years[1], Euratom is also interested to a lesser extent in research both on reactors of already proven types and on the development of entirely new kinds of reactor (in particular a variety known as SUSPOP 'fog-cooled' reactors; and advanced water reactors).

The Treaty provided for an initial five-year research programme, which is due to come to an end in 1962: a programme for a further five years has been drafted and was due to be approved by the Council of Ministers in the summer of 1962. The first programme involved the expenditure of $215 million, and as it took time to get the research programme under way most of this was spent over the last two years. It is therefore a very similar rate of expenditure which is planned in the second programme for which the Commission is proposing a total of $480 million (likely to be whittled down somewhat by the Council).

[1] At the time of writing it looks as though these figures, proposed by the Euratom Commission, may be slightly cut by the Council of Ministers.

At all events the scale of the second programme would clearly have to be revised in the event of British accession.

THE COMMON RESEARCH CENTRE

It was early decided that the Community's own research should not be concentrated in a single centre, which might prove unwieldy and therefore less efficient, and would fail to give a stimulus to research throughout the area. The Common Research Centre therefore comprises in fact a series of four centres (in Italy, Belgium, Germany and the Netherlands), each specialising in some particular aspects of the overall research programme.

The most important unit is at Ispra, formerly the Italian national atomic research centre, and now made over to the Community: some 150 Italian research workers still remain, and work closely with the 1,200 or more members of the Euratom research teams. It is the work at Ispra that is centred around ORGEL, although it will also work on some aspects of the fast reactor schemes.

Secondly, at Geel in Belgium a Central Bureau of Nuclear Measurement—a vital necessity for any research programme—has been established. Thirdly, a European Transuranian Institute[1] is being set up at Karlsruhe in Germany, closely linked with the atomic centre already existing there. One of its major tasks is the development of fuel elements based on plutonium. Lastly, the fourth branch of the Common Research Centre is at Petten, where work will be centred on a high flux reactor taken over from Reactor Centrum Nederland, the Dutch national research centre. The Petten Centre will also devote its activities amongst other things to the use of thorium in connection with the BBC-Krupp project. Neither of these branches came fully into operation until 1962, and indeed the whole of the Common Research Centre is in the very early stages of activity. No fresh additions are planned in the present member countries.

The balance between direct expenditure on research and the sum spent through research contracts reflects the policy of stimulating national activity. At least 60 per cent of the $215 million of the first programme will have been spent under research contracts, 250 of which had been signed by May 1962. About half the budget of the second research programme will also be spent through contracts. At present there are twelve major 'contracts of association' covering a wide

---

[1] 'Transuranian' is the technical term for plutonium and other elements with a greater molecular weight than uranium.

field and extending for periods up to twenty years, and the rest are either for small specific projects or are intended to promote the use of nuclear energy. The contracts are concluded with the national research organisations, with universities and research institutes, and also with industrial firms (either metallurgical or chemical firms, or groups interested in the development of nuclear energy).

It is not possible here to do more than list the various fields in which Euratom is active: they cover the production of radio-isotopes and marked molecules and their use in medicine and industry; the biological applications of nuclear energy (e.g., the use of radiation to fight cattle diseases), and research on controlled nuclear fission (which constitutes a whole programme in itself, with contracts to the Italian national centre, work by a combined France-Euratom team, contracts to two German institutes, and co-operation with CERN, a non-governmental pure research centre in Geneva). Work is being done, both under contract and at Ispra, on the automatic treatment of scientific data and on the development of translating machines for scientific texts. In a quite different direction Euratom is promoting and assisting work on developing a nuclear-powered vessel. Besides the contracts under Euratom's own programme there are others under a joint research programme with the United States.

ENCOURAGING THE DEVELOPMENT OF POWER REACTORS

Another agreement with the United States signed in 1960 was intended to stimulate the building of power reactors. Firms in the Community were invited to submit projects which would qualify for joint aid under the programme. In the event the response proved disappointing: only an Italian firm, SENN, took advantage of the offer, with a project for a boiling water reactor. A second invitation launched in September 1961 met with a slightly better response: one project was submitted by SENA (the Franco-Belgian Nuclear Company of the Ardennes) for a reactor on the border between France and Belgium at Chooz, another by a German firm, and another is still expected at the time of writing.

It was in 1960 that the idea gained momentum of direct action by Euratom itself in the field of power reactors. The argument behind it ran like this: in the not-too-distant future (and before 1970 according to some estimates) nuclear power stations could start providing energy at costs competitive with traditional fuel and power resources; yet to wait until then would be disastrous, for only practical experience gained in the operation of such plants on an industrial scale could serve as a basis for a viable programme of production—and such experience takes years to acquire. The finance and backing which Euratom could give would enable private firms in the Community, which would otherwise find the financial risks not worth taking, to undertake experimental programmes and gain experience which later would benefit the Community as a whole.

A programme drawn up in 1961 met with a favourable reception all round and was approved by the Council of Ministers. By the end of 1962 two contracts had been signed, a third was being prepared, and other applications had been received.

Lastly it is worth recording that the Euratom Commission has taken a number of important steps to meet the new responsibilities which the development of nuclear energy thrusts upon society. As one of its first tasks it worked out, with the collaboration and approval of other Community bodies, a set of 'safety standards'—indicating safe 'doses' of radioactivity, and maximum permissible levels in the atmosphere, water and soil—which now apply throughout the Community, and are kept constantly under review, changes being submitted to the Parliament and the Economic and Social Committee for their views. When a special convention on third party liability for nuclear accidents (providing for government guarantees) was worked out under OEEC the Euratom countries decided it was not adequate, and have themselves drawn up a more far-reaching additional convention.

It is difficult to estimate the true importance of Euratom. Certainly it has not yet succeeded in welding the activities of the member States (in particular of France) into a single coherent whole. On the other hand it has succeeded in encouraging a considerable degree of co-operation in specific fields, and by 1962 the shape of a concerted programme for concentrating on the development of a limited number of reactor types was taking shape. Once the work of the Common Research Centre gets into its stride it should provide a major impetus to research. Although in absolute terms the Community still lags far behind the U.K., Russia or the United States in its nuclear development for peaceful uses, the scale of its research activity has now overtaken Britain. It is too early, however, to say what the practical results of this research effort will be.

As far as nuclear power is concerned, the existence of Euratom should provide a guarantee that when it does become competitive, perhaps in the next decade, with power from traditional sources, it will be developed under a single co-ordinated programme for the Community. Moreover it can be assumed, as we shall see below, that by then the Community will have a common policy for the whole vital field of fuel and power.

(ii) The Coal and Steel Community

The Coal and Steel Community was the forerunner of the Common Market. The motives that presided at its birth were perhaps more openly political than in the case of EEC and Euratom: the avowed aim was to end for ever the possibility of war between the countries of Western Europe, by pooling two basic industries essential to any war effort.

From the economic point of view, ECSC is a common market, run by a nine-member body, the High Authority, which in the prevailing atmosphere of enthusiasm for this first experiment in integration was given considerable powers. Free movement of the products coming under the Paris Treaty by which ECSC was set up—coal, coke, iron-ore, scrap, pig-iron, and steel—was achieved almost at once: in 1953 the import duties on steel (amounting to as much as 20 per cent in some cases for finished steel), and quotas and other restrictions on the other goods, were removed. There is no common external tariff: the Community is an exporter rather than an importer of steel, and for coal the member countries retain control over their import policy. Scrap exports have been banned for most of the period since 1952.

The major task facing the High Authority was thus less to create a free trade area than to ensure the application throughout the area of the principles of free and undistorted competition on which the Treaty is based. In addition it has played some role in shaping—or at least guiding—the development of the industries for which it is responsible. In the steel sector its task has been made easier by a steady run of progress and expansion: the coal economy on the other hand has run into a major crisis which raises such vast problems that they can only be dealt with in the framework of a policy for the whole fuel and power sector.

The removal of trade barriers for coal and steel had two main results. Trade in all ECSC goods expanded at unprecedented speed, far outstripping both the growth of trade with other countries and the trade between the Six in other goods: from 1952 to 1955 alone the rise in intra-Community trade in coal and steel amounted to 93 per cent, whereas during the same three years trade in all the sectors liberalised under OEEC rose by only 53 per cent. Under the stimulus of this increased trade—combined of course with the general economic boom —the Community's steel output rose by 93 per cent from 1951 to 1960 as against an average increase in world production of no more than 66 per cent. Despite the rapid development of new steel-producing areas, the Six's share in the total went up steadily (from 17·9 per cent to 21·3 per cent), whereas the U.S. share fell drastically from 43·3 per cent to 26·3 per cent and that of Britain also fell slightly (from 7·5 per cent to 7·2 per cent). Owing to the increased efficiency of the Community industry as a whole—for which the common market in steel was at least partly responsible—European steel prices remained stable at a time when world prices in general were rising.

A second major consequence of the common market was a rationalisation of the flow of trade in coal and steel. A map of coal and iron-ore deposits in Western Europe shows a triangle taking in the Ruhr, Lorraine and N.E. France: yet the hazards of history had divided this area between no less than five sovereign countries each with its own industrial economy. Trade increased so rapidly because it was now able to find its natural course between areas complementary to each other —Ruhr coal now going to Lorraine, to take only one instance, instead of all the way to Southern Germany.

Ensuring free competition in this highly cartelised branch of the economy was one of the High Authority's most difficult tasks, and remains one of its major concerns. All firms in the Community are required to submit to the High Authority price schedules for their goods, and to sell to all customers, at the prices set, without discrimination. The prices are given for specific areas and firms may align their prices in these areas on those of their competitors: but no unpublished rebates are allowed, and the High Authority can and does take firm action, imposing fines on offenders, to prevent the coal and steel companies infringing the pricing rules. In the coal sector price alignment on competitors is only allowed where the producer is the natural supplier for the area, for geographical reasons, or has a standing link with customers. In Germany and Belgium joint selling agencies exist, under strict conditions laid down by the High Authority, to organise the sale of coal.

The corollary to price control and the presentation of price schedules (which the High Authority need not publish but which any potential competitor may consult) is full knowledge too of the rates charged for transport: if transport rates remain secret the railways in particular can accord national firms advantages over their competitors. The High Authority has been trying for years to achieve an open market in transport: discrimination in the rates charged is banned by the ECSC Treaty, and after failing to get the governments to agree to compulsory publication of rates and conditions (or their notification to the High Authority) the latter issued in 1960 a 'directive' both requiring the States to accept the principle and laying down the means by which they were to do it. The Court of Justice, to which two member States appealed, ruled that the High Authority had no power to issue a directive, and so in 1961 the High Authority issued instead a recommendation (which is binding as to the ends to be achieved, but leaves the means to the discretion of the governments) to the same effect. Both Italy and Holland appealed against the recommendation but in July 1962 the Court upheld the action of the High Authority; its ruling is clearly of great importance in relation to the EEC Commission's plans for achieving fair competition in the whole transport sector.

The other aspect of the High Authority's role as watch-dog of fair competition is its anti-cartel activity. All cartels in the coal and steel industries have to be registered, and many of the seventy or so that were in existence when this provision came into force in 1953 were soon dissolved, though smaller ones (such as joint selling bodies in the smaller coalfields) were granted extensions. Major conflicts lasting several years took place before the biggest cartels—such as GEORG, which sold all the Ruhr coal—could be abolished or brought into line by compromise settlements. A dispute over the powers of the three coal-selling cartels into which GEORG was split up continued until May 1962 when the Court of Justice finally upheld a High Authority decision that it would be contrary to the Treaty for them to link up again in a single selling agency.

New mergers and concentrations, too, are subject to the High Authority's approval. Since one of the aims of the common market was to bring about an adaptation to a larger scale of output, the High Authority has been fairly lenient in interpreting the requirement that new groupings must not acquire a dominant position on their sector of the market or on part of it. A large proportion of the mergers planned in the last ten years have been approved. Each case is examined strictly on its merits and the High Authority has sometimes required the firms to break off their links with other groups, or has made it a condition that future plans for expansion must be submitted for approval.

AN ACTIVE POLICY

The High Authority is not merely a sort of policeman enforcing the rules of the Treaty, as might be supposed from the above. There are many ways in which it plays a positive role, both in promoting the balanced progress of the common market and in improving conditions for the workers in the coal and steel industries.

Its role of guidance finds its most immediate expression in 'General Objectives' for coal and steel. Drawn up after a major study involving consultations with innumerable experts in all the sectors involved, they are in fact detailed forecasts of supply and demand trends, intended to indicate the lines along which the industry should develop if a reasonable equilibrium is to be maintained. New General Objectives for iron and steel were published in February 1962, covering predictable trends up to 1965. New General Objectives for coal are also due and will probably be cast so as to set future developments for coal in the context of trends in the energy sector as a whole.

It is in the light of the General Objectives that the High Authority examines the investment projects of the ECSC firms, which have to be submitted to it in advance. It cannot prevent a firm from carrying out an investment project, but may publish a negative 'opinion' pointing out that it does not fit in with the pattern of development outlined in the Objectives and may disturb the balance of supply and demand or create surplus capacity.

The High Authority does not limit itself to guidance: it also pursues an active policy of its own. In this it is helped by the fact that unlike the EEC Commission (which is dependent on the contributions of member States, and risks having its financial estimates cut by the Council of Ministers) it has funds of its own. They are obtained from a levy of up to 1 per cent on the annual business turnover of all ECSC firms (except the iron-ore companies): for 1961–2 the levy stood at 0·35 per cent and for 1962–3 the satisfactory financial position of the High Authority enabled it to be cut to 0·2 per cent. The levy rate is decided by the High Authority (which must however get the agreement of the Council by a two-thirds majority if it wants to raise the rate above one per cent). Hesitatingly at first, but more confidently in recent years, the High Authority has followed a financial policy of its own: by careful placing of its funds, and by building up a substantial 'reserve fund', it has established its credit on the international markets and is now in a position to raise any funds it needs by loans.

It was in 1955 that the High Authority first obtained a $100 million loan from the U.S. Export-Import Bank. Since then it has successfully floated loans on the Swiss market, the American market several times, and more recently inside the Community also. It uses the funds obtained to grant loans to aid investment projects by Community firms, giving first priority to investments intended either to increase productivity or to bring about an adaptation to new market conditions. Together with the General Objectives, the loan policy constitutes a means of 'steering' private investment in the coal and steel sectors.

A special case where the High Authority took direct action to guarantee the stability of the common market was the 'Scrap Perequation Fund'. During the early years of ECSC there was an acute scrap metal shortage and the idea of the Fund was to keep scrap prices in the Community below the soaring levels on the world market, sharing the burden of doing so equally amongst all the firms using scrap. Any steel company which was obliged to import scrap from the rest of the world to meet its requirements received from the Fund the difference between the price paid and the price in the Community: and the total paid out was collected from the more fortunate firms not obliged to import, by means of a levy on all scrap transactions inside the member countries. Despite administrative complications (and a series of frauds which were discovered later, with scrap from ship-breaking being passed off as imported scrap in order to qualify for a refund!) the scheme served its main purpose and helped to keep scrap prices, and thus steel prices, steady.

LOOKING AFTER THE WORKERS

Investment is not the only sphere where the High Authority is active: it has taken a lively interest in living and working conditions. The basis of its social policy, under the Treaty, was due to be free movement of miners and steel-workers, but attempts to ensure this by granting an ECSC 'worker's card' failed resoundingly because the card was only made available to skilled workers who in any case were in demand at home, or if they wanted to move could always obtain work permits and good conditions without difficulty.

More important by far have been High Authority grants for industrial reconversion. An early scheme, which came to an end with the transitional period in 1958, applied only to cases where it was the direct effects of the common market and increased competition which had put the firms in difficulties. A new scheme now in operation enables the High Authority to use its own funds to make grants towards the re-training or re-settlement of workers when this is made necessary by structural changes on the coal or steel markets: the obvious case is that of miners from mines which have to be closed down. During the 1958 coal crisis the High Authority also paid out millions of dollars from its reserves under a scheme to keep the wages of miners on short-time (above all in Belgium and Germany) up to a certain minimum level.

Of all the High Authority's activities the one with the most imme-diate efficacity is perhaps the workers' housing schemes. Since this was not something which figured in the Treaty (and the High Authority could therefore use neither the proceeds of the levy, nor the reserve fund) special loans have been raised to help provide adequate housing conditions for the workers—many of them migrants—in the coal and steel industries. Since a first pilot scheme in 1958 proved successful the High Authority has undertaken four other programmes. By January 1st, 1962, over 43,000 dwellings had been built under the scheme, and those under construction will bring the total up to 56,400. The total sum provided either directly by the High Authority or as a result of its initiative is over $110 million.

Lastly, the High Authority had been active for many years in the fields of safe working conditions and industrial medicine, making grants to encourage research, co-ordinating the work of existing bodies, and promoting collaboration between workers and employers.

INSTITUTIONS

About the institutional framework of the Coal and Steel Community little needs to be said. The Consultative Committee plays a role very similar to that of the Economic and Social Committee in EEC, carrying on the whole probably rather more weight with the Executive. The European Parliament continues to maintain the tradition of close super-vision of the High Authority's activities which it established as the Common Assembly from 1952 to 1958. Members of the High Autho-rity regularly attend meetings of parliamentary committees and there is a steady flow of parliamentary questions about the coal and steel sector.

The Court of Justice has played an extremely important part in the history of the Coal and Steel Community. It has frequently had to give rulings on cases with the widest economic and even political implications. Thus right at the beginning it quashed a decision by the High Authority authorising steel firms to sell at a certain margin above or below their scheduled prices. In 1961 it turned down as being contrary to the Treaty the text of a revised version of Article 65.2 (on cartels), worked out jointly by the High Authority and the Council of Ministers and designed to make it possible for the High Authority to be more lenient in authorising joint selling on the crisis-stricken coal market: this meant that the only way to achieve the desired end would be a major revision of the Article in question, involving ratification by the national parliaments—a procedure which both the High Authority and some member governments are unwilling to risk in current political circumstances. Another major case where its ruling will be of far-reaching importance is that concerning compulsory publicity for transport rates.

Also in the institutional field it is worth mentioning that there has been close liaison with the U.K. in the Council of Association, and that the Community has agreements with Switzerland and Austria about conditions for the through transport of ECSC products.

In the iron and steel sector, it can reasonably be said that the Community has proved a success. The same is hardly true for coal. When the Treaty was signed there was a fuel shortage and every effort was made to expand output and encourage coal imports. Then the tide turned and the coal-mining industry faced a crisis, with short-time working, stocks at the pit-heads piling up to unprecedented levels, and output far exeeding demand. The situation was aggravated by a flow of cheap American coal under long-term contracts concluded during the period of shortage. Trying to introduce solutions which would be applied by the Community as a whole, the High Authority found itself unable to rally the support of the governments. A plan for production quotas and limitation of imports failed to pass the Council of Ministers. Instead the High Authority had no option but to leave it to the member countries to solve their own problems: Germany put import restrictions on coal from non-member countries, and the High Authority was obliged to agree to temporary isolation of the Belgian coal market from the rest of the common market (a measure which has still not been rescinded in 1962 despite the return to a more normal market situation). The High Authority's own action was limited to direct assistance to the miners hit by the crisis.

This failure of the supranational machinery, though in part symptomatic of the low ebb reached by the supranational idea at that time—the governments preferring the formula they had just adopted for the Common Market—also reflected the fact that coal was facing a structural crisis resulting from the competition of fuel oil. Coal policy could no longer be considered separately from energy problems as a whole: it began to be realised that the Community needed a common energy policy.

(iii) A COMMON ENERGY POLICY

As a result of the historical development of European integration, the different sectors of the fuel and power economy come under the authority of three different Communities: coal under ECSC, atomic energy under Euratom, and oil and natural gas under the general provisions of the Common Market. Yet the problem facing the Six—the same as has arisen in Britain—is one that can be solved only by a single policy covering the whole energy economy. Simply stated it is this: coal, which formerly dominated the fuel and power market, has lost ground so rapidly over recent years to fuel oil and natural gas that, a M. Marjolin of the EEC Commission put it in a speech to the European Parliament, it has 'lost not merely its monopoly but even its absolute majority'. At the same time as the new cleaner and more efficient fuel drove it from many of its traditional markets in industry and elsewhere in the economy (heating, the railways, etc.) it has also faced growing competition from cheaper imported coal, especially from the United States, even on the markets where it remains the only suitable fuel.

At the same time as oil products gained ground at the expense of coal, the Community as a whole has come to be more and more dependent on imports for its total fuel and power consumption. Most of its imported oil comes from the Middle East, but in recent years a growing proportion has been imported from the Soviet bloc, and this raises the problem of ensuring that Western Europe does not become dependent on supplies which could be cut off for political reasons: reliable sources of energy are an essential condition of the Community's economic expansion. Lastly, there looms on the horizon the possibility of economically competitive nuclear power stations, which according to some recent estimates should start contributing to the Community's energy supply from 1970 onwards.

One result of the division of the energy sector between the three Communities is that none of the Treaties contains any provision for a common energy policy. The recognition that one is needed is merely the logical conclusion from the need for cheap and reliable supplies of energy as a basis for expansion in a Community which will be developing as a unit thanks to common or co-ordinated policies in other sectors. As with transport, major divergencies from one country to another in the prices of the various forms of energy, or in the way they are treated as regards taxation, or, again, in their relative competitive position, could distort competition in the market as a whole.

It is therefore easy enough for the Six to agree on the need for co-ordination of their policies or even for a common policy: but there is a fundamental clash between their interests. Germany, as the country with the biggest coal output and the largest mining community, has to defend the interests of the mines; France has had a special interest in finding European markets for Sahara oil (but also has her own coal-mining industry to think of); and Italy, who has no coal interests to protect, and has built up her economy on the basis of the cheapest available imported energy and more recently on the new forms—her own natural gas, and imported oil of which she is a major refiner—is primarily interested in ensuring energy supplies at the lowest possible price.

As early as 1957 the Council of Ministers of the Coal and Steel Community entrusted the High Authority with the task of working out a common energy policy for the Six countries. When the other two Communities were set up, the work was taken over by a group of members from all three Executives, known as the Interexecutive for Energy. Analysing the situation and working out proposals which might serve to reconcile the various interests involved proved a lengthy and laborious undertaking, and it was not until early in 1961 that a first set of proposals was laid before the Council of Ministers of ECSC. They indicated the general lines along which a common policy might be worked out, and also contained suggestions for drawing up without delay the kind of emergency measures which would clearly be needed to protect the coal industry from disaster should there be an economic recession—experience having shown that once the crisis had begun it would be far more difficult to get the member States to agree to Community measures.

Those proposals formed the subject of a great deal of public debate, but nothing was done to put them into effect, for they were never formally adopted by the Council of Ministers, although it debated them at length on many occasions. Meanwhile various industrial groups, such as the organisation which groups the coal-consuming industries of Western Europe, made urgent calls for steps towards a common policy. In January and February 1962 the European Parliamentary Assembly held a marathon debate which reflected in its range and confusion the complexity of the problems to be faced, but resulted in the adoption of a resolution calling for a policy roughly corresponding to that proposed by the Interexecutive.

At last, in April 1962 in Rome at an unofficial meeting of the Ministers responsible for fuel and power in the member countries, a first major step forward seemed to have been made. For the first time there was all-round agreement on the need not just for co-ordination of national policies but for a genuine common policy, to be applied at the Community level, and to be based unequivocally on the long-term aim of ensuring adequate energy supplies for the Community at the lowest possible cost to the consumer—though taking into account of course the need to guarantee the coal-mining industry a smooth adaptation to the changing situation on the energy market. The Interexecutive was instructed to work out a time-table for the elaboration and implementation of such a policy. A first set of proposals were due to go before the Ministers in the summer of 1962, but decisions are unlikely before the autumn.

BLUEPRINT FOR AN ENERGY POLICY

It is possible, however, taking as a starting-point the proposals of the Interexecutive, to predict the general lines along which the common policy is likely to take shape. The first basic principle is that, as the 1961 Interexecutive report put it, 'nothing should be done to give the more costly forms of energy *lasting* protection against the more economic forms', for this would mean deliberately putting a brake on economic progress. The objective will rather be the adaptation of the Community economy to the new conditions on the energy market. (In this connection it has often been pointed out that the price reductions made by the oil companies for petroleum products which compete directly with coal are sometimes tactical ones aimed at persuading a given group of users to change over to oil products, and that prices might rise again later; it would be a mistake to close down coal-mining capacity which might turn out in the long run to be economic. The Interexecutive points out however that should the Community's coal needs ever come to exceed output it would be easy to import coal cheaper than it can be produced in the member countries.)

The second principle is however that the re-adaptation must be a gradual one, giving the coal-mining industry time to re-organise. To leave the problem to be solved by the free play of market forces would have disastrous social consequences in areas still largely dependent on the mines for employment.

In the light of these two principles, several practical steps are envisaged. The first would be the introduction of a common commercial policy for the whole energy sector. Coal at present moves freely between member countries (except that the precarious Belgian market is for the moment isolated) but there is no uniform external trade policy. It is therefore proposed to harmonise tariff and quota policies (as laid down in Article 72 of the ECSC Treaty) and work out a common approach to coal imports from State-trading countries (especially Poland); in addition there would be prior consultation on transactions such as long-term contracts) with non-member countries. Trade in oil and petroleum products between member countries will of course be freed gradually under the Rome Treaty: but so far the common external tariff (refined oil figured on List G) has not been set, and it would have to be determined as an integral part of the common policy.

Secondly, there will undoubtedly have to be steps to bring the rules of competition covering oil and coal into line. At the moment coal is subject to the strict rules imposed in the ECSC Treaty (publication and strict observance of price schedules), with the result that its price structure is inflexible and tactical changes cannot be made to meet competition from fuel oil: the duel between the two is thus unequal from the start, since oil can be sold at unpublished prices which the companies can and do vary at will to drive coal from one or other sector of the market. The proposals for remedying this situation are at the heart of the debate on energy policy. It has been suggested that there should be an 'orientation price', which would in fact be a 'guiding price' rather than a target price. It would be calculated on the basis of estimated demand and supply and would be set at the level which if observed would keep the market in a healthy state, saving coal from ruinous competition but not protecting inefficient mines. Firms would of course be allowed a margin of variation around the price. It is far from clear however whether the scheme will ever form part of the common policy.

As a complement to this the Interexecutive has been considering a comparison of all national policies affecting fuel and power prices including direct setting of prices or special taxes on fuel oil such as have been applied in Belgium and Germany. Efforts would be made to narrow the gaps between national price levels. Lastly legislation on the levels of stocks of oil (for supply reasons) and on air- and water-pollution should be brought into line.

National measures of various kinds for subsidising the coal industry should gradually be complemented and then replaced by measures operating at the Community level. At the same time every effort should be made, in particular by co-ordinating the re-adaptation schemes of EEC and ECSC, to set the coal industry on a sounder economic basis by the closing-down of uncompetitive mines and by other means; one minor suggestion was a cut in the retiring age for miners.

Lastly there should be, as suggested above, a flexible but complete plan for meeting major difficulties which may occur before the long-term re-adaptation of the coal-mining industry has been completed. Such a plan would come into action automatically when the situation fulfilled a number of objective criteria also to be worked out in advance: there would thus be no delay and no scope for refusal to co-operate on the part of one or other government.

I should perhaps emphasise that what I have been describing is not a policy already drawn up or adopted, but merely the form which such a policy may take when eventually agreed upon. The outline programme which the Interexecutive is due to submit to the ministers for the elaboration and implementation of a common policy in fact provides for a preparatory period—to last until the beginning of 1964, thus in all probability allowing new member States to play their part—during which the detailed measures for the transition period and the outline of the eventual common energy market would be drafted.

The transitional period itself, beginning in 1964, would see the first practical steps, with measures of national policy gradually being replaced by Community policy (as in the case of subsidies or commercial policy) or else brought into line (taxation, etc.).

At the end of the transitional period (1970 at the latest), the common energy policy would come fully into effect, taking its place amongst the other common policies of the Community and closely linked with them. Energy policy has been a slow starter, both because of the complexity of the problems, and because there was nothing in the Treaties to oblige the member countries to take action: but once again the interaction of one aspect of the economy on another—the logic of integration, one might call it—seems bound to have its way.

5

African Partners and European Associates

At a late stage in the negotiations on the Treaty of Rome, the French proposed that their overseas territories should be accepted as a joint responsibility of the Common Market, and with them the Belgian Dutch and Italian territories too. It was a brilliant tactical move France's partners, too far committed to risk a break-down of the whole Common Market project by refusing, gave way.[1]

The aim of linking all these under-developed areas closely with the Community was to promote their economic and social development or, to look at it from a different angle, to share out some of the burden formerly borne by the member countries with which they had immediate ties. There were two sides to the Association. First, the creation of a free trade area: all the member countries opened their frontiers to goods from the associated countries and territories at the same rate as to other member countries, whilst the overseas areas applied to the Community as a whole the trading system previously reserved for the 'parent' country (though retaining the right to apply whatever duties are necessary to protect developing industries). The most important aspect of this system was of course the opening up of the whole Community—and in particular the German market—to exports of tropical products and other commodities from the associated countries, and the creation of a preference (through the application of the common ex-

[1] The areas thus associated with the Community were: (a) Madagascar and the fifteen African States due to participate in the new Association, viz.: Senegal Mauretania, Ivory Coast, Dahomey, Upper Volta, Niger, Togo, Cameroun Gabon, Congo-Brazzaville, Centrafrican Republic, Tchad, and Mali (all formerly French), Somalia (formerly under Italian trusteeship) and Congo-Léopoldville (formerly Belgian) (b) Guinea, which refused to continue the association (c) Ruanda-Urundi (due for independence from Belgium very soon) (d) the various small French overseas dependencies (the overseas Departments are considered as part of France) (e) Dutch New Guinea.

In addition the Dutch West Indies will have the status of an Associated State under the new Association, as will Surinam (Dutch Guiana).

ernal tariff) against the exports of other primary producers.[1] It was this which provoked vigorous protests in GATT from the Latin American countries and from Commonwealth countries such as Ghana, who argued that this preference would be bound to lead to their losing markets in the Community. To this the Six replied that for one thing there was no statistical proof available of any such development; and that the growth of demand in the increasingly prosperous Community was such that other primary producing areas need suffer no reduction in the absolute size of their markets even if trade with the associated countries rose.

The second, equally important leg of the Association agreement was the commitment by all the member countries to help finance the economic and social development of the former colonies. In regularly increasing slices over a five-year period they committed themselves to pay a total of $581 million (of which France and Germany each contributed 200 millions) into a Development Fund to be distributed over the same period, with the French territories receiving the lion's share: $511 million. The funds were to be divided between projects for social development—especially hospitals and dispensaries, schools, and training establishments of all kinds—and economic development schemes of general interest: bridges, roads, ports, waterholes, etc. The projects were to be presented by the local administrations through the European states with which they were linked.

The Development Fund took a long time to get into its stride—partly because of the shortage of qualified personnel on the spot, and the consequent dearth of viable projects, and partly owing to the long and complicated procedure involved in the presentation and approval of projects. Nevertheless by 1961 and 1962 the Fund was providing a steady flow of aid for the most pressing needs of economic and social development.

The Association was concluded for an indefinite period, but the Convention fixing the details of its application was due to be revised and renewed after five years, i.e., at the end of 1962. Long before then the situation had undergone a radical change. During 1960, the 'Year of African Independence', all the African countries formerly under French rule, plus Madagascar, the Belgian Congo and Italian Somaliland

---

[1] Germany was, however, granted a substantial duty-free import quota for bananas, to continue even after the end of the transitional period at 75 per cent of the quantity imported in 1956; Italy was granted a duty-free quota on similar lines for unroasted coffee.

achieved autonomous status. With the sole exception of Guinea, they chose to retain their ties with the Common Market: but it was clear that when the Association was reviewed it must take on an entirely new form. Future co-operation and aid must be on a basis of strict equality.

Since the African countries obtained their independence one of the most successful aspects of the Common Market's relations with them has been in the parliamentary field. The European Parliamentary Assembly had taken an active interest from the start in the link with the overseas countries, sending a number of missions to study its problems on the spot. In 1960 the idea of a Eurafrican parliamentary conference was launched, and after a preliminary meeting in Rome a full-scale conference took place in Strasbourg in June 1961, with members of the Assembly and African and Malagasy M.P.s taking part under the joint chairmanship of Herr Hans Furler, President of the E.P.A., and M. Lamine Gueye, the brilliant and dignified President of the Senegal National Assembly.

The real decisions on the future of the Association lie, however, in the hands of the governments of the Six European and the Sixteen African states. The EEC Commission presented precise proposals in the summer of 1961, but when talks began amongst the Six it became clear that there were major differences of opinion, especially between the Germans, who felt that the preferences accorded to the associated countries as against third countries should be reduced and replaced as far as possible by commodity stabilisation schemes, and the French who insisted on the maintenance of preferences. A first meeting with the Ministers of the African countries in Paris in December 1961 yielded little more than a statement of aims couched in the vaguest terms, and the problem was thrust on to working parties of European and African experts. Progress in the early months of 1962 was slow, largely owing to differences of opinion amongst the Six. The prospect of Britain joining the Community complicated the issue: the African countries backed by the French, were anxious to shape the new Association and ensure the maintenance of preferences before any decisions were taken on linking the African Commonwealth countries with the Community. The Dutch on the other hand held that the new Association could only realistically be established by taking into account the terms on which Commonwealth countries might be associated. In May, however, when the Six met the African Ministers for the second time it proved possible to reach a wide measure of agreement on the 'trade' and 'aid' aspects of the new Association with the prospect of a first draft of the new Association agreement by mid-June 1962: at all events, the general shape of it is now clear.

The basic form of the present scheme is to be retained. The Association will remain a free trade area, although with the African States still at liberty to impose customs duties or quota restrictions to protect their developing economies. On the other hand the duties on tropical products in the Common External Tariff of the Community will be cut, in some cases by as much as half, thus reducing discrimination against other tropical producer countries. Special steps will be worked out to ensure that the flow of coffee and bananas from the associated countries to the Community is maintained; there will be inter-governmental co-operation in an attempt to agree on a joint policy for the marketing of tropical products; and some direct aid to producers is allowed. The Community will commit itself to take steps to increase the general level of consumption of tropical products.

The member States will take on a new commitment to provide a total sum of aid (the amount of which is likely to be around $860 million over five years). The Development Fund through which the aid will continue to be channelled will be recast so as to make it more flexible and enable it to give aid in a wider range of forms: subsidies and loans for the development of the social and economic infra-structure (schools, hospitals, communications, etc., as under the present scheme); grants for the development of agriculture, industry and trade; and straightforward loans at economically viable interest rates. Secondly funds will be available to assist local price-regulation schemes aimed at combatting short-term price fluctuations. Under the heading of technical assistance the programme will include preparatory work for investment schemes, aid with operating projects already financed, and an expanded programme of educational grants and training.

On the institutional side there is likely to be a ministerial Council comprising the member States of the Community and all the associated States, and with alternate European and African chairmanship, an administrative body in which the African countries will play a part, and also a parliamentary body along the lines of the Conference held in 1961.

It is of course not possible to predict how far British membership of the Community, and the consequent association of Commonwealth countries or territories, will alter the shape of the Association. The British delegation to the Brussels Conference did indicate however in April 1962 that it found the prospective outlines of the new scheme satisfactory as a basis for offering associate status to the Commonwealth countries in Africa and the West Indies.

The balance between trade and aid in the new Association is of course important for the Community's relations with the rest of the world: the United States and the Latin-American countries would prefer to see all preference brought to an end. Here we again run into the problem of future world-wide agreements.[1]

Politically, the value of the Association has been and remains hard to evaluate, and its future development is even harder to forecast. In so far as the Common Market can keep free of the stigma of 'neo-colonialism' it is likely to retain the allegiance of the Africans, whose cultural ties are chiefly with Europe. The double link between the present associated States, the African Commonwealth countries and the enlarged Community could be a valuable factor of stability in the world: but it is too early to see how far the common link with the Community, the basis for which is largely economic, can counteract the divergent political trends in Africa.[2]

THE WILY GREEKS—AND OTHER CANDIDATES

No picture of the Common Market system can be balanced or complete unless it gives some account of the Communities' relations with non-member countries. We have seen how the development of a common commercial policy involves dealing as a unit with the rest of the world; and in Part III below Michael Shanks will be dealing at length with the Community's role in the world. There are, however, one or two links which have already been given a precise form, and other cases where non-member countries are seeking to establish a specific relationship with the Community, and these must be described briefly here.

Thus Euratom has signed Association Agreements with the United States, Canada and Brazil (as well as with the U.K.) and is negotiating another with the Argentine. ECSC, besides its Association with Britain, has agreements with Austria and Switzerland covering ECSC goods in

---

[1] See Part III, Chapter 3, below.
[2] Twelve of the sixteen associated States are linked in a Western orientated Organisation for African and Malgasy Economic Co-operation (OAMEC). The four others are Mali and Togo, which are planning their economic development along more socialist lines, with a policy of international non-alignment; Somalia; and Congo-Léopoldville.

ransit. Since the Common Market was set up, a steadily growing number of countries have established direct diplomatic representation with the Communities in Brussels; and only French obstruction has prevented the Community from having its own diplomatic representatives in London and Washington.

The creation of the Common Market, and the setting up two years later of the European Free Trade Association left a small number of backward Western European countries isolated, and threatened with exclusion from the advantages of tariff cuts inside the two industrial groups. Greece was one of these unfortunates, and wasted no time in applying for association with the Common Market under the terms of Article 238.[1] The application was received in June 1959 and there followed twenty-one months of laborious negotiations between the EEC Commission, acting on behalf of the Six under a mandate from the Council, and the Greek government. The Greeks fully lived up. to the reputation as a tough and wily bargainer which the individual Greek enjoys in neighbouring countries, and could be well content with the terms of the Association Agreement finally signed. It is to lead in the end, when Greece is economically prepared, to full membership: for the moment it provides for a customs union—though with a number of important exceptions where Greece will not apply the Common Tariff for twenty years. Greece is guaranteed markets for the tobacco and agricultural products which are the mainstays of her export economy, and the Community is to provide her with $125 million of financial aid over five years through the European Investment Bank. Although from the point of view of the Six the determination to reach an agreement, despite all the difficulties, was first and foremost a political one, dictated by a desire to prove the open character of the Community and a more general feeling that to link Greece to them was to strengthen the West, the Common Market also stands to benefit considerably in the long run. For one thing Greece may to some extent replace Italy as a source of migrant labour to meet the Community's shortage. More important in the end will be the additional market for Community industries as the Greek economy expands.

The Turkish government, which made a similar application for association not long after the Greeks, has not been so lucky. The Commission was not able to carry on two sets of negotiations at once; and

[1] Article 238 runs: 'Any European State may ask to become a member of the Community. It shall address its application to the Council which after taking the advice of the Commission decides unanimously'.

it was firmly laid down all along that the generous terms granted to Greece were not to be considered a precedent for future negotiations. Negotiations began again in 1962 but it looks as though the agreement with Turkey will be a far more cautious one, with the possibility of a real Association including a customs union only after a five-year period in which a vigorous attempt will be made to strengthen the Turkish economy.

Although there have been no more formal applications for association (other than those of the three EFTA neutrals—Austria, Sweden and Switzerland[1]—and Portugal, who has now specified that it is association that she is seeking, and Spain) there is quite a queue of countries waiting at the door of the Community. Israel has said she would like some form of agreement to protect her trade with EEC and there has been some talk of a trade agreement with Iran. Under the terms of the Treaty Morocco, Tunisia and Libya can seek special arrangements with EEC, and it is not improbable that an independent Algeria may want to do the same.[2] Thus, as is not surprising, many of the countries around the Mediterranean are interested in establishing special relations with their big new Northern neighbour.

Clearly these and any other applications will have to be left until the Community has accomplished the difficult task of absorbing new members, and of defining its relationship with the European industrialised countries which have applied for Association. In the long run, however, the attraction of the Community is likely to be such that most of the neighbouring countries find it useful to achieve a sound working relationship with it. It could become the centre of a network of agreements of various kinds—though not, it is worth underlining, preferential trade agreements.

[1] See also Part III, Chapters 2 and 3, below.

[2] Under the Evian agreement an independent Algeria will in any case enjoy very close economic links with France, and therefore indirectly with the EEC as a whole.

6

The Common Market and . . .

(i) . . . THE BUSINESSMAN

THE PREVIOUS chapters may have served to give an idea of the scope and complexity of the Common Market undertaking, and of the importance of the changes it is meant to bring about. They give little or no indication of what it has meant in practical terms, or what it is going to mean, to the various sectors of the economy. How has it affected the economies of the member States and the scale of their trade? What has it meant to individual firms and how have they reacted? What has it meant for the workers, and how far have its effects been felt by the man in the street, either as consumer or as citizen? To these questions I shall try to reply.

We saw that in the coal and steel sector the abolition of restriction led to increased intra-Community trade, accompanied (at least for steel, which faced no crisis) by rising output and general stability. In the Common Market the same thing has occurred, although clearly the degree to which the rapid and favourable expansion of the economies of the Six countries can be attributed to the creation of the Common Market is impossible to ascertain. It must be recognised that the member countries were amongst those with the highest rates of expansion throughout the post-war period: they had lower starting-levels (as compared for instance with the EFTA countries) and benefited to a greater extent from reconstruction. Similarly, the expansion of the Community's trade has to be seen against a background of more rapidly increasing world trade between industrialised countries than with commodity-producing countries.[1]

Whatever the real importance of these provisos, the facts about the expansion of the Common Market's trade are clear. During the period 1959–61 trade between the member countries increased more rapidly and more steadily than their trade with other countries. During the first two years, which marked a period of expansion for world trade as

[1] Cf. the GATT Annual Reports for 1960 and 1961.

a whole, the difference was not particularly marked. Thus during the first six months of 1959, immediately following the first 10 per cent tariff cuts (which were in any case extended to third countries and therefore created no Community preferences) intra-Community trade was 14 per cent higher than in the same six months of 1958, and Community imports 11 per cent higher. The following year the gap widened: for the period January–June 1960 intra-Community trade rose by 34 per cent compared with the first half of 1959 (with even higher figures in some countries: 56 per cent for imports and 59 per cent for exports in the case of Italy, 49 per cent and 45 per cent respectively for France) whereas Community exports rose by 23 per cent and imports by 21·7 per cent. Overall figures can be misleading, however: intra-trade in foodstuffs had risen by 33 per cent as against a stand-still for imports from EFTA and only a 9 per cent rise for imports from other non-member countries; intra-trade in raw materials rose by 42 per cent as against 19 per cent for imports; and for manufactures the figures were 36 per cent and 35 per cent respectively.

It was in 1961, when activity in world trade slackened, that the effects of the Common Market could be unmistakably distinguished. For the first six months intra-Community trade rose by 17 per cent compared with the 1960 figures, whereas imports rose only 6 per cent and exports only 3 per cent. It was clear that the tariff cuts, which reached 30 per cent on January 1st, 1961, were beginning to take effect, particularly as what little increase there was in imports was attributable mainly to investment goods or manufactures for which demand inside the Community exceeded supply.

With the further 10 per cent tariff cut on January 1st, 1962, under the terms of the Treaty, and the 'accelerated' cut on July 1st, bringing tariff protection down to exactly half the level it was when the Common Market started, there can be no doubt that the increase in trade within the Community will continue to outpace the growth of trade with the rest of the world. There has been much discussion about what is the 'crucial' level of cuts (after which the duty still applied is not big enough to have any significance for trade because traders start basing their calculations on the final duty-free price): it may well lie around or somewhat above 50 per cent for most goods.[1] In this case the coming

[1] It clearly varies however from product to product: in May 1962 the Federal German government was still able to use a major cut in import duties on cars as an instrument of economic policy—thus indicating that the remaining protection was still considered important.

years will see the freeing of trade in goods having its maximum effect. (From another point of view this level also marks the time when the tariff cuts start really hurting at sensitive spots in the economy; moreover, the rapidity of the recent succession of tariff reductions may have taken firms by surprise before they have time to adapt to the increase in competition.)

The striking maintenance of the growth in intra-Community trade whilst world trade practically stagnated reflects another factor which can certainly be attributed in part to the Common Market, namely lessened vulnerability to cyclical fluctuations in the level of activity, to the ups-and-downs of expansion and recession, boom and slump. Genuine co-ordination of national business cycle and budgetary policies remains something for the future, but the indirect stabilising effects of the lowering of barriers are not to be under-estimated. Similarly the fixed investments made at an increasing rate by Common Market firms during the early years in an attempt to prepare for both a wider market and keener competition themselves contributed to expansion. All these and other factors too—such as the freer movement of capital—will be bound to gain in impetus as they are taken further under the Common Market time-table: and in addition there seems a likelihood of first steps towards co-ordinating national policies (at least as far as preparedness to deal with the beginnings of a recession is concerned).

NO TIME FOR SPILT MILK

These indisputable though unmeasurable good effects on the general economic situation provide the background against which to look at what the Common Market has meant to individual firms and how they have reacted. One point seems to me to be fundamental: whatever their original attitudes may have been to the idea of a Common Market—and many were fearful, still more doubtful—from the moment the Treaty of Rome was signed and ratified, the businessmen of the Six countries wasted no time in recriminations. They were faced with a near-automatic, irreversible process, leading in twelve years (or fifteen at the most . . . and perhaps, they soon found, even less than twelve) to a single market of 160 million consumers within which all protection would have disappeared. In every possible way they set out to adapt themselves—some to make the best of a bad job, others to exploit to the utmost the new possibilities now open to them. It was typical of this state of mind that in the second half of 1959 industrial and trade circles in the Six countries came out overwhelmingly in favour of the EEC Commission's proposals for speeding up the time-table for tariff cuts and for the Common Market in general. Having found that tariff cuts in an expanding economy were not to be feared, they preferred to obtain the advantages of the common market as rapidly as possible and to face the necessary adaptation whilst the boom conditions, which made it far easier, still persisted.

What in fact were these advantages, what was this adaptation, and how have they set about it? The notion of a market of 160 million consumers belongs to the realm of economic theory: to the business-man, the removal of trade barriers has two foreseeable effects. First, that markets previously closed to him, either by quota restrictions or by protective customs duties rendering his products uncompetitive, are now progressively opened to him. Clearly the lower his production costs in relation to his competitors, the sooner the tariff reductions will have reached a stage where it becomes possible for him to sell on the market in question. The reverse of the coin, however, lies in his being gradually subjected to keener competition as the barriers behind which he has sheltered are removed.

Firms in the Common Market reacted in several ways. The first and most obvious step, taken by a large number of firms, was to engage in investment programmes intended to improve their ability to compete, either by modernisation of equipment or by the extension of produc-tion capacity, or both. Again it is impossible to estimate at all accurately to what extent the wave of private investment which has been the principal driving force behind the boom in the Common Market countries in recent years has been prompted by such motives; but it is significant that it occurred not only in Germany and Holland, where a labour shortage drove firms to modernise or to invest in labour-saving machinery in an attempt to raise their productivity, but also in France and Italy, the two high-tariff countries where the firms could expect the biggest increase in foreign competition as a result of the common market.

GETTING TOGETHER

A second reaction to the common market was to seek to achieve, by mergers or other forms of concentration, a scale of activity better adapted to the bigger market. Not surprisingly it is in France, where industry had been most vociferous in its fears and protestations about the Common Market that one of the most striking waves of concen-trations has occurred: having most to fear they have reacted the most vigorously. Amongst the smaller firms, which are extremely numerous in France, the most popular form of action has been the straightforward merger, either between two smaller firms in the same area, or between two firms specialising in the same sector and no longer able to afford the luxury of competing, or again with a larger firm taking over, by mutual agreement, one or more smaller ones to achieve a more rational organisation of output. Whilst smaller firms may be animated by a general realisation of the need to achieve a more rational and efficient scale of production, in order to be sure of being competitive, the big firms, which are already efficient, often have a slightly different kind of incentive to get things ship-shape. The removal of trade barriers brings them up against specific competitors, whose size, scale of activity and level of efficiency they know: to take an example, it is clearly the prospect of competition with other similar giants which has prompted the link-up of Péchiney and Ugine in France and the creation of the vast new group Union Chimique Belge in Belgium, for the standard size for heavy-weights in the chemicals sector is set by Bayer in Germany.

There have been interesting cases, again mainly in France, of a large number of firms in a given sector grouping together for mutual aid. Thus in 1960 the French metallurgical, mechanical engineering and electrical engineering industries set up two joint undertakings: one was to provide advice to firms in the sectors concerned on adaptation to new conditions (mergers, modernisation, specialisation agreements); and the other, with the backing of several large French banks, was to provide the funds needed for the operations decided on. The scheme was highly successful and by the end of 1961 had given advice to over 30 firms and provided funds on a large scale. Similar groups have been created by forty textile firms in N.E. France and by a dozen or more of the major firms engaged in the manufacture and distribution of various kinds of processed foodstuffs.

Even more striking than the efforts of firms to adapt themselves within their home market has been their readiness to extend their activities to other member countries and to link up across the frontiers which are due to disappear. They have been doing this on a steadily increasing scale and in several ways. Perhaps the most significant is the specialisation agreement, which has seemed to many firms the most rational way to lessen the threat of foreign competition: it is seldom enough that the range of production of the bigger firms corresponds very closely, and there is therefore scope for co-ordination of production programmes, with each partner specialising in its major branches. The two together can then offer a more complete total range than either could alone, and each sells the full range on its home market, thus increasing its own sales and neutralising a possible source of dangerous competition. The EEC Commission, commenting on the wave of mergers in its 1960 Annual Report, noted this trend and suggested that the tendency for producers to make the most of their natural advantages would result in structural changes 'not at the level of whole branches of industry, but at the level of products, with each country coming to concentrate on certain specialities and abandon others'.

Another similar kind of agreement between firms in different member countries covers technical co-operation and the pooling of research (one example is an agreement between Mercedes and Citroen). It may be accompanied by reciprocal use of distribution networks (as in the case of Renault and Alfa Romeo, whose ranges of cars are complementary rather than competing: they went on from a reciprocal selling agreement in 1960 to the creation in 1961 of two joint subsidiaries in Southern Italy, one to build Renault tractors and the other cars).

Creation of joint subsidiaries is another course open: in some cases it has been a way of combining the know-how of one firm with the sales experience and production capacity of the other; alternatively, the two may link up to exploit a new and expanding sector. The removal of customs duties of course lessens the incentive to manufacture abroad, except in order to cater for a local market, and a large proportion of the fully-owned subsidiaries which have been set up in other member countries are intended to run sales and servicing networks.

The movement of economic inter-penetration between the member countries shows no signs of abating: it may indeed be reasonably expected to increase, aided by free movement of capital and the gradual freeing of the right of establishment, and stimulated by increasing competition and rising living standards. Already in these first few years it has assumed remarkable proportions. A study published in October 1961[1] recorded, in the period up to September 1st, 1961, the setting up of 880 subsidiaries in other member countries (105 of them by German firms), the conclusion of 610 agreements on technical co-operation across frontiers, and 480 cases where EEC firms had taken shares in businesses in other member countries.

[1] By the *Deutsches Industrie- und Handelstag.*

The threat of keener competition naturally brings with it the temptation to protect existing markets or to find some way of agreeing to limit competition. The EEC Commission said in its 1961 report that whilst in general most of the agreements being concluded seemed to fit in with the objectives of the Treaty some of them might call for investigation in connection with the rules of competition. The essential aim of the Regulations which came into effect in February 1962 is precisely to give the Commission an instrument for ensuring that advantages resulting from the movement of inter-penetration are also advantages for the consumer.

CASHING IN ON THE COMMON MARKET

One of the most attractive possibilities open to firms out to strengthen their competitive position is that of agreements on technical co-operation, use of patents, or manufacture under licence for efficient and advanced firms outside the Community, and particularly in America. More important still, very large numbers of American, Canadian and British firms have sought to get a foot-hold in one way or another in the Common Market area. The desire to cash in on a rapidly expanding market, which offers seemingly endless scope both for developing new sectors of production and for starting output in new sectors, has provoked an unprecedented flow of American capital into the Community. In 1958–60 608 American firms set up new subsidiaries in EEC (either independently or in collaboration with European firms) or else bought out existing European firms in the Six countries. Many more took important minority holdings in European firms, and others again established themselves in Switzerland. The flow of U.S investment increased still further in 1961 and has shown no signs of abating in 1962.

Inside Europe again, the movement of inter-penetration has not failed to evoke a response from banking and financial circles. A wide range of investment trusts have been created; in a number of cases the fund has been formed by one bank from each member country, and holds securities of leading firms throughout the Community.

It may be objected that this is too happy a picture of rapid and successful adaptation to be true. The Common Market is bound to claim its victims amongst the inefficient firms which only protection enabled to survive, but so far they have been rare. Undoubtedly this is due to a large extent to the steady expansion of the economy, which has left scope for adaptation; again, it might conceivably be that the real havoc will be wrought only by future tariff cuts, when the level of protection is cut by more than 50 per cent.[1] Certainly, any kind of economic recession would make marginal or near-marginal firms more vulnerable. In fact, the process of structural change has indeed begun —as is shown by the rising scale of applications for aid from the Social Fund to help finance the re-settlement or re-training of workers under reconversion schemes. If difficulties on an important scale were to be experienced by particular sectors or areas, the Fund and the Investment Bank between them should provide a guarantee that the situation will be kept under control.

THE BUTCHERS, THE BAKERS . . .

If individual firms in the Common Market have not been behind-hand in their reactions, nor have the various industries as such. I have described how the Commission when working out its various proposals for the implementation of the Common Market takes care to obtain the views of industry. In general, however, industry has not waited to be consulted. During 1958 and 1959 especially, the national federations or employers' organisations of every conceivable branch of trade and industry got in touch with their opposite numbers in the other member countries. As a result, the Butchers, the Bakers, and in all probability the Candlestick Makers, have their Common Market organisation. Up to March 1961 140 such bodies had been set up, 89 of them in the industrial sector, 42 between traders' organisations. Some are specialised committees within already existing organisations covering a wider area; others, though occasioned by the creation of the Common Market, are not limited to the Six countries. Thus the Manufacturers of Farm Machinery have a body taking in Austria, Switzerland and the U.K., as well as the Six, and the Toy Manufacturers of the Six have the U.K. industry in their organisation.

The scope and influence of these Community-wide groupings varies enormously. At one end of the scale are organisations like the Banking Federation of the Six countries, or COLIME, itself an EEC sub-section inside ORGALIME, which groups the national federations of metallurgical and mechanical and electrical engineering industries of Western Europe—a sector of industry which by January 1959 already counted

[1] It is worth recalling that in a number of cases member States have been allowed to apply temporary escape clauses to enable firms or sectors of industry (such as the Sicilian sulphur industry) to adapt themselves to meet the shock of tariff cuts.

eighteen more specialised Common Market groups for its various branches. At the other are such worthy bodies as the International Union of Makers of Sanitary Appliances and Hydraulic Apparatus in General, or the European Raw Hides Council. Yet all have similar aims and operate in similar ways: they study jointly the repercussions of the Common Market on their particular sector—both its effects on internal structure and conditions of competition, and its implications for trade with the rest of the world—and follow closely the activities of the institutions, making their interest, and their views on matters which concern them, known to the EEC Commission. They tend to hold general assemblies once a year, may have standing committees or specialised study groups, and in very many cases have a Secretariat established in Brussels.

When the EEC Commission wants to ascertain the views of Common Market industry on its various proposals, however, it turns not to these organisations—which are basically pressure groups defending their own special interests just as they do at the national level—but to two bodies whose names have become familiar to those who have followed the first four years of the Common Market: Unice, and Copa. UNICE is the Union of the Industrial Federations of the European Community (the bodies which correspond to the Federation of British Industries in the U.K.). From the first it has studied and debated the whole range of problems and opportunities of the Common Market from the point of view of industry, working out detailed policy statements on everything from aid to under-developed countries to the harmonisation of the tax on business turnover or the need for a concerted anti-dumping policy: in 1961 it sought to be as closely associated as possible with the work of the Business Cycle Policy Committee, and it has carried out its own analysis, to take one instance, of the trend towards concentration in industry. Its influence in the Common Market, like that of any sectional interest, is balanced against that of other sectors by the play of the Community machinery: but it is an effective spokesman for the views of industry, outside the limited consultative bodies of the Communities. COPA (*Comité des Organisations professionnelles agricoles*) is the equivalent to UNICE in the agricultural sector, and channels the views of farmers' organisations in the member countries. It played an important and constructive part in the elaboration of the common agricultural policy, being consulted at every turn of the complex process—although its views were often so little in accordance with those of the Commission that it was wryly remarked that Dr. Mansholt consulted it only in order to do the opposite of what was suggested.

A third overall body, less influential than the others, is the Permanent Conference of the Chambers of Commerce of the European Community, which has also made detailed studies of all aspects of the Community's emergent commercial policy and has made known to the Commission the views of the trading world about them.

(ii) ... THE WORKERS

What have the first four years of the Common Market meant to the workers? How have their interests been furthered, and how will they be furthered and defended in the future?

First and foremost, it must be recognised that the economic expansion of the Community economy—for which the Common Market is partly, though not of course wholly, responsible—has benefited the workers in terms of rising wages and increased living standards. In countries where demand has outstripped the increase in production capacities (the Netherlands and Germany especially) unemployment has virtually disappeared, and throughout 1961 and the early part of 1962 offers of employment have remained three or four or even more times as numerous as the numbers seeking jobs: the strength of the workers' position has been reflected in both countries in a marked reduction in working hours. By contributing to cyclical stability, and maintaining a high level of activity, the Common Market has effectively ensured workers against the threat of unemployment. Most striking of all of course is the case of Italy, where the steady expansion has meant a change from unending and hopeless under-employment for over a million workers who have been absorbed into the Italian industrial economy or have found work in other member countries.

In this connection the plans now afoot for co-ordinating the economic policy measures of the member States in the event of a threat of recession are of immediate significance for the workers.

Such indirect but none the less important effects apart, the Common Market can directly affect working conditions, or open up new opportunities for the workers, in a number of ways, and seems likely to do so to a growing extent. There is no need to do more than recall the steps being taken to ensure equal pay for men and women in the five member countries where the principle was not fully accepted. The application of the principle is not going through without some difficulty—there being a certain unwillingness to admit that it should be interpreted in a broad sense, and not as applying solely to men and women doing specifically the same job (some employers have sought to get around the problem by simply creating new job classifications reserved for men or for women only)—yet its acceptance is a major step. Again, the whole system of free movement of labour represents a practical gain: and for the many workers who in any case would have gone to jobs in other member countries (and also for seasonal and frontier workers) the guarantees of continuity in social service provisions and the right to settle with their families are valuable measures.

Workers in the sectors covered by the Rome Treaties have yet to benefit from any such direct aid as is represented by the High Authority's workers' housing schemes—and the Social Affairs Committee of the European Parliament, which in February 1962 went to look for itself at the living conditions of migrant Italian workers in Holland and Germany, suggested that a similar programme under EEC was urgently needed. Workers in the Coal and Steel Community have also benefited more so far than those in other sectors as regards research on safer and healthier working conditions, and industrial medicine. As we saw above the activity of the Commission in these and other fields has hardly begun; and it has done little to promote harmonisation of labour legislation in general or conditions for collective bargaining in the member countries.

A major field in which the workers undoubtedly have good reason to be grateful for the creation of the Communities is that of re-training and re-settlement. In the coal industry above all the structural crisis would have meant the closing down of mines in any case, common market or no, and the High Authority has provided millions of dollars in direct aid and towards protecting the miners from the effects of this major economic upheaval. In the general Common Market the Social Fund—whatever criticisms may be levied, with reason, against its method of operating—is a practical safeguard for the workers against suffering ill-effects from the creation of the Common Market, and the Commission's proposals for a common vocational training policy complement its work.

THE T.U.S

Such have been the effects of integration on individual workers in the early years of the Common Market. Meanwhile, organised labour has not been slow in establishing fruitful co-operation in order to advance the claims and defend the rights of the workers at the Common Market level.

It is worth noting here certain important ways in which the trade union structure in the Six countries differs from that in Britain. In all the member countries there is both a Catholic-orientated 'Christian' trade union organisation and a 'free' or lay organisation (though in Germany the 'free' trade unions are in the overwhelming majority and it was not until 1955 that a Catholic splinter group broke away). In addition there are Communist trade unions, which are very powerful in both France and Italy; and in Holland there are also Protestant unions. From the point of view of European integration, however, these differences have not been important, and save in the case of the Communists, who have been determinedly anti-European, the common tradition, derived from the Internationals, of thinking in terms of workers' unity across national frontiers has led them to make common cause on the side of progress towards unification.

Apart from the Communist organisation, there are two major international trade union movements. One is the ICFTU (International Confederation of Free Trade Unions), which when ECSC was set up already had a European Regional Organisation: the Common Market Committee which ICFTU set up (it is known by its French initials as CISL) has become as we shall see the co-ordinating body for all the free trade unions in the Six countries and their mouth-piece on European affairs. The other world-wide movement, the International Federation of Christian Trade Unions (IFCTU) set up in 1955 a Federation of Christian TUs for ECSC, and this was later transformed to deal with Common Market affairs.

During the years before 1958 it was chiefly the central national trade union organisations, and to a growing extent the liaison bodies which they had created at the level of the Six, which defended the workers' interests in matters of integration. It is interesting to see how their attitudes evolved, for those years were in the nature of a dress rehearsal for the Common Market. On many questions the national trade union organisations tended at first to take the same line as the employers' federations in their particular industries, on the grounds that their own interests were best defended by protecting the interests of the industry where the workers were employed: thus the German miners' unions opposed the break-up of the joint coal-selling cartels, and the French miners were worried principally about the fate of their national mines.

On other points, however, such as working conditions or social security benefits, it was not long before the unions realised that their interest lay in helping the High Authority to bring about harmonisation—which would always mean alignment on the best prevailing conditions. This desire for harmonisation was particularly marked on the part of the Belgian unions, though for a slightly different reason: having already obtained about the best conditions in the Community, they saw that they could not now persuade their employers to agree to further improvements unless there were to be a levelling-up of conditions throughout the Community, so that they were not placing themselves at a disadvantage in relation to their competitors.

They soon managed to convince the other unions of the need for uniform conditions throughout the Community as an argument in bargaining.

In general, there was agreement on working through the two regional organisations, which themselves co-operated closely, in all dealings with the Community institutions (including for instance the nomination of workers' representatives for the Consultative Committee). Gradually a joint approach on many problems was evolved, and the general principle of alignment on the best prevailing conditions was applied at every turn, with the High Authority's detailed statistics on real wages, purchasing power, social security schemes, and so on, providing useful ammunition. The climax to this movement came in 1954 with the agreement to press at the supranational level as well as on the home front for the adoption of a 45-hour week in all ECSC industries.

THE UNABASHED PRESSURE GROUPS

By the time the Rome Treaties were signed—the unions having been fully consulted during the process of drafting—the two central trade union bodies had established a tradition of joint action to which the national movements gave their full backing.

Given the general political circumstances in the member countries during the early years of the Common Market, with conservative-minded governments generally in power, it is not surprising that the action of the trade unions in the Communities has taken very much the form of 'pressure group' activities—a description which the ICFTU

Common Market Committee (or at least its Secretary-General) entirely agrees with.

These activities all centre around the two small Secretariats in Brussels, which serve the Executive Committees of leaders from the union organisations in the member States; there are also full-scale annual Assemblies which debate the development of the Common Market and the workers' position in it. These Secretariats—which also work in liaison with each other—co-ordinate activities at the national and the Community level. The trade unions are represented on most—though not all—of the advisory or consultative bodies in the Communities: the Consultative Committee of ECSC, the Economic and Social Committee, the Consultative Committee on the free movement of workers, the Consultative Committee for Transport Questions, and the Committee for the Social Fund. It was realised at an early stage that the mere presence of individual trade unionists was not enough to ensure the furthering of the interests of labour, and it was the Secretariats which undertook to ensure the necessary collaboration. In this the unions contributed to the effectiveness of the Economic and Social Committee which, being already unwieldy, could hardly work usefully at all unless the groups were to co-ordinate their activity in advance.

Representation on the official consultative organs, although useful, was considered by the unions to be inadequate as a means of making their presence felt. A second, more important form of action has developed: the tradition of consultation of the trade unions by the Executives at the various stages of work on drawing up Common Market legislation. As far as the limited resources of their present Secretariats allow[1] the unions use the classical pressure group tactic of being fully informed and ready to make constructive proposals on matters which concern them. Apart from the consultations on specific projects (when Commission 'round tables' with UNICE representatives are paralleled by similar meetings with the unionists) M. Marjolin, the member of the EEC Commission responsible for general economic questions, regularly holds meetings with them to discuss the development of the economic situation in the Community economy.

The unions are no more ready than any other pressure group to sit back and wait to be consulted: the real strength of the two groups (and

[1] The contrast between the extremely modest scale of their organisation and the highly-organised way in which corresponding federal pressure groups work in the United States is a striking one.

more particularly perhaps of the free trade unions, since the Christian trade unions have virtually no influence in Germany, and relatively little in Italy), lies in their ability to mobilise pressure of various kinds and in various quarters throughout the Community. Thus when a question is due to come before the Council of Ministers the action of national T.U. movements is brought to bear in all the member countries, pressure being exerted through the tried and traditional channels at the national level. Their strength in most national parliaments is of course considerable, though probably a good deal less in the U.K., and so are their links with the European Parliament: there are a number of trade unionists amongst the active members of the Parliament—mostly in the Socialist group, of course, but also amongst the Christian Democrats, so that there are two channels for getting trade union views put across in debates and in committee.

In general the pattern is one of links between the central organisations at the national level: but as with the employers, there are also direct horizontal links at a lower level. Specialised Committees link national (free) trade unions of farm workers, transport workers, general workers and bulding and wood workers. Unions in the textiles, food, and metallurgical industries are due to set up such Community-level bodies.

In conclusion I cannot do better than quote the words of a report to the Third General Assembly of the Free Trade Unions of the member States, held in Brussels in January 1962: 'despite all the difficulties and despite all the limitations, the influence of the Trade Unions is an established fact, particularly as regards everything having to do with the EEC Treaty'. The unions are not of course satisfied with the scope of their influence, but they have succeeded in actively defending the interests of the workers, helped by the buoyant conditions which have characterised the labour market in the Six so far. The methods they use are those of persuasion and of influence on the decision-making process: if the notion of direct action is ever mentioned it is, significantly enough, not in connection with economic or social claims but with the idea that the member governments might one day think fit to envisage admitting Franco's Spain to associate membership of the Community.

There is no doubt, of course, that the unions could—given the favourable bargaining conditions created by full employment—have achieved even more had their national organisations been stronger. Co-operation with the British T.U.C. may in future help to strengthen their position and build on the foundations already laid.

(iii) ... THE INDIVIDUAL

What does the Common Market mean to the man in the street—first in his economic existence as 'the consumer', and secondly as an ordinary citizen of a member country?

A constant improvement in the standard of living (and working conditions) of the peoples of the member countries is set out in the preamble of the Treaty as *the* essential aim of the whole undertaking. Nor can it be questioned that the aim has so far been achieved in the steady economic expansion which has occurred in the Community since 1958.

From the immediate implementation of the Treaty, there are two advantages which the consumer has a right to expect: lower prices, and a wider choice of goods. Once again, as far as prices are concerned, it is impossible to assess to what extent trends which have occurred can be attributed to the Common Market: however, the general price stability which has reigned, with few exceptions, in the member countries over the last few years can certainly be attributed in part to lower duties on imports and in part also to increasing competition or the threat of it. If prices are maintained when, in the general context of economic expansion, they might have been expected to rise, or else are raised less than they might have been, the retailer, even were he to be aware of it, is unlikely to indicate on the price tabs that it is due to the Common Market. (Yet there have been one or two cases where exactly this was done: in 1959 a Brussels department store held a publicity week when prices were marked down to what they would be if all customs duties had already been removed). Nevertheless, what little evidence there is would seem to show that the consumer has reaped some direct advantage: at a meeting of heads of department stores from the member countries, called by the EEC Commission early in 1962, it transpired that on the whole there had been a tendency for prices to fall more than they rose, which could in fact be attributed largely to the Common Market. One of the problems of the Common Market, which the rules of competition are intended to solve, is indeed to ensure that the economic advantages are passed on to the consumer.

As to wider choice, there is no way of measuring it. It does not result automatically from the removal of trade barriers, but depends on the initiative of retailers in seeking a wider range to suit customers' tastes, and even more on the extent to which firms start competing on new markets. The process when it does occur is a gradual one, and the average consumer is unlikely to have been struck as yet by a marked increase in the goods available to him—although durable consumer goods, and cars in particular, where foreign makes are already known, may provide the exception. The process will undoubtedly be hastened by the tendency of firms to rely on reciprocal use of distribution net-works, to which we referred above.

In his everyday life and habits as a citizen, the Common Market has meant very little change for the average inhabitant of the member countries—nor is it likely to mean any drastic changes in the future. He still has to produce an identity card (not a passport it is true) on crossing a frontier, and his luggage is still liable to be searched; and to send a parcel from one country to another, to get a work permit, or to take up residence in another member-country, still involves time-wasting form-alities, with everything in triplicate or quadruplicate. Such minor steps as uniform postal rates are proving hard to achieve: nor is this to be wondered at, for minor administrative bureaucracy will surely be one of the last bastions of discrimination against foreigners.

Where the citizen does increasingly run up against the effects of the Common Market, and will do more and more, is in his work, for the break-down of barriers has repercussions which filter through to every aspect of economic life, from banking to green-grocering and from lorry-driving to farming.

7

Problems of Sovereignty

FOR A country about to take the major step of joining the European Communities when they have already been in existence for over four years (and in the case of ECSC for more than ten), and obliged by the existing members to accept unchanged the basic structure and institutional framework established by the Treaties, there is one question which must inevitably loom large: that of sovereignty. The word has come to have a certain emotive force, and arguments about 'surrender of sovereignty' can be misleading and dangerous. It would perhaps be more accurate to talk about transfers of decision-making powers, or a 'changing political centre of gravity'—but it serves adequately to designate a whole series of changes involved in joining the Communities, the importance of which is worth analysing. (I intentionally leave aside here the whole question of whether whatever limitation of sovereignty is involved in membership is or is not outweighed by the advantages in the economic and political fields which may result from integration, and which Michael Shanks examines in Part III below: this is a question on which the reader will have to make up his mind in the light of the book as a whole.)

Clearly the very act of signing—and ratifying—the three Treaties involves in itself a 'surrender of sovereignty': they are concluded for an unlimited period (Art. 240 of the EEC Treaty) and no provision is made for a member country to withdraw. The texts lay down a number of targets to be achieved over a period of years, to which the signatories are formally committed in advance. Some of these are set out in precise terms (e.g. the customs reductions), others have to be worked out by common agreement (e.g. the common policies): but the commitment is unequivocal.

The actual commitments written into the Treaty are of course voluntarily accepted, and must be ratified by the national parliaments. Of much greater practical importance is the degree to which membership, and participation in the process by which the Treaties are implemented, involves the surrender—or more accurately the *sharing*—of control over both the everyday conduct of economic affairs and the formation of national policies. Only an analysis of the practical experience of the Six since the Treaties came into force can show what is really involved, and what the implications are, for all member countries (founder members and newcomers alike) in the future.

There are in fact several ways in which the relationship of the member States to the Community institutions involves a limitation of rights which have hitherto always been exercised only at the national level, and are therefore referred to as 'sovereign'. A distinction must be made between restrictions on the independent action of the national governments on the one hand, and the removal of decision-making processes from the sovereign control of national parliaments (and through them of the electorate) on the other.

The national governments surrender in many fields their right of unfettered and autonomous decision-making, and take part in return in the joint decision-making machinery of the ministerial Councils. Secondly, they accept the right of the two Commissions and the High Authority to take executive decisions with immediate effect throughout the area of the Community. In addition they accept the right of the same bodies to keep check upon the observance both of those decisions and of the terms of the Treaties in general. Lastly, they accept the final jurisdiction of the Court of Justice of the Communities in any dispute between them and the institutions of the Communities.

The question of the derogation from the sovereignty of the national parliaments is a more complex one, and more fundamentally important because it involves the whole basic question of democratic control. It results essentially from the fact that, as we saw in Chapter 1, the ministerial Councils, being organs of the Communities, are not responsible to the national parliaments: nor are they responsible on the other hand to the European Parliament (which in any case is not yet qualified by its composition or its powers to take the place of the national parliaments).

SHARED DECISION-MAKING

As we saw in examining the institutional machinery of the Common Market, the Council of Ministers is the sole decision-making body, even though it can never itself take the initiative but must always work on the basis of a draft prepared by the Commission. Although in fact made up of ministers sent by the governments of the member States, the Council is an organ of the Community: it has a collective identity of its own irrespective of what ministers are taking part on a given occasion. The process by which it takes its decisions differs fundamentally from the round-the-table negotiating of traditional diplomacy when the meeting is no more than the sum of its independent parts. It is a body existing in its own right which has the essential function of achieving that balancing-out of national interests which was reflected in the Treaty and continues at every stage of its application.

The actual debates in the Council leading up to any decision merely represent, after all, the culminating stage in a process of consultation and compromise which I have traced in some detail in Chapter 1. They have been foreshadowed, with the same arguments advanced on all sides, first in the meetings of national experts, then in the Permanent Representatives' Committee. Thus the member governments are already part authors of the text which the Commission lays before the Council, and in which their particular interests have been taken into account as far as the interests of the others, or of the Community as a whole, permit.

The real significance of the fact that the Council is a Community body, and of this detailed process of preliminary synthesis, is that there is a prior commitment to reach agreement. Any particular decision by the Council is merely one element in a continuing process involved in the implementation of the Treaty: it may be delayed, but failure to reach agreement is no more taken into account than is the possibility that a national Cabinet might fail to decide on some major element of national policy.

Nor does this apply only to matters where the Treaty specifically requires a decision, and there is thus a contractual element involved. There is a more general 'moral' commitment to take the decisions necessary for the overall progress of the process of integration; and to this will be added to a growing extent the pressure of economic necessity, as the implementation of decisions in one sector of the economy makes co-ordination in another sector essential.

This particular character of the Council of the Communities grew up during the years before 1958 in the Council of the Coal and Steel Community. The story is told of a meeting of the ECSC Council to discuss transport problems[1]: at one point there was an adjournment whilst the ministers of economics, who were old Council hands, took aside the transport ministers, attending for the first time, and explained to them the way the Council worked, and the fact that they could not go on refusing to make the concessions needed for a compromise agreement. The same tradition has held from the start in the work of the EEC and Euratom Council, which has met with increasing frequency, and with a membership which has changed relatively little: the Foreign Minister, the Ministers of Agriculture, the Ministers of Economic Affairs, and a number of others have now considerable experience of the way the Community works and of the process of balancing-out concession against concession.

The true nature of the Council process, and the way national interests are reconciled, is only really revealed where the conflict is a major one and the interests involved vital to several of the member countries. Then it can be seen to what extent any member State may hold out against the others or, alternatively, may have to make concessions. During the first few years of the Common Market there have been relatively few major conflicts or deadlocks in the Council, although the reconciling of national interests over the customs duties for products in List G often required many hours of discussion. Two cases are worth examining in some detail. One shows how a member State which is isolated and has the weight of Community opinion against it may be required to make concessions on what it maintains to be a vital interest in order to permit a major agreement; the other shows the bargaining process at work on a major problem where all the member countries have interests at stake and a complicated overall compromise is required.

The first case is that of the original 'acceleration'—the decision to make an anticipated tariff cut of 10 per cent, and to speed up the application of the Treaty in general, which the Council took in May 1960. The country with the special interest to defend was Holland, who wanted the additional 10 per cent cut to apply also to trade in foodstuffs. Germany, which had already found the cuts made in duties on agricultural products hard to swallow for internal political reasons, wanted no acceleration in the farm sector; and the other member countries tended to be on the German side. At the beginning of the

[1] Cf. E. B. Haas, *The Uniting of Europe* (Stevens & Sons Ltd., 1958); the analysis of decision-making in the early years of ECSC, on pp. 492 et seq. of this book is particularly interesting.

meeting the Dutch were stating their readiness to veto the acceleration on industrial goods unless they got satisfaction on foodstuffs. But they were under heavy psychological and political pressure, since all the member countries were agreed on the acceleration in principle and considered it an invaluable step in strengthening the Common Market; moreover economic opinion throughout the Community was in favour. Twice the Council sat late into the night before the Dutch, complaining bitterly that the Germans had shown complete lack of 'Community spirit' and that they had only given way for the sake of the Community as a whole, accepted a compromise whereby there was a 5 per cent additional cut, limited however to those agricultural products not yet freed from quota restrictions (and representing in fact a fairly limited proportion of the trade in foodstuffs). Clearly the Dutch had made a major concession: but on the other hand the final solution was a compromise which granted them some part of what they had asked.

It was the decisions at the end of December 1961 and the beginning of January 1962 which provide the classic example of the Common Market decision-making process. All the elements were present: the decisions to be taken (farm policy above all) involved issues of vital importance to all the member States and affected major vested interests in each country; at the same time they were essential to the further progress of the Community (above all the move to the second stage of the transition period); and lastly the Council was under pressure both because of the need to take a decision within a rigid time-limit, and because political circumstances (above all the negotiations with the United Kingdom) made it essential to avoid a failure.

The situation is worth looking at in some detail. Under the terms of the Treaty the Council had to take a unanimous formal decision by the end of 1961 on the move to the second stage of the transitional period (which has important implications for Community policy in many fields); if not taken by December 31st, the decision had to be postponed for a year. Taking that decision was however conditional upon the Council's concluding that reasonable and balanced progress had been made in applying the Treaty during the first stage. The French made it clear that they considered agreement on the cartel Regulations, evidence of general progress in other countries towards equal pay for equal work, and above all agreement on the basic elements of the common farm policy all to be indispensable conditions for coming to that conclusion. With the cartels decision satisfactorily out of the way, the Council still had before it twelve sets of farm policy regulations, each extremely complex and each containing points on which major differences of opinion remained, requiring decisions which could only be taken at ministerial level. Without going into the complexities of the problems, suffice it to say that the differences of opinion did not at all follow the same pattern in each case: each country had interests to defend, and knew where it would have to make concessions; each was in a minority in some cases, and had allies in others (the Dutch for instance were particularly glad to find themselves for once the allies rather than the opponents of the French when it came to the pigmeat regulations!). All the same, the biggest single clash was undoubtedly between France and Germany over cereals.

In the circumstances it was a striking fact, on which all observers were agreed, that the ministers tackled the problem from the outset in a 'Community spirit'. The 'political will to succeed', which has become one of the catch-phrases of the Common Market, was clearly in evidence. In every case the solutions reached, around 5 a.m. on January 14th, 1962, were compromises. Significantly, they corresponded very closely to the compromise proposals which the EEC Commission had put forward before the end of the year. The last ten days of tough bargaining (after the Council, at the suggestion of M. Pisani, the French Minister of Agriculture, 'stopped its clock' in order to be able to take the decision on the move to the second stage when it finally reached agreement) seemed to have served as much as anything to prove to the farmers in the various countries that the governments had really done their best, and that if agreement was to be reached at all then no more concessions could be won. No one country lost face by an obvious surrender of vital interests: concessions were made on all sides; and there was never any question of 'steam-rollering'. It was suggested that perhaps the French did best out of the deal, but simply through superior negotiating skill; and the French Minister of Agriculture was often instrumental in achieving a compromise. Even more so the agreement was a triumph for the EEC Commission, and for Dr. Mansholt in particular, who was ready at every turn with a valid proposal for solving each deadlock. Lastly, the way the decisions were received by the farmers was significant: with the kind of realistic acceptance of the inevitability of the integration process to which I referred in the previous chapter, they wasted little time on recriminations and at once began to examine the practical significance of the new policy.

MAJORITY VOTING

The move to the second stage of the transitional period involves one major change with apparent implications for sovereignty: the move from unanimous voting to qualified majority voting for most of the Council's decisions. The 'qualified majority' system means in effect weighted voting: each of the three big States has four votes, Belgium and the Netherlands have two each, and Luxembourg has one: twelve votes are required for a qualified majority, and the favourable votes of at least four countries are required for decisions not being taken on the basis of an EEC Commission proposal. The point of the scheme is to ensure that whilst one of the three big countries can be over-ruled by its partners, two of them (or even one if it has the backing of Belgium or the Netherlands) cannot be.[1]

An interesting light is shed on the possible significance of the change by what happened in the case of the anti-cartel Regulations adopted in December 1961. Only a qualified majority was needed (because the decision had not been taken by the end of 1961, as the Treaty required —cf. Art. 87). When the Commission's final draft came before the Council in November, after long and tedious debate at other levels, agreement was reached on all aspects except one (the question of sector-by-sector enquiries). On this point France was in a minority, and the other member States could have passed the measure by a qualified majority. The Council decided however to make a further effort to reach unanimity, and the Permanent Representatives did succeed in working out a compromise which the Council unanimously accepted in December. The lesson to be learnt from this seems to be that every effort will always be made to achieve unanimity on major issues. The Commission in particular can be expected to work for unanimity wherever possible, since it must co-operate closely with the member States in elaborating the detailed measures for the implementation of the Council's decisions. The more important the decision, therefore, the greater the efforts that will be made to reach a compromise. Nevertheless occasions may well arise where a government may prefer for reasons of internal tactics to be over-ruled by its partners on a point

[1] The re-casting of the 'qualified majority' system to accommodate new member countries may prove one of the most delicate points in the negotiations.

where it is subject to heavy interest group pressure, rather than to accept a compromise which it would have difficulty in defending at home.

THE SCOPE AND SIGNIFICANCE OF THE COMMISSION'S POWERS

The EEC Commission has a wide range of tasks to perform, and various instruments at its disposal in dealing with the member States. In quite a number of cases it is charged directly with taking action to ensure the implementation of the Treaty, and it may issue 'opinions' and 'recommendations' (which are in no way binding) reminding member States or individual firms of their obligations. It can however take strictly executive decisions only in those cases where it is specifically empowered to do so either by the Treaty or within the framework of directives which the Council has issued (binding only as regards the end to be attained) or decisions which it has taken (binding as regards both means and ends).

It is worth looking at the kind of powers the Commission has (though the list cannot be exhaustive). Thus, in the framework of the common commercial policy, it has the power to grant import quotas duty-free or at reduced duties. Under the anti-cartel Regulations, it is the Commission which is empowered to rule that an agreement or an association between firms is illegal and must be terminated; alternatively it can allow the agreement to be concluded or maintained. Also, under the same Regulations, the Commission's agents have the right to carry out direct investigations into the affairs of firms in the member countries, though they have to inform the national authorities and will in practice collaborate closely with them. It is worth noting that the High Authority has had, and has used fully, a similar right of investigation under the ECSC Treaty and that it has not caused any major difficulties. Under the terms of the Regulations, and foreseeably under other Regulations yet to be drawn up (e.g., on transport) the Commission can impose fines on firms in member States; again the High Authority has had similar powers in connection with infringements of ECSC price schedule regulations.

In general the powers of direct action of the EEC Commission are fairly limited. The EEC Council is in fact careful to retain for itself any decisions which are of importance in their effects on national interests. The Regulations on the common farm policy are typical in this respect: it is the EEC Council itself which will take the vital decisions each year setting the target prices for grain and for other foodstuffs.

The power and importance of the Commission in fact resides not in a right of decision—which is not its function in the institutional framework—but in its right of initiative. It has the power to make proposals to the Council concerning any aspect of the Common Market, and this gives it great scope: one has only to remember that the crucially important work on the harmonisation of direct taxation was undertaken under the terms of the vaguely worded article about harmonisation of legislation. The shape of the Commission's proposals on any given matter is unlikely to be radically changed by the Council, especially since, as we have seen, it draws them up in full knowledge of the views of the member States.

The conclusion which emerges therefore is that the activities of the Commission hardly represent a threat to national sovereignty, save in the sense that it is the source of the multiple proposals which are bound to require a gradual transfer of the decision-making process from the member-States to the Community. The jibe that the Common Market is run by technicians and bureaucrats is not strictly accurate. The activities of the Commission—both the proposals it draws up and everything it does to implement the Treaty—are subject to lively scrutiny by the Parliament, which fulfils this role of supervision and control very effectively. As for the High Authority, which has it is true far greater direct powers than the Commission, it exercises them to stimulate and guide the evolution of the coal and steel market in a way which can hardly be said to infringe on national sovereignty. When the High Authority has clashed directly with entrenched national interests—e.g., over Belgian coal—it has come off second best.

One other aspect of the Commission's functions is worth recalling: its role as watch-dog of the Treaty and the Regulations. It keeps check on the one hand to ensure that the States do not introduce new measures which infringe the Treaty, and on the other hand to ensure that they do carry out their new obligations. The procedure in the event of an infringement being discovered is in no way arbitrary, however: the Commission first sends a 'reasoned opinion' explaining the grounds for considering that the Treaty has been violated—and to this the State in question may reply, giving its reasons. If the Commission is not satisfied with the arguments it issues a recommendation calling on the offender to put an end to the infringement. If this recommendation is not acted upon it can then bring a case against the member country in question before the Court of Justice, and the Court's ruling is binding. During the early years of the Common Market the first steps of the

ifringement procedure were applied in many cases, especially in con-
ection with the reduction of trade barriers. In 1961 the first cases were
rought before the Court; and early in 1962 the Court ruled for the
Commission against the Italian government in two cases. There seems
very indication that the Commission will be vigilant in ensuring the
pplication of the Treaty: but this hardly implies any limitation of the
overeign rights of the States, which are under an obvious obligation
o carry out their Treaty commitments. Vice versa, the governments
ave of course the right to appeal to the Court against the Commission
a any case where it is felt to have exceeded its legitimate powers under
he Treaty or under the terms of Council decisions. In the Coal and
teel Community the member countries have not hesitated to take
uch action against the High Authority.

The idea that the national governments should be subject to a ruling
y the Court, without any right of appeal, must ring strangely on
British ears. It can hardly be considered in itself to represent an aban-
onment of sovereign rights. The abandonment, as we saw, comes in
he signing of the Treaty: once formal commitments of the general
ind to be found in the Rome Treaty are accepted, it is essential that
here should be some authority independent of both the member
tates and the other Community institutions capable of ruling on the
iterpretation of the Treaty.

WANTED, A PARLIAMENT!

On most of the major decisions taken in the Common Market, then,
he member governments have to make concessions—and with quali-
ied majority voting in the Council of Ministers it becomes at least
heoretically possible for even one of the bigger member countries to be
bliged to bow to the wishes of its partners on a matter which concerns
vital national interest. There are far-reaching implications here for
he national parliaments.

The Council, as a Community body, is not responsible to the
ational parliaments. More explicitly, a body with the power to take
ecisions which have force of law in all the member countries is not
ubject to parliamentary control in those countries. Although when
bliged to make concessions in the course of a Council meeting a
Minister may make the formal passage of the decision dependent upon
he agreement of his government (this was the procedure adopted by
he French Minister of Agriculture when the decisions on the common
arm policy were taken in January 1962) there can be no question of

making it dependent upon parliamentary approval.[1] To take a strikin example, the anti-cartel Regulations, which apply directly in th member countries, and which, moreover, the national courts have t apply, never came before the national parliaments.

In general the Six national parliaments have taken relatively littl interest in the affairs of the Communities. There were naturally ful scale debates before ratification on the implications of the Rom Treaties, and there are from time to time foreign affairs debates in whic Common Market matters are touched on. But only the Dutch Parlia ment has regularly debated the affairs of the Community. Certainl there is no question of the national parliaments exercising a detaile parliamentary control—which would in any case have to be *post fact* —over the decisions of the Council. Interest has inevitably bee growing, and Common Market affairs have begun to come up mor frequently, but it has been the plans for political union rather tha economic decisions which have attracted the most attention in th national legislatures.

Yet the last thing that the authors of the Rome Treaty intended to d was to remove the operation of the Common Market from any kin of democratic control. In the Coal and Steel Community until 1958 was perhaps just possible to suggest that the Common Assembly exer cised democratic control, since it was the High Authority, which it ha the power to dismiss (once a year, on the basis of the Annual Report which had the power of decision. When the jurisdiction of the Assem bly was extended to the other two Communities, however, the gapin hole in the system of democratic control became evident.

For in the Common Market the role and importance of th Commission (which the Assembly can still oblige to resign, by vote of censure at any time) is very different from that of the Hig Authority: and the Council, which is not subject to the nation parliaments, escapes entirely from control by the European Parliamen also.

It is worth recalling briefly what I wrote in Chapter 1 about th present position of the Parliament: its role is officially one of consulta tion and supervision, and both these activities it carries out well an

---

[1] The Federal German government did tie its hands in connection with th 'acceleration' decisions by making certain commitments of a more or less form nature beforehand to the Bundestag. Acceleration is however to some extent special case since there is no binding obligation on the governments to reac agreement.

conscientiously. Yet the Council is quite capable of ignoring its advice —as happened in 1960 over the budgets of the Communities, when the Assembly unanimously backed the Executives in requesting the full amount indicated in the estimates, and the Council went on and confirmed the drastic cuts recommended to it by a group of experts. In relation to the Executives of all three Communities the position of the Parliament is stronger. Yet this is not due at all to the very limited power it has over them—the power of causing them to resign, which in any case it would have little interest in using since it has no say in their replacement—but rather to the tradition of close interest and co-operation which has been established. In the history of ECSC and the Common Market so far, the Executives and the Parliament have been natural allies.

From the first the Common Assembly insisted on being consulted on the High Authority's policies before they were put into effect; and in the Common Market, of course, this right of consultation is formally recognised and works well in practice. Indeed the Parliament does not content itself with a detailed analysis and criticism of the official propositions sent to it by the Council. In a number of fields, the Parliament has taken the initiative in elaborating its own ideas ahead of the Commission's own proposals. The most striking case was that of transport policy, where two voluminous reports by a Dutch M.P., Mr. Kapteyn, which the Parliament adopted, constitute a major contribution to the solution of the problems raised by working out a common policy. Again, in the case of the anti-cartel Regulations the Commission actually replaced parts of its own proposals, defeated in the Assembly, by the latter's own text.

All this is important, and serves to emphasise that the European Parliament is an active and conscientious body carrying out its functions to the best of its ability. But it does not change the fact that the Assembly has no real democratic powers over the Commission, let alone over the Council, which is not even theoretically responsible to it. Nor does it change the fact that it is only chosen indirectly, and thus has no valid mandate from the electors of the member countries. Not only are large groups of national voters not represented even directly—no Communist members being sent to Strasbourg, despite the importance of the Communist Parties in France and Italy. Because its powers are limited—and membership takes up a lot of time—it attracts only very few of the leading figures from national politics: one reason why the Socialist group in the European Parliament is more impressive in its performances than the other two is that the Socialists, having been in opposition in most of the member countries most of the time since the Common Market was created, have been able to afford to pay more attention to the European Assembly. Precisely because it is not elected the debates of the Parliament, however high a level they may reach, have little appeal to public opinion. In short, the Parliament in its present form resembles nothing more than an active parliamentary committee, composed almost entirely of back benchers and largely ignored by public opinion.

EUROPEAN ELECTIONS?

There is one obvious solution to this lacuna in the Community system. Both the ECSC Treaty and the two Rome Treaties contain express provision for the Parliament to be elected by direct universal suffrage throughout the Community. Not unnaturally plans were made almost at once to implement this clause. In 1959 a special sub-committee of the Assembly's Political Affairs Committee started work on a draft Treaty, and after discussing in detail with the six national parliaments, as well as with the governments, the political and technical problems involved, it drew up a draft which the Assembly approved. It was submitted to the Foreign Ministers of the Six, and it was optimistically imagined that the first elections might take place in 1962, or in 1963 at the latest.

Since then, as we shall see in the next chapter, the plan has run up against French opposition and has become just one element in the dispute over the shape of future political union. Nevertheless, since direct elections remain one of the primary objectives of the 'federalists'[1] and there is every reason to think that they will eventually be held, it is worth looking briefly at the outlines of the Assembly's plan. It represents in fact a compromise designed to make the change from the present system less radical, and therefore more acceptable to governments and national parliaments alike. At least at first, some of the members of the European Parliament would continue to be delegated from the national Assemblies, only the rest being directly elected. Secondly, the elections would not be held according to a single uniform voting system (as a strict interpretation of Art. 138, s. 3 of the Treaty would require): instead each member State would elect a given number of members using its present national system. Only at a later stage

[1] See Chapter 8 for the importance of direct elections in the context of the dispute over the shape of any future political union.

would a uniform system be substituted, for it poses immense technical problems, some of the member States at present having proportional representation and others a system more like the English one. There would be a two-fold increase in the number of members bringing it up to 284, but even then the electoral constituencies would be vast by national standards.[1]

What really interests us in this chapter, however, is the repercussions such a scheme would have for the role and status of the national parliaments. Whether or not the directly elected European Parliament were given increased powers at once, the very fact of being representative would immediately give it a far greater say in the affairs of the Communities. The draft plan did not indicate whether an M.P. would be allowed to be a member both of his national parliament and of the European Parliament, but in any event sheer pressure of work would make it practically impossible to be an effective member of both. Politicians would therefore face a major choice: whether to choose election to the European Parliament, with a limited but expanding say in the affairs of the Community, or to stay in the national parliament.

Here however I am venturing into the realms of the fairly distant future. If ever such a choice does become a real one it will mean that a crucial stage has been reached in the shift of the economic and even the political centre of gravity from the national to the Community level. These are still for the moment theoretical problems. Yet they may well have to be faced: indeed it is a recurrent theme of this account of the developing Community that the end of the transitional period is destined to see that transfer of the level of decision-making very far advanced. For Britain and the Scandinavian countries above all (as for Holland too) the primordial importance of parliament in the institutional system makes it indispensable for any wider body which they join to have a genuine and effective system of democratic control—it is certainly no coincidence that it is the Dutch M.P.s who have done the most to establish in the European Parliament the traditions and

---

[1] The inadequacy of sticking to the national systems rather than adopting a uniform system is emphasised by the case of the Grand Duchy of Luxembourg which under the project in question, which keeps the present proportions, would have almost as many members of the European Parliament as national M.P.s— whereas under a system of uniform constituencies the 300,000 Luxembourgers would not even elect one member! Strangely, the idea of a bi-cameral scheme has hardly been looked at.

procedure of a genuine parliament. Yet development of the European Parliament to its rightful position with democratic control over the Council would mean the decline of the national parliaments. These are matters which are going to prove taxing: but it is also without any doubt the field where Britain and the Scandinavians can make their biggest contribution to the development of the Community.

8

Towards Political Unity

THE BASIC motives behind the creation first of the Coal and Steel
Community and then of the other two Communities were political:
and although these were undertakings entirely justifiable in terms of
the economic advantages they would bring, both those who took part
and those who stood aloof were fully aware that the long-term aim was
the political unification of Western Europe. Similarly, as we saw in
Part I, the motives behind the British move towards Europe were a
mixture of the economic and the political.

In his speech in Paris in October 1961, opening the negotiations for
membership of the Common Market, Mr. Heath clearly stated
Britain's full acceptance of the political aims of the member countries
underlying the Treaties of Rome, and also the objectives of the plans
for political co-operation which were then under discussion amongst
the Six. During the months that followed both the Lord Privy Seal and
the Prime Minister made statements to the effect that the Government
was willing to join in political co-operation if invited by the Six, and
would sign a Treaty of Political Union if one existed when Britain
joined the economic Communities. Then, on April 10th, 1962, at a
meeting of the W.E.U. Council held in London, Mr. Heath informed
the Six of the British government's active desire to play its part in the
work of the member countries on drawing up plans for some form of
political union.

Towards what form of political union, then, has the Community of
the Six been moving since it was set up, and what real progress has so
far been made? The present complex and in some ways paradoxical
situation, and the possible trends of future development—in which
Britain will have to play her full part—can only be understood in the
light of the disagreement between two basically conflicting concepts
which has been bedevilling the efforts of the member countries to
achieve closer unity for more than two years.

At the time the Rome Treaties were signed and the Common Market came into being, all those concerned were in basic agreement about

the way it was intended to develop. Political unity was to grow gradually out of economic integration. The three Communities, the 'Europeans' felt, could form the nucleus of and the basis for the development of federal forms of government to which the powers at present exercised by the national States would gradually be transferred, not only in the economic but also in the political and other fields.

The situation in 1962 is not at all so simple, and the way ahead no longer seems so clear and obvious as it did to the 'Europeans' back in 1957. For the 'integrationist' views which prevailed when the Common Market was created have since run into head-long collision with the attitude of General de Gaulle, who conceives of European unity only in terms of co-operation between the governments of independent sovereign States.

The kind of progress the 'Europeans' were—and still are—hoping for is to be based on the development of the three existing Communities. Two steps are of basic importance to their plans: direct elections to the European Parliament, and the merger of the High Authority and the two Commissions in Brussels into a single European Executive.

Throughout the ten years of its existence, first as the Common Assembly of ECSC, then as the Parliamentary Assembly of the three Communities, the European Parliament has been the most outspokenly 'European' of all the Institutions, doing its best to act as a 'driving force' towards European unity. In ECSC it was constantly urging the High Authority to exert to the utmost its supranational powers, encouraging it in clashes with the Governments, and criticising it when it failed to adopt an active policy. In the Common Market the same tradition has been broadened and developed; never accepting any limitation on the scope of its debates, the Parliament has adopted *avant garde* positions in a steady flow of reports and resolutions on all aspects of integration. Yet, as we have seen, it remains but the shadow of a Parliament in the true sense of the word.

Direct elections could not fail to bring a vast increase in the influence and importance of the Parliament, giving it a new authority—*de facto* if not at first *de jure*—in its relations with the Council of Ministers and its control over the Executives. In short, it would fill the dangerous void in the Community system, by ensuring genuine democratic control over the Institutions which run it. At the same time the holding of direct elections would be the biggest single step possible in bringing home to the man in the street the meaning and importance of the Common Market, by involving him in its operation.

The other step the 'Europeans' had been counting on was a merger of the three Executives. Even without any change in its formal relationship with the Council of Ministers, a single body running the affairs of the three Communities, and wielding the powers at present held by the High Authority and the Commissions (for it is generally accepted that the High Authority's supranational powers in its particular field should not be levelled down to correspond to the more limited ones of the Commissions), would gain at once in prestige and influence, as well as being able to deal more efficiently with such joint problems as energy or transport policy. Just as 1960 saw the final drafting of a Treaty for direct elections, so in the same year a plan for merging the Executives had been drawn up and awaited the approval of the Governments.

Another move which it was hoped to make towards unifying the Community was to choose a single seat for all the Institutions—with the implication that it would one day become the administrative 'capital' of a united Europe. The process by which the various Institutions have come to be spread throughout Europe forms part of the complicated history of the Community, but the facts and their consequences are clear: the High Authority and the Court of Justice are in Luxembourg, the Common Market and Euratom are centred on the Commissions in Brussels, and the Parliament meets in Strasbourg but has its Secretariat in Luxembourg. The cost of this arrangement in terms of money, time spent on travel, and reduced efficiency is easily imagined. There is a continual coming and going of officials between Brussels and Luxembourg, and when the Assembly meets a whole administrative apparatus has to be transferred from Luxembourg and Brussels and set up in Strasbourg for perhaps a week or less. More important still, the choice of a single seat would have a considerable psychological impact on public opinion. In 1959, although urged persistently by the Assembly to take a final decision, the Foreign Ministers of the Six shelved the whole question for three years, ostensibly to 'put an end to the uncertainty hanging over the Institutions', but in fact because of their inability to reach an agreement, with both Belgium and Luxembourg ready to use a veto against the loss from their capital cities of the Institutions to which they were well-requited 'temporary' hosts.

Nor were these the only moves afoot to build up the identity and importance of the Community. In the summer of 1959 plans were well advanced for establishing diplomatic representation in London and

Washington; and a scheme for a European Community flag was being seriously considered.

More important by far, plans had been drawn up, and in the summer of 1960 were on the point of being approved, for setting up a European University, under clause 9, para. 2 of the Euratom Treaty. What it was planned to create was a post-graduate university, taking students from all the member countries and from other countries as well, to spend two years studying for a diploma in law, economics, history, sociology, mathematics or applied physics. The subjects would be taught from the European rather than the national angle, and the University would thus complement, not compete with, the national universities. It was thought of both as having a practical value in providing the highly trained élite, thinking in European rather than national terms, which the Community will be needing, and as a major contribution to the development of a united Europe aware of itself as a unit. A phrase in a report on the University, by Professor Geiger, which the Assembly adopted in 1960, expresses this feeling quite clearly:

'The reasons which bring the European Communities to create a new University scarcely differ, basically, from those which—at least since the Reformation—have been at the origin of most universities: the promoters of a political movement seek a sort of apotheosis and a symbol in the foundation of an institution of culture and research; they hope thus for a sort of spiritual consolidation of their political achievements.'

Alongside the setting up of the University, a major effort was planned to develop university co-operation and student exchanges, and the equivalence of degrees and diplomas, which would enable a year spent studying abroad to be counted towards a degree in a national university. Specialised institutes which took a given proportion of foreign students would be classified as 'European institutes'.

Thus the trend which the 'Europeans' had foreseen seemed in the early years of the Common Market to be well under way. Moreover, in addition to these various schemes, the Foreign Ministers of the Six member countries started in November 1959 holding regular quarterly meetings, outside the framework of the Communities, at which they discussed the whole field of foreign policy. These meetings were generally looked on as being 'a political extension of the Communities', and M. Couve de Murville, French Foreign Minister, stated at the time 'the solidarity which is emerging as a result of the Common Market leads the Governments almost automatically to concert their action in other fields, and particularly in the field of international policy'. Although the meetings certainly never went beyond a general discussion and exchange of views there was, as Signor Pella of Italy put it, 'an enthusiasm which makes it possible to hope that in the future something can be achieved, even beyond the wide but well-defined limits of the Rome Treaties'.

Yet the disagreement which was soon to break out between the members of the Common Market was already latent. With General de Gaulle in power in France it was bound to occur sooner or later. In the appointment as Prime Minister of M. Michel Debré, who as a member of the Common Assembly had been for many years a lone but courageous opponent of the ideas of supranationality and a federated Europe, the 'Europeans' saw a confirmation of their fears.

Yet the early years of the de Gaulle régime—which were the first years of the Common Market too—saw no obvious change in the French attitude. De Gaulle had firmly stated his intention of carrying out to the letter his country's commitments under the Treaties setting up the three economic Communities: and France did indeed loyally apply the Treaties. It was not until the summer of 1960 that a distinctive French policy about the future development of European unity began clearly to emerge. The first suggestion of it came in a speech by M. Debré to the French National Assembly, in which he referred to the possibility of setting up, as a first step towards political unity, an independent Political Secretariat. Gradually the de Gaulle-Debré scheme was revealed: the essence of it, to quote M. Debré himself, was to 'ensure by organised co-operation between governments, the legitimate and responsible authorities of the nations, a joint action in certain essential fields'.

The contrast between the spirit of this statement and that in which the Rome Treaties had been signed is clear. To the 'Europeans', the future lies in the gradual cession of sovereignty to central, supranational institutions paving the way eventually for a federation. This was the view held by the governments of the other member countries, and by leaders of political parties of all tendencies throughout the Community—as their membership of Jean Monnet's Action Committee for a United States of Europe shows.[1]

De Gaulle's attitude, on the other hand, cannot be better summed up than in his own phrase—l'*Europe des patries*: the Europe of separate sovereign countries. In view of the crucial importance his attitude has

[1] See the next chapter for an account of the role of the Action Committee.

had for the development of European unity, it is worth quoting his own words as he explained it at a press conference in Paris in September 1960.

'To build Europe, that is, to unite it, is clearly something essential: that is a commonplace. . . . However, in such a field as this we must proceed not according to rules but according to the realities of the situation . . . the realities, the pillars upon which we build, are the States. The States, which are very different one from another, which each have a soul and a history and a language of their own, their own values and glory and ambitions. . . . The States are the only entities which have the right to give orders and the power to be obeyed. To imagine that something can be built up which can act effectively and be approved by the peoples outside or over and above the States, is an illusion. It is true that in the meanwhile . . . it has been possible to set up certain more or less extra- or supra-national bodies: these bodies have their value technically, but they have not and cannot have political authority, and consequent political effectiveness. As long as nothing serious occurs, they work, without very much difficulty, but as soon as some dramatic event occurs, a major problem to be solved, then it is seen that this or that high authority has in fact no authority over the various national groups, and that only the States do have . . . it is natural that the States of Europe should have at their disposal specialised bodies, for the problems they have in common, to prepare and if necessary to follow up their decisions. But these decisions are theirs to take, and can only be theirs, and they can only take them by co-operation.

'If we enter upon this course, then links will multiply, habits will be formed, and with the passage of time, little by little, it is possible that we may come to make some further steps towards European unity . . . that is what France is proposing: it is all that, and nothing else.'

By the summer of 1960 the practical implications of this attitude for the future of the Communities had begun to make themselves felt. It became clear that whilst France would fulfill her strict Treaty obligations, she would systematically and unrelentingly block any steps designed to strengthen the prestige or authority of the Communities. Merger of the Executives was opposed; the direct elections plan met with a blank French refusal; the proposed diplomatic representation had to be dropped, as did the idea of a Community flag. Sometimes the *volte face* was strikingly sudden: it was at the meeting of the

Euratom Council of Ministers actually due to take the final decision on the creation of the European University that the French delegate suddenly voiced a series of major objections to a project which had until then had the full approval of French experts and officials. The most open expression of French hostility to the Communities was to come at the end of 1961 when the French government refused to renew the mandate of M. Etienne Hirsch, the gifted, energetic President of the Euratom Commission, who was too ardently 'European' for the General's liking, and replaced him by M. Paul Chatenet, a Gaullist, who was prepared to run Euratom strictly as a technical organism without political implications.

Yet at the same time there was no denying that de Gaulle had taken the initiative. The 'Europeans' had not put forward any plans for a separate political organisation—precisely because they felt that it was too early for the kind of supranational political institution which they hoped for. In the autumn of 1960 de Gaulle undertook an active diplomatic campaign—which coincided with the diplomatic soundings about eventual British membership of the Common Market—to bring the leaders of the other countries round to his propositions. These were for regular meetings of the heads of government and the creation of an inter-governmental political secretariat. Italy and the Benelux countries were against the institutionalisation of political consultations outside the framework of the Communities; the German attitude was less hostile because any steps which could strengthen the political cohesion of Western Europe seemed precious to the German Government.

De Gaulle's meetings with the Prime Ministers of the other Common Market countries were accompanied by a criss-cross of consultations between these countries themselves on the attitude they should adopt. The French proposals put them in a dilemma. In view of the French attitude it was clear that they could no longer count on economic integration leading gradually but autonomously towards political integration. Although the basic concept behind de Gaulle's notion of unity was far removed from theirs, and represented in effect a step back to the kind of inter-governmental co-operation which they were hoping to leave behind, they could not adopt a wholly negative attitude; the only possible attitude was to attempt to reach a compromise which would guarantee the future of the existing Communities and be such as to leave the way open for development along federalist lines in the future. It is worth remembering that de Gaulle's fervent wish to restore French authority and prestige in the world corresponded—

though it took a more nationalistic form—with the ambitions of the 'Europeans' for a politically united Europe. It was a major achievement of the 'Europeans' to have channelled de Gaulle's ambitions into the framework of the Six. Their task now was to ensure that French leadership did not mean the end of that Community as they conceived it.

The final outcome of the first round of talks was a meeting held in Paris in February 1961. The participants were de Gaulle, Adenauer, the Belgian, Italian and Luxembourg Prime Ministers, and Mr. Joseph Luns, the Dutch Foreign Minister. The latter, arriving to find that de Gaulle and Adenauer had met the previous day and agreed on a text which their partners were expected to accept without argument, put his foot down and obstinately refused to sign, arguing that the smaller countries had not been adequately consulted, and were faced with a *fait accompli*. More important still, he held that the plan endangered the future of the existing Institutions, which by their supranational character were the smaller countries' guarantee against big power domination. This first clash accurately foreshadowed the debate which was to go on throughout the succeeding year. A further period of consultations was agreed on, and in these the Dutch continued to remain more or less isolated in their opposition to the French plans.

When the heads of the six governments (and Mr. Luns) met again it was in Bad Godesberg, near Bonn, on July 18th, 1961. There they reached agreement on a high-sounding declaration, stating their desire to create a 'Union of European peoples', which would 'give shape to the desire for political union, already emphasised in the Treaties instituting the European Communities'. They agreed to organise their co-operation 'with a view to creating institutions', and to hold regular meetings. A commission of diplomats under the chairmanship of the French Ambassador to Denmark, M. Christian Fouchet, was set up and instructed to present proposals for giving the union of the peoples of Europe, as soon as possible, 'a statutory form': in other words, a new Treaty was to be drafted.

A separate declaration dealt with cultural co-operation; the European University was now to be created, not within the framework of the Communities, but by the Italian government with the backing of the member countries; and conventions on other aspects of cultural co-operation were to be drafted.

The Fouchet Commission, which met during the autumn and winter of 1961, ran up against the basic conflict about what kind of Union it was the Six wanted, which had been glossed over but not resolved at Bad Godesberg. Moreover in the autumn the ranks of the 'integrationists' were markedly strengthened when M. Paul-Henri Spaak, veteran of the Common Market negotiations, and doughtiest of the Europeans, again became Belgian Foreign Minister. At the early meetings of the Commission all the delegations presented their views, but only the French submitted a draft Treaty, to be known subsequently as the Fouchet Plan, which formed the basis for the talks. On certain elements of the future Union there was a measure of agreement: it would be instituted by a new Treaty, and its major characteristic would be regular meetings of the heads of State or government; it would cover not only foreign policy, but also defence and culture. About many important aspects, however, there was disagreement— for instance, should the voting always be unanimous? What role should the Assembly play in the new set-up? Should there be a political secretariat? How should the new institutions be linked with those of the existing Communities? On some points the French made concessions, and before Christmas agreement seemed in sight. Then, in the new year, all the concessions were withdrawn, and a new text presented, taking no account at all of the views which the Assembly had expressed in December in a constructive and conciliatory resolution, voted almost unanimously, and intended to indicate the minimum the 'Europeans' could accept.

The result of this move was to crystallise the divergences. France's five partners agreed on an alternative text, taking the Assembly's views into account. Further work then reduced the main differences to three. Distrustful of de Gaulle's desire to act independently of the Atlantic Alliance, the Dutch insisted on the inclusion of a clause stating that the Six's co-operation on defence should take place in the framework of NATO. Secondly, all the other Five wanted a clause stating in detail the aims of the Union and specifically guaranteeing the existing Institutions. Lastly, most important of all, since they were to accept something involving no real supranational elements, the Five wanted a specific commitment that when the Treaty was revised after three years there should be positive moves to give the Union a federal shape. This above all the French would not accept. In the background to the discussion was the Dutch insistence that since Britain was to join the Communities she should also join the political Union.

A Foreign Ministers' meeting in Luxembourg in March 1962 brought no agreement. There were then talks between de Gaulle and the Italian Prime Minister Fanfani, and between the latter and Chancellor Adenauer, in hopes of compromise. A further meeting in Paris on April 17th yielded a compromise on the first two points, but deadlock on the third—the revision commitment—upon which all the Five were adamant. It was at the WEU Council meeting in London a week earlier that Mr. Heath had stated the British desire to take part in the talks and now both M. Spaak and Mr. Luns called for British participation in any future talks. Since progress along the lines they wanted was in any case blocked by French intransigence, they preferred to hold open the door for Britain, although British government thinking was known to be more in line with that of de Gaulle than with their own: for in the British presence they saw a safeguard for the interests of the smaller countries against French desires to dominate the Community. Mr. Luns, at least, hoped, as he told the Dutch Senate, that Britain once in the Community would come round to the idea of moving towards supranational political integration. (Nor is it lost upon the 'Europeans' that the accession of three or four new countries will be bound to increase the power of the Commission, and its influence and prestige in relation to individual member countries).

Thus a first long phase had come to a fruitless end, leaving a question mark still hanging over the future political co-operation and eventual political unity amongst the member countries of the Common Market. Whilst the wishes of the Five are clear, there are now two unknowns. First, what attitude might a future French government adopt? The latest indications are that the supporters of integration are numerous even in the present National Assembly in Paris. I should go so far as to prophecy that the whole episode of de Gaulle's resistance to integration may one day be looked back on as the last serious manifestation of the obsolescent notion of the sovereign nation State—at least in Western Europe. Surely post-Suez Britain will not be joining the Communities in order to shape them along the lines wanted by de Gaulle?

The second unknown is indeed the direction in which Britain and other new members will cast their influence. At the time of writing the two questions—political unity and British membership—seem, thanks to the ambitions of de Gaulle, to be more and more closely linked. By the time this book appears it may be clear how far if at all the General has tried to use his veto on British entry to win support in the dispute over the shape of future political co-operation.

One point is worth making however. Time is undoubtedly on the side of the 'integrationists'. The steady and irreversible progress of economic integration will go on linking the destinies of the member countries more and more closely. Common policies in such vital economic spheres as foreign trade, transport and above all agriculture cannot fail to make co-ordination necessary throughout the economy —and even probably some form of flexible planning at the European level. The decisions involved, as General de Gaulle himself has recognised, are essentially political ones. Thus, whatever institutional forms of political unity are or are not worked out, there will be a spill-over from the economic into the political sphere. Were the French position to change, and not to be replaced by an equally rigid position on the part of another member, some of the measures planned by the 'Europeans' might be expected to be applied, in particular direct elections or a merger of the Executives, and this would hasten the process.

Whatever the form of political co-operation adopted—and some form at least seems likely before very long—the pressure of events would tend to make it develop along federalist lines: and the weight which any political union of the enlarged Community would carry in world affairs might reasonably be expected to convince doubting partners of its value and of the need to reinforce and develop it.

9

Europe as an Ideal

OUR DISSECTION of the Community of the Six is now almost complete: we have looked at its institutional skeleton, its commercial and industrial flesh and blood, and its economic and political habits and behaviour. What we have so far failed to locate is its soul. Yet beyond any shadow of doubt it is more than just an advantageous economic arrangement, more even than a realistic political adaptation to the changing scale and balance of power in the modern world. It would be a mistake for any country to enter the Community without realising the idealism which contributed to its creation and which continues to underly it—and which is not confined to those who are closely associated with the process of integration itself, but is shared by people in all walks of life throughout the Six member countries. My picture of the Community would not be complete without an attempt to convey the scope and importance of this undercurrent of belief in the intrinsic value of a united Europe which seems very largely to have passed our island by.

To appreciate its significance one has only to realise that 'the European idea'—*la construction européenne*—has always been taken perfectly seriously, since the last war, in the member countries. The men who have propagated it, like those who have now begun to give it practical shape, have been idealists but never cranks, far-sighted optimists but never mere dreamers. The leaders and members of the various movements for European unity which sprang up after the war—the European Movement itself, or the *Nouvelles Equipes Internationales* of the Christian Democrats, to take only two examples—were in many cases active politicians, resistance fighters, influential and responsible people of all shades of political opinion who saw in the destruction of the old order on the Continent a chance to create a new framework, to rediscover the spiritual unity of Europe and remove out-dated barriers; they were convinced that it was only by uniting that Europe could defend her values and her way of life, threatened by the ideological conflict, and at the same time make her rightful contribution to the post-war world.

Here perhaps there is a clue to the strength of the appeal which the idea of unity has had on the Continent: despite the violent and destructive nationalisms of the nineteenth and twentieth centuries, the memory, or rather the awareness, of Europe as one spiritual and intellectual whole is still a very real one. Whilst the English stayed safely looking on from behind the Channel, which served them only too successfully in the office of a moat, many of the ancestors of the Common Market's present inhabitants were fellow-citizens of the Holy Roman Empire, or more recently were willing or unwilling fellow-subjects of Napoleon. The Channel remained, but frontiers in Europe moved this way and that: numerous are the areas which even in recent times have changed their official nationality, if not always their allegiance, and sometimes have changed back again within the space of a lifetime. Of the six member States, only France and the Netherlands date back as independent sovereign States for more than 130 years—and even then their boundaries have not remained unchanged.

Not that such feelings are consciously behind the spread of the European ideal. Far more immediately responsible is the deeply-felt disgust with modern war, and with the ugliness and suffering which only the occupied or the defeated can really know (all the Six were one or the other), and which we in Britain (and *a fortiori* the neutrals) can never fully appreciate.

At all events the European idea took root and flourished after the war in this group of countries. True, the political parties, to the disappointment of the idealists, returned more or less to their pre-war patterns and habits; the institutions of the nation State rose again. Yet the idea of European unity did not wither as a result: it was not abandoned either by individuals or by parties. Nor was it an ideal to which they paid merely lip-service: in many cases it was one of the practical planks in their policy, and the parties which advocated it had the backing, for the general emotional and psychological reasons to which I have referred, of a large proportion of the electorates. How else could the ECSC Treaty have passed the national parliaments, the European Defence Community Treaty have been sunk only by the unholy alliance of the Communists and the nationalist extremists in the French National Assembly, the Rome Treaties, with all that they imply, have been ratified by sweeping majorities? To look at it from another angle, if successive British governments held cautiously aloof from the doings of the Six it was basically because there was no corresponding movement of public opinion in Britain attached to these ideals.

Considering how the European idea flourished whilst it was no more than an expression of unrealised aspirations, it was only to be expected that it would widen and deepen its hold once it began to assume practical shape. The organisation and working of the Communities, it is true, are in most cases too technical and too remote to fire the enthusiasm of the man-in-the-street. As Professor Hallstein told the European Parliament, at the ceremony held in April 1962 to mark the fifth anniversary of the signing of the Treaties of Rome:

'The European Community has no emblems, it has no flag, no anthem, holds no parades and has no sovereign. It has no instruments of integration which appeal to the senses, to the eye or to the ear.

'That is in keeping with the style of our Community, a style of realism, of hard prosaic work, which even leads to our being taxed with being a technocracy. The ground on which we work is common sense rather than emotion, our strength reasoned conviction rather than myths, our tactic discussion rather than the sway of passion.'

Moreover, as we saw in a previous chapter, the average citizen has been little touched in his daily life by the Common Market's practical effects.

Yet in those five years since the Treaties were signed, the Common Market has nevertheless found its way—however vague its image may still be—into the public mind. It is still seldom enough that it hits the headlines, but on the other hand it is years now since even in the popular press 'MEC', 'Euromarkt' or 'EWG' had to be spelt out to Italian, Dutch or German readers. The Common Market has become one of the accepted facts of the political and economic scene—no more exciting, or interesting, or comprehensible than other elements, but no less so. And occasionally, all the same, it does hit the headlines. Few things did more to catch the public imagination than the story of the marathon negotiations on the common agricultural policy, with over a dozen ministers sitting late into the night, the fiction of prolonging 1961 until a decision was reached, the news of a Secretary of State for Economic Affairs collapsing from sheer physical and nervous exhaustion, and being carried from the conference chamber, and decisions affecting the price of food throughout the Community for years to come being taken at five o'clock on a Sunday morning in January. It is rarely enough that national affairs are settled in such a dramatic manner.

I mentioned in an earlier chapter that the implementation of the economic dispositions impinges on an ever-widening circle of citizens in the course of their daily work: businessmen seeking to increase exports find customs barriers are falling before them at the blast of the EEC Council's trumpet; garage-owners find they can sell more Volkswagens in France or Fiats in Germany; and greengrocers can offer their customers cheaper Italian fruit and vegetables. We saw how industrialists in every branch of the economy, and trade unionists too, have sought out their opposite numbers in other member countries to negotiate agreements or to plan joint action in defence of their mutual interests. It would be wrong to suppose that those who thus react to the practical pressure resulting from the Treaty are unaware of its wider significance. Most of them see beyond the immediate advantages—bigger markets, greater stability, rising living standards—and realise that integration will also mean improved understanding, or a stronger bulwark against Communism (whichever they find more important). For a combination of reasons, at all events, the trade, industrial and above all the trade union organisations at the Community level are almost invariably staunchly 'European'. Both major trade union organisations, for example, regularly adopt resolutions dealing not just with economic or social affairs but also with the problems of integration in general. The following passage[1] is not at all untypical: 'It is not only the fact, in itself very important, of wanting to obtain economic and social advantages which caused the Trade Unions to rally to the European idea, but also the fact that they recognised the political aspect of that idea; and it is that which has brought them to associate themselves with it with such conviction.'

I suggested above that the political parties are generally 'European' in their outlook. There is no single organisation in the Community more significant of the existence of a genuine and wide-spread commitment to European unity than the Action Committee for the United States of Europe. In 1955 Jean Monnet, the *éminence grise* of the movement for European unity, who had conceived and helped to plan the coal and steel pool, resigned from his post as President of the High Authority, disillusioned by its inability to play a genuinely supra-national role in the face of the attitude of the Governments. He proceeded to devote all his energies to working once more behind the scenes for the further development of European unity, and played his part in creating the Common Market. Immediately it was set up he began thinking about the next step, and in 1959 he founded the Action

[1] From a report to the General Assembly of the Free Trade Unions of the Six member States of the Community held in Brussels January 10th–12th, 1962.

Committee, a purely unofficial body including the leaders of all the major non-extremist political parties and of the non-Communist trade union organisations from each of the countries of the Communities. Its resolutions, based on research done by Monnet and his staff, reflect the views of the leading 'Europeans' and—at least until the period of French obstruction—were a reliable guide to what was likely to be achieved in practice in the not-too-distant future.

Apart from the politicians, and apart even from those who have a direct interest in the workings of the Common Market, a large number of organisations at the national and the Community level have expressed their views on European unity—it has become a topic on which every group seems to want to make its position clear; almost inevitably, these declarations are in 'federalist' or 'integrationist' terms. Another index of public interest is the ever-increasing flow of groups, above all from youth organisations of every kind, which visit the Institutions to learn how they work and what they do. The Common Market and its effects are becoming increasingly important subjects of university studies. Yet, rather surprisingly, little has been done to lay the foundations for European unity in the schools and universities, either by bringing courses into line or by active teaching in the schools.[1] Moreover, as we saw, equivalence of degrees and other qualifications remains for the moment at the planning stage.

The conclusion which I think can be safely drawn from all this is that the European Communities are not just the creations of the politicians or the economists, who may have put up the outward framework, but could build on sound foundations of public support—not just apathetic acquiescence but a positive desire for and interest in unity. This is certainly not to suggest that there was no opposition to the whole idea of unity, or that there is no disagreement or criticism. With of course the vital exception of the attitude of de Gaulle—which as I have suggested is a minority one in the Community and almost certainly in France also[2]—the criticism is aimed rather at the speed at which shared

[1] At the post-graduate level the proposed European University was foreshadowed by the College of Europe in Bruges, and other institutions in Turin, Nancy and elsewhere with a specifically 'European' course, but the scale of their activity is very limited; nor are they specifically limited to the Community.

[2] The resignation of M. Pflimlin and four other M.R.P. Ministers from the Pompidou Cabinet in May 1962 in protest against de Gaulle's re-affirmation at a press conference of his views on unification, and his slighting remarks about the Communities, reveals the strength of feeling about Europe in French political circles.

goals are being reached, or the fairness to one or other group of the methods being used. To a very marked extent the opposition which existed at the time the Treaty was drafted and signed has faded quietly away now that the Common Market is a *fait accompli*. Much of it came from economic interest groups which have now changed over to pursuing their ends by pressure group activities within the framework of the Communities.

A slightly different case, and one perhaps not without its special significance in the context of the present study, is that of the German Socialist Party, which was distinctly anti-European, and even voted against the ratification of the ECSC Treaty, but which after working with the other Socialist parties in the Common Assembly was converted—to such an extent that the leader of the militantly pro-European Socialist Group in the European Parliament is now a German Socialist, Herr Birkelbach.

No referendum has ever been held about European unity, but an interesting side-light on public attitudes has been provided from time to time by the militant wing of the European Movement[1] which favours direct elections for a Constituent Assembly, and the sudden and revolutionary replacement of the national governments by a federal authority. On a number of occasions this movement has held 'mock elections' in a number of European cities—and without official backing, campaign machinery or great publicity has succeeded in persuading people to turn out in strikingly large numbers to express their support for unity.

Here I must make two provisos. It should not be concluded that everyone in the Six countries is a 'convinced European' in any active sense: there are more than 160 million people in EEC, and though probably by now almost all of them have heard of the Common Market very many doubtless still have very little idea about how it works and many still distrust it. Nor should it be assumed that the unity of 'little Europe' is already virtually achieved. The High Authority and the Commissions continue to run up against the entrenched conservatism of one or other national civil service; pressure groups seek to shape the policies of the Communities; and each government has points about which it will make concessions only with the greatest reluctance (the French over social services or the former colonies, the Dutch over transport, the Germans over coal, and so on). The national

[1] In 1961 this movement under Sig. Spinelli split from the more moderate European Federalist Movement.

governments are tenacious of their power and prerogatives. Moreover, it should not be concluded that the traditional hatreds and enmities of Europe have been obliterated, or that they will be obliterated tomorrow. The average Frenchman has not lost, for example, his suspicion of the German, his traditional enemy. Psychologically, Europe cannot be made overnight. Old doubts and suspicions remain; a new crisis could bring them once more to the surface. The making of Europe proceeds against great obstacles—the obstacles of conservatism, of chauvinism, of inertia, of a legacy of hatred and distrust. And yet astonishingly it moves forward. The balancing-out of interests increasingly takes place within the framework of accepted common goals. Despite the disputes over the form of political unity, the move to the second stage has had a profound psychological effect. Any doubts which may have lingered during the first four years are gone: the problems the Community still has to face are no less, and may even be more difficult than any encountered so far, but few can doubt that they will be solved.[1]

All that I have set out to convey here is that the idea of European unity as a valid ideal to be striven for has a far more serious and respectable tradition behind it than it has in Britain. (The very fact that there is no need inside the Community for those tiresome inverted commas around the 'Europeans' is significant.) The years since 1957 have given the peoples of the Six countries a considerable grounding in the process of adding a new political and psychological dimension over and above the nation (but not instead of it) to their view of the world. That process may not have gone very far, but it has deep roots; and it is one which the peoples of new member countries will find themselves undergoing—and which they must undergo if the Community is to be successfully welded into one.

For some time yet the economic and institutional framework which sustains the predominance of the national outlook will remain intact: but the 'Europeans' are at work skilfully and with little fuss, like beavers. Some barriers—like customs duties, or restrictions on establishment—will soon topple altogether, and others are being undermined: more important still, the foundations of a new edifice are being laid. On January 1st, 1967, there should be no more customs duties on trade between six, seven, eight . . . or more countries of Western Europe. If

[2] There is a distinct fear, however, in some quarters that the admission of new members who have not lived through this first tough preparatory stage will weaken or 'dilute' the Community.

not tomorrow then the day after a Treaty of Political Union will be signed, and the press will report on talks about 'the Community's foreign policy'; if not tomorrow then the day after millions of citizens will go to the polls to elect their representatives to the European Parliament; and before many years have passed the first students of the European University will be receiving their post-graduate diplomas. None of this is in the Treaty of Rome: but nor is it the mere fantasy of a few pro-European cranks. These are things which politicians and businessmen, trade unionists, university professors and taxi-drivers are prepared to accept as a practical goal; for they will mean that the Europe towards which the Common Market is a first step is well on the way to being achieved.

I doubt whether any major long-term undertaking of a human society can genuinely succeed unless it reflects and embodies basic wishes of the peoples involved. There are two powerful feelings common to present-day Europeans: one is impatience with the divisions between them which have brought nothing but waste and suffering and evil; and the other is a vague but powerful desire for Europe to have a position at least of respected equality in a world which has adopted the material aspects of Europe's civilisation and has been partly shaped by her culture. It is these feelings that the idea of a united Europe promises to satisfy, and perhaps we British—who certainly share those same feelings—are now in our undemonstrative way coming to realise it.

Part Three

BRITAIN'S ROLE IN EUROPE

Problems of Adjustment

E.F.T.A. AND AGRICULTURE

SUCH, THEN, is the Community to which Britain is seeking admission. Clearly, British membership poses greater problems of adjustment than any it has had to solve so far. At this stage, it would be folly to predict in detail what solutions will be found for the three major issues in the current negotiations—namely agriculture, the EFTA and the Commonwealth. But it is perhaps worth while indicating the general lines along which solutions must be found if the negotiations for Britain's entry are to succeed.

In principle, 'Efta' need not present any serious problem. Under the London Agreement of May 1961, Britain is committed to 'full consultation' with her EFTA colleagues on the progress of her negotiations with the Six, and the following month the EFTA ministers agreed that the organisation must stay in being until satisfactory arrangements had been made for all members, 'thus enabling them to participate from the same date in an integrated European market'. The exact implications of this pledge for Britain are far from clear, nor is it easy to assess how closely the Seven will in fact be able to stick together in the negotiations over their future. Two of them, Denmark and Norway, have decided to seek full membership of the Common Market with Britain. Portugal presents a more difficult problem. Economically the appropriate solution would be the sort of associate status accorded to Greece, leading eventually to full membership. But the Six may well have political reservations on Portuguese membership under the Salazar régime. The other 'Efta' countries are unlikely to stay out of Europe for Portugal.

Associate membership would be the best solution too, one would think, for Eire, which has also expressed willingness to join, though she is not a member of the EFTA. On the other hand, there is quite a chance that Eire may get full membership. Austria and Finland are debarred from full membership of the Common Market, for political reasons. Finland dare not offend Russia, while Austria is bound by treaty to remain neutral as between East and West. The best solution therefore would be for these two countries to become EEC associates, sharing the economic rights and obligations of the Common Market members, but not the political ones.[1] Clearly they would be debarred from taking part in policy-making, and as the Community tightened its political links and moved nearer to a United States of Europe, they would increasingly be left out in the cold—failing a general easing in world tension, which would allow them to seek full membership. To offset this, the Community should assume an explicit responsibility for seeing that the integration of Western Europe does not involve any weakening in the economic conditions of these two countries.

Austria and Finland are neutrals by necessity. Sweden and Switzerland are neutrals by choice. They too would clearly like associate status with the Common Market on the same lines; but they may have difficulty in persuading the Six to let them have it. The U.S.A. has made it clear that she will oppose what she would regard as favouritism to two countries which have done nothing to incur the special loyalty of the West. Why, argue the Americans, should the Swedes and Swiss have preferential treatment to them in the Common Market, if they are not willing to pay the price of membership which they could so easily do? Swiss neutrality made sense when it was neutrality between France and Germany; it makes no sense today, when France and Germany are on the same side. The Swedes justify their neutrality by arguing that without it Finland would be dangerously isolated and in danger of absorption by Russia. If satisfactory arrangements can be made by the Community for Finland, this justification for Swedish neutrality will go.

French voices have also been raised to say that one must either be in the club or outside it—unless one can plead special circumstances. If associate membership is made too easy, why should anybody be willing to pay the price of full membership—and how then can the club hold together? And in any case, it is argued, the economic obstacles to entry for the Swedes and Swiss are far less than for the British.

There is much in these arguments, and it would certainly be tragic if Britain's entry were to be blocked by Swiss or Swedish stubbornness. Nevertheless, there is the awkward fact that Britain is committed to seeing that satisfactory provisions are made for her 'Efta' colleagues

[1] The exact form of the agreement would depend essentially on the Russian attitude. If Russia refuses to be discriminated against, it may be necessary to go back to the free trade area formula and the use of certificates of origin to prevent Soviet goods entering the Common Market via Austria and Finland duty-free.

before joining the Six. And there is much to be said, too, for not letting the Common Market become absorbed into the cold war. The Association with it of countries like Sweden and Switzerland, who are not NATO members, would help to prevent the line rigidifying, and it would be a pity for these countries therefore to be dragooned under threats of economic pressure into a West European military bloc against their will.

The answer surely is to allow for a breathing-space in which Sweden and Switzerland can decide freely where their future lies, and in which the full members of the EEC can decide how strictly to apply the rules of membership in their case. This can best be done by giving them associate membership on a probationary basis for a strictly limited period, after which the issue must be considered afresh. My own guess is that eventually both countries will in fact opt for full membership, but it would be wrong to try to force them into it prematurely.

The problems presented by British agriculture hardly look insuperable. Plainly, Britain must accept the agricultural policy hammered out by the Six. This will mean adjusting present British farm support prices—the price the Government pays the farmer for his produce—to the target prices of the Six. Since these target prices have yet to be determined, it is hard to say what difference this will in fact make. But in any case Britain will have a say in deciding what the levels are. The Community negotiators have decided to adopt the present British practice of an annual farm price review.

More important is the question of how the difference between the Community target price and the price on world markets is to be paid for. In Britain today the Government pays the difference; the farmer enjoys a direct State subsidy. In the EEC this will not be possible. Protection will be achieved through duties or levies on imports, bringing their price up to the Common Market price. Leaving aside for the moment the most important question—namely the future of Britain's imports from the Commonwealth—what will this mean for Britain? It will mean a rise in the cost of living, which has been assessed as a maximum of 3 per cent, spread over a period of six years. This is hardly a major burden, especially as it will be offset by equivalent cuts in Government spending on farm subsidies, which are currently running at some £350 million a year.

One would think that a saving of this order in the Budget would be welcomed by Conservatives. After all, when they took over from the Socialists in 1951, one of their first acts was to reduce the general level of subsidies on the grounds that Government spending and taxation were too high, and that if people were taxed less they could afford to spend more. The same argument surely applies today, especially when the Government is under so much pressure to reduce taxation. The farm support system is in fact an anachronism, which would probably not survive—to judge by hints thrown out by Ministers—even if Britain did not go into the Common Market. The money saved by the State could go into other ways of reducing the cost of living, or it could be spent on more welfare services to the poorer section of the community to compensate them for the higher cost of food.

As we have seen, the proceeds of the import levies will eventually go into a common EEC agricultural pool, to be used to finance investment in new equipment and methods for EEC farmers and export subsidies for European farm products. Britain, as the biggest food importer in the Community, will account for a substantial part of these levies, and it is fair that she should be allowed to use a large part of them to help those parts of her agriculture which will be particularly vulnerable to Common Market competition. In particular, redeployment will be needed on a large scale in British horticulture, which cannot compete without large-scale investment and structural changes. But apart from horticulture, there is no reason why British farmers as a group should not hold their own in a Common Market which aims at agricultural self-sufficiency. It would be different if the Six believed in agricultural free trade; but they do not, except among themselves. Because of their large peasant populations, the Six have a much greater stake in agricultural protection than Britain has. A European Community of which Britain is a member will still be a net food importer at least for a considerable number of years, despite the growth in agricultural productivity on the Continent, and despite the probable accession to the Community of agricultural-exporting countries like Denmark and Eire. British agricultural efficiency compares favourably with most, though not all, of the Six. It is hard, therefore, to see British agriculture as a whole suffering serious adverse effects from Common Market membership even after the transitional period.

Nevertheless, adjustments will be needed. As we have already seen, Britain's horticulturists will need special assistance to enable them to modernise or switch to other forms of farming, and a special sum should be set apart for this out of the import levies Britain has to pay. The cost of British farmers' feedingstuffs will also go up in the Common Market, thereby reducing their profit margins; there is probably not much that can be done about this without infringing the Treaty

But the crucial issue will be the levels at which Community target prices and import duties are fixed. It seems certain that this will involve a tug-of-war between Germany and France, the former wanting high prices and the latter—probably supported by the Commission—cheaper prices. British influence in this struggle could be of crucial importance; one's guess is that British ideas on the right level of prices will be somewhere between France's and Germany's, but rather nearer to France's.

COMMON MARKET AND COMMONWEALTH

The biggest series of problems surrounding Britain's entry are those affecting the Commonwealth. Economically, these problems divide into five main sections, and the simplest procedure is to take them in order.

First, and least important, are the manufactured exports from the 'white' Commonwealth—mainly from Canada, to a lesser extent from Australia and New Zealand. These goods make up less than 2 per cent of all British imports from the Commonwealth, and it has been agreed that the common external tariff shall be applied to them progressively over a period of eight years, with provision for further discussions in 1966 and 1969. This will hardly make a major difference to the economies of the countries concerned. Their best hope lies in general liberalisation of world trade through GATT.

Second come the industrial raw materials which make up 40 per cent of Britain's imports from the Commonwealth. For most of these there is no problem, because the common external tariff of the Community on these materials is zero. But there are twenty-seven materials which Britain now imports duty-free from the Commonwealth, but which are subject to tariffs in the Common Market. The most important are wood pulp, newsprint, aluminium, lead and zinc. Britain has asked for the common external tariff in each case to be reduced to zero, and at the time of writing commodity-by-commodity negotiations with the Six are in full swing in Brussels. Plainly, the British negotiators are not going to get all they want, and a compromise of some sort is inevitable. No great issues of principle are involved here, so agreement should not be too difficult to attain.

A more important question concerns the future of trade with the tropical Commonwealth countries of Africa and the West Indies. As things stand now, these countries are liable to face discrimination in the British market in favour of the associated overseas territories of the Six, which as we have seen have special access to the Common Market. The obvious solution is for all Commonwealth countries that wish it to apply for associated overseas territory status on the same terms as the French Union countries. The Six have indicated unofficially that they would not stand in the way of such a solution for the Commonwealth countries of Africa, the Caribbean and the Pacific, and it seems probable that similar arrangements will be made for the smaller surviving British colonies.

No difficulty, therefore, should arise here over principles. The problem is rather one of politics. Dr. Nkrumah of Ghana has branded AOT status as 'neo-colonialism', and this attitude is bound to make it difficult for other African countries to accept it. It is desirable, therefore, that the door should be left open for a fixed period, so that the African leaders, including Dr. Nkrumah himself, should have time to think the matter over carefully.

The future of India, Pakistan, Ceylon and Hong Kong poses more intractable difficulties. No problems are likely to arise over the commodity exports of these countries—as a gallant concession to British tastes, tea looks like getting into the Community duty-free; but with manufactures it is a different story. The Six have refused to entertain the idea of AOT status for these countries, nor are they prepared to lower the common external tariff for them. On the other hand it is widely recognised that the West has an obligation to help the Asian countries to pay their way by selling their goods. The obvious solution is to assure them of guaranteed quotas for their manufactures in the advanced industrial countries—quotas which will more than compensate for their loss of tariff preferences in Britain. (For these countries with their very low costs, the problem is in any case not whether their goods can get in over a tariff, but whether they will be allowed in at all or whether they will be kept out by quota restrictions.) This is best done on a world-wide basis, on the lines of the international agreement on cotton textiles, undertaken on President Kennedy's initiative. The trouble with international agreements of this sort, however, is the lack of adequate institutional machinery to enforce them in most cases; and it may be necessary in the short term for Europe to go ahead on its own. This means, in effect, that the Community would accept an obligation to find a market for a minimum fixed amount of the main categories of Asian export manufactures provided they are competitive in price and quality. It remains to be seen if this can be achieved.

The final Commonwealth problem concerns what are inelegantly known as 'temperate zone foodstuffs'—Canadian and Australian wheat, New Zealand meat and dairy products, and so on. Here the problems are bafflingly complex. New Zealand represents a special case, for her whole economy has been built up to supply the British market. Something like three-fifths of all New Zealand's exports go to Great Britain, and over 80 per cent of her three main exports of butter, cheese and lamb. If these products are kept out of Britain in favour of Continental competitors, New Zealand faces ruin, for there is no alternative market in sight for her in the world. New Zealand is the one country for whom a reasonable solution to the Common Market problem is literally a matter of life and death. Britain could not sign the Treaty of Rome without first taking care of New Zealand.

Fortunately this is understood in Brussels, and it seems certain that special arrangements will be made. What form they will take is not clear. New Zealand might be given special quotas for imports either into Britain or the Community at large, perhaps coupled with some form of revenue guarantee for her butter sales, at least for an interim period until an international agreement can be worked out.

For Canadian and Australian cereals the solution would seem to lie in allowing them to retain a degree of preference in Britain during the transition period to 1970; thereafter these special measures will have to be replaced by world-wide commodity agreements. So far as wheat is concerned, the problem is more acute for Australia than for Canada, for Australia produces the same 'soft' wheat as Europe does, while Canadian 'hard' wheat is not grown on any large scale in Europe. An interesting new alignment took place shortly after the start of the Brussels negotiations. France and Australia, both wheat exporters, joined forces in campaigning for a world wheat agreement which would stabilise prices at a fairly high level. Britain, as a major importer, at first threw up her hands in horror at the prospect of having to pay higher prices, but at the time of writing is showing signs of coming round to favour the idea. Similar world agreements are being considered by the experts of the Six for beef, mutton and lamb, though the perishable nature of the commodities concerned obviously makes this a more difficult project, and nobody can guarantee that it will succeed.

Although the technical problems to be surmounted are immense, the outlines of a temporary agreement on the main Commonwealth trade problems are emerging, and it is clear that none of the problems involved are insoluble, *given goodwill on both sides*. But one must stress the word 'temporary'. As we have seen, in almost every case the ultimate solution can be seen to involve world-wide agreements, rather than bilateral agreements between Europe and the Commonwealth countries concerned. The Six themselves stress that the eventual solution for Asian manufactures and Commonwealth temperate zone foodstuffs must be found in agreements on a world scale. The same applies, in rather different degree, to 'white' Commonwealth manufactures, where the solution lies in a general lowering of world tariffs—and also to tropical commodities. The extension of AOT status to Commonwealth countries can only be a temporary solution. It is unpopular with the Americans, and with those tropical countries—in Latin America for example—who are excluded. The perpetuation of AOT status will introduce fresh divisions into Africa and the under-developed countries generally. Once again, the ultimate solution must be a world-wide one.

The eventual relationship between a United Europe and the rest of the world—including particularly the Commonwealth, the U.S. and the under-developed countries as a whole—is something to which we shall return later in this book. For the moment, the point to make is that a temporary reconciliation *can* be achieved between the needs of the Commonwealth and the requirements of the Common Market. Moreover, in the long run anything which strengthens the British economy should benefit the Commonwealth. The more prosperous Britain is, the more Commonwealth raw materials she will import, and the more capital she will have available for Commonwealth investment. These are not small matters.

CAN WE COMPETE?

But *will* Common Market membership make Britain more prosperous? Will we be able, in other words, to compete effectively? Plainly, the view of the Government and of industry itself is that we will. There would be no point in going into Europe if the prospect it presented for British industry was one of permanent decay. But industry, as we have seen, has throughout been on balance strongly in favour of British entry.

The first point to make is an obvious one. The faster the Six keep expanding, the bigger market they will offer. We have seen that in recent years Britain's exports to Europe have been going up much faster than our exports to the Commonwealth, precisely because Europe's rate of growth has been faster. This process looks like continuing, though the pace of growth may well slow down somewhat in the sixties (and this, as we shall see, will present new opportunities as well as new challenges for the under-developed world).

Moreover, the very sluggishness of the British economy in the fifties could now redound to our advantage in Europe. For in the last few years Continental labour costs have been catching up with, in some cases overtaking, Britain's. For standards of living depend on, and follow, industrial growth. Before the war Britain had perhaps the highest standard of living in Europe. Today we rank below Switzerland, Sweden and probably Belgium, while Germany and France have just about caught us up, and the Netherlands and Northern Italy are not far behind. By 1970, on current trends, British living standards will be below those of France, Germany, Holland and the three Scandinavian countries, as well as Belgium and Switzerland.

This is a depressing picture, and one hopes that it will be averted by a faster rate of growth in British industry. But it has a brighter side. Apart from Italy, none of the Six is really still in a position to undercut Britain on wage-costs. Moreover, the reserve of industrial manpower has now virtually disappeared among the Six except in Italy, having been sucked up by the rapid expansion of industry. The conditions of labour shortage which have hampered British industry for so long now exist, on a more acute scale, over most of the Common Market. It is significant that one of the reasons why British firms have been winning orders on the Continent recently is that they can quote quicker deliveries than their competitors.

Third, despite her weaknesses, Britain has a number of industrial advantages. The range of her industrial production is broader than that of the Six. In the City of London she has a network of commercial and financial intelligence and services which is still without rival on the Continent. One might say, in fact, that Britain has all the necessary ingredients for success if she could only organise them.

This is not the place to describe in detail the reforms needed to organise the latent potential of the British economy. The ramifications of the class system, which increasingly threaten to divide the country into warring sections of 'We' and 'They', are a major obstacle, intensified as they are by an ossifying trade union structure.[1] Weaknesses in management are all too frequent. Insufficient competition, lack of social mobility, and an educational system which not only perpetuates inequality but has in the past failed to devote enough attention to training

[1] I deal with these matters at greater length in my book *The Stagnant Society* (Penguin, 1961).

scientists and technologists, and still refuses to provide for management training at university level, are largely to blame. Add to this a lack of any effective planning at govermental level, and the crushing burden of trying to maintain Great Power status and the role of sterling as a world currency on an inadequate industrial base, and one has a rough-and-ready diagnosis of the main ills from which Britain has been suffering. What is needed is a society which provides genuine equality of opportunity, a far more professional approach to management, a more comprehensive educational system, and effective national planning such as the National Economic Development Council is setting out to provide. Then Britain will prosper, for the necessary conditions of success are all here.

But these changes will take time, and there is no denying that the first impact of the Common Market on British industry may be far from pleasant. In order to catch up with the tariff cuts the Six have been making among themselves, Britain will have to halve her tariffs against the Six on joining;[1] in return, of course, tariffs against British goods in the Six will also be halved, but on balance British tariffs are today somewhat higher than those of the Six, so that our cuts will be rather more extensive. Adjustment to the common external tariff of the Common Market, which will take place over a period of years, will also involve a slight reduction in the total level of British protection against non-European competitors like the U.S. or Japan.

It is doubtful, however, how important tariff protection is in most of the highly-complex industrial goods which make up the bulk of the trade between the advanced industrial powers. Other factors—design, specification, delivery times—are important as well as cost, and it may be that the main effect of tariff cuts is to reduce profit margins rather than alter the actual pattern of trade. It does not therefore follow that because a particular British industry—chemicals for example—has higher tariffs than its opposite numbers on the Continent, that it will do badly in the Common Market.

The ending of Commonwealth preferences will both harm and help British industry. Obviously industries like cotton textiles will welcome a greater degree of protection against imports from the Asian Commonwealth. On the other hand, higher tariffs on Commonwealth raw material imports will tend to push up production costs in British in-

[1] Remaining tariffs will then be progressively whittled away to zero in line with the cuts which the Six make in their own internal tariff structures during the transitional phase to the full implementation of the Common Market.

dustry, and if food prices go up this may involve firms in paying higher wages in compensation. Also, the loss of British tariff preferences in Commonwealth markets may have some temporary effect. In the long run there is little doubt that what is lost in the Commonwealth will be more than made good in Europe, but the transitional process of adjustment—transferring sales forces, gearing oneself up to supply a market with very different tastes and traditions—may not in all cases be an easy one.

It is not very profitable to try to draw up a list of which industries will gain and which will not in the Common Market. In every industry some firms will benefit, while some will suffer. The firms that will benefit are those which are able to exploit the techniques of mass production, or which offer a product of special quality. The firms that will lose are those whose products are neither of particularly high quality, nor particularly cheaply or efficiently produced. In short, the firms which will do well in the Common Market are those which would do well in any case, while those which will do badly are those which on the whole deserve to do badly. British entry to the Common Market will accelerate and intensify changes which would otherwise have taken place more slowly; it will not change or distort the general pattern of growth, but will force it through more quickly.

The weakest sector of British industry at present lies in the field of mass consumer goods, and it is here that the Common Market may well claim its biggest number of casualties. Cotton and rayon may benefit from the easing of Asian competition, but they may still find it hard to hold their own against the Continent. The cheaper end of British wool textiles will face stiff competition from Italy, while the higher-quality products should enjoy expanding sales in Europe.

In clothing and footwear, too, Italy—and to some extent France—may gain in the British home market, though in men's clothing Britain should do well. In carpets, pottery, glassware, toys, cameras, scientific instruments, clocks and watches competition is going to get a lot keener, and while some British firms will do well others almost certainly will not.

In the motor industry, British commercial vehicles, tractors, sports cars and components and accessories will do very well, but the car manufacturers themselves face a very stiff struggle, and the number of independent firms may decline. Two other industries where competition in Europe will be very keen are chemicals and paper manufacture, though in each case the best British firms should more than hold their own; the paper manufacturers will benefit from the fact that Scandinavian competition will no longer be directed overwhelmingly at Britain, as it has been in the EFTA, but instead dispersed over Western Europe as a whole. In appliances the position is less clear, and the gains and losses from Britain's point of view may be fairly evenly balanced. British refrigerators may do rather badly, but washing machines should do reasonably well. Radio and TV sets should be little affected. In engineering there are strong and weak sectors, with the strong slightly predominating.

The British industries which look like doing really well, in addition to those mentioned already, include electronic and automation equipment, office equipment (outside the special fields dominated by Grundig and Olivetti), farm machinery, certain types of plastics, and multiple tailoring. But Britain should also gain a great deal of business in the 'service' sector of industry. It has already been pointed out that the services of the City of London—in banking, insurance, commercial intelligence and so on—are unrivalled on the Continent. The Six are also some years behind Britain in development of the latest forms of retailing. 'Shall I tell you which British firm will do best in the Common Market?' a leading industrialist said to me the other day. 'In my view it's a toss-up between Jaguar and Marks and Spencers.'

But this rough balance-sheet of likely gainers and losers is based on one's assessment of the industries concerned *now*. This must be stressed, for the comparative efficiency of different industries is continually changing. In costs, in technology, in native ability, Britain and the leading Continental countries are today roughly level. They are all competing to supply a market whose present rate of growth is dramatic, and whose future potential is enormous. Where Britain is behind, it is usually because of weaknesses in design, sloppy sales techniques, insufficient drive, costs marginally higher than her competitors. These are all faults that can be remedied. British designs need to be more exciting to appeal to Continental buyers. British industry as a whole needs to concentrate more on salesmanship. Too few British firms are prepared to write their sales literature in the language of the country they are trying to sell to, to quote prices in the currency of the customer country, to use metric measurements. These are familiar complaints, but none the less important. The sooner Britain goes over to a metric system and to Continental weights and measures, the better for her foreign trade. British industry is changing fast, and on the speed of her adjustment will depend whether the onset of the Common Market brings prosperity or crisis. The knife-edge between success and failure is as keen as that.

So far as the two smaller European Communities are concerned, membership is unlikely to pose any particular problems for Britain. Britain's lead in nuclear energy should stand us in good stead in Euratom, once the Continental nuclear power programme gets off the ground. In the ECSC British coal and British steel should both on balance gain business, though in neither case on a very large scale. The most important question here is the evolution of a European energy policy, which is discussed below.

There are however a number of factors which will affect British industry's ability to compete in Europe, which are outside the control of industry itself. Energy costs, which have just been mentioned, are one. The general tenor of Government policy towards industry—rates and methods of taxation, planning, use of controls, and so on—is another. The competing claims on sterling are a third. And finally there is the question of transport costs and the distribution of industry.

All of these, however, impinge in one way or another on the 'unfinished business' in the Common Market's in-tray. Since the future of Britain and British policy will increasingly be linked with that of the Common Market, it is best to consider all these questions within the context of Europe rather than of Britain alone.

'UNFINISHED BUSINESS': ENERGY POLICY

Europe's search for a common energy policy, as we saw in Part II, has so far been pretty unrewarding—though there are some signs that this may at last be beginning to change. This is only partly because of the division of responsibility for energy between three separate Communities. An administrative reform would not solve the problem, but it would probably help. And two possible solutions—both of them have been canvassed in Brussels and Luxembourg—suggest themselves.

The first would be to merge the three Communities in one. This is by far the best solution, and the one which will eventually have to be adopted. But, as we have seen, it is at present anathema to the French Government. There may be a case, therefore, for adopting the second-best alternative, which is to replace Euratom and the ECSC by an Energy Commission, which would also be responsible for oil, natural gas, hydro-power and secondary forms of energy. The administrative organs of Euratom and the ECSC could be absorbed into this Commission without appreciably altering their internal structures. Steel might perhaps be transferred to the EEC in exchange for oil and natural gas. The constitution of the Energy Commission should be such that it could easily be absorbed into the EEC as and when circumstances permitted it.

This is an administrative reform which in British terms would make sense; the British Ministry of Power covers all forms of energy, and also—though largely as a historical accident—steel. But the mere establishment of an Energy Commission would not by itself make a European energy policy. It would not overcome the basic conflicts between the coal-producing countries like Germany and Belgium, the energy importers like Italy, and France with her *dirigiste* energy policy and her need to find an outlet in Europe for the products of the Sahara.

What is Britain's position in this? Like most of the Six—but unlike Italy and the Netherlands—Britain bans all imports of coal. (Germany imports some coal, but on a very limited and restricted scale.) Once in the ECSC, of course, this will cease to apply to coal imports from the Six. But this is unlikely to make much difference in practice, for Continental coal costs are on average at least as high as they are here. The only exporters of really cheap coal in the world are the U.S., Poland and the Soviet Union. And the coal interests in the Six will amost certainly want Britain to continue her ban on these imports, if only because British coal displaced by U.S. imports is liable to find its way on to the Continent.

So far as oil is concerned, Britain imposes no tariff or other restrictions on oil imports, but she does have a tax on fuel oil—as do Belgium and Germany. This tax is highly unpopular with industry, and if British industry is to get its costs down there is a strong case for removing it. In fact British coal is staging such a strong recovery at the present time that the tax will probably be removed within the next few years, whatever happens in the Common Market.

Unlike most of the Six, Britain has a strong interest in both coal and oil. Not only is she a major refiner of imported crude oil, but she has a big financial stake in Middle East and Caribbean crude. Britain, therefore, would presumably oppose any attempt to restrict oil imports from non-Communist sources into the European Community, though she would probably support a stiff attitude towards coal imports.

On the whole the oil companies in Britain have not pursued anything like such a ruthless price-cutting policy as they have, for example, in

Germany. One reason for this may be the knowledge that if they embarrassed the Government by making too savage inroads into coal markets, the Government might retaliate—for example by opening the door to direct imports of Russian oil, which would undercut the British and American companies.

It seems clear, therefore, that Britain has no special interests in the energy field which would conflict with the sort of energy policy the Community is likely to evolve. Such a policy is bound to involve a good deal of 'give and take', and Britain with her wide range of interests is in some ways well placed to act as a natural mediator between Germany (in this case supported by Belgium), Italy (who may get the support of any of the other EFTA countries joining the Six, since none of them has much indigenous coal or oil) and France. In all countries coal faces a natural long-term contraction, and in all countries State aid of one sort or another will help to soften this process. In Britain the ending of the fuel oil tax should be accompanied or preceded by a writing-off of the Coal Board's accumulated deficit and a moratorium on interest payments for a fixed period. This would give the Coal Board the room for manoeuvre it needs to get its prices down so that it can meet oil competition effectively on equal terms.

Britain's energy policy requirements can be summed up thus:—

(1) Energy prices in Britain must not be higher than those on the Continent if our industry is to be competitive. If the Six are determined on a cheap energy policy, Britain cannot afford to be left out. There is already something deeply ironic about a situation in which Italy, having no indigenous energy resources of her own apart from some natural gas and hydro-power, nevertheless gets her energy far cheaper than her competitors by relying on imports. This is a product of a situation in which it is cheaper to mine coal in America and ship it across the ocean to Naples than to mine it in the Ruhr or Rhondda for use in a factory at the pithead.

(2) At the same time, Britain has an interest in seeing that the rundown in demand for coal is not too sudden or too drastic. A planned contraction in coal can be far more effectively carried out on a European than on a purely British scale.

(3) It is in Britain's interest that Europe should not be too heavily committed to Saharan or Soviet oil, but that markets should be kept open for the Middle East and Caribbean crudes in which Britain has both a financial and a refining interest. For political and technical reasons, the Six are likely to accept this. But the international oil

companies will have to learn to live with Signor Mattei of ENI[1], which may mean allowing him the interest in Middle Eastern production which he has always wanted; and some cuts in the overall level of published oil prices in Europe—as distinct from the discounted prices which tough-bargaining customers can usually get—may be inevitable.

A good deal of very hard bargaining lies ahead before Europe gets the planned energy policy she is groping towards. But there is no reason to think that Britain will do badly out of the policy when it emerges, and both Britain and the Six should find it easier to hammer out an effective energy policy together rather than in isolation.

'UNFINISHED BUSINESS': TRANSPORT

After energy, the next big item in the field of European integration looks like being transport policy. And this is an issue in which British interests are much more closely and painfully involved; for transport costs look like being Britain's Achilles heel in the Common Market.

To see why, one has only to look at the map. Geographically, Britain lies at the perimeter of Europe. It is obviously much easier to supply the Italian market, for example, from Germany or France than it is from Britain. Transport costs can be an important item in a product, such as a motor-car, which is not only comparatively bulky but subject to very keen price competition.

Clearly there is not much that can be done about this, other than to try to minimise one's natural disadvantages by making one's transport facilities as efficient as possible. Unhappily, since the war Britain has lagged badly in investment in transport. The amount spent on new road construction, as is well known, has been a good deal less as a percentage of national income than in most of the Continental countries. An effort is now being made to catch up, but we have still some way to go. Similarly, despite the amount spent on railway modernisation, British Railways compare unfavourably for efficiency with those on the Continent—partly because most of the Continental countries made railway modernisation a high priority immediately after the war, whereas we waited for ten years before starting ours.

The same deficiencies apply, perhaps even more markedly, to our port facilities. Turn-round time for ships in the Port of London and

---

[1] *Ente Nazionale Idrocarburi*, the Italian nationalised oil and natural gas monopoly which has been a thorn in the flesh of the international oil companies, and Europe's coal industries, since the war. E.N.I. is the channel through which Soviet crude oil enters the Community.

other big British ports compares unfavourably with those in major Continental ports like Rotterdam and Hamburg, which have better labour relations and more modern equipment and lay-outs. It is not just a question of modernising facilities at the docks themselves, but also of improving road and rail approaches to the ports. Customs procedures also need to be streamlined. At the Export Council for Europe conference at Eastbourne in the autumn of 1961, the director-general of the Federation of British Industries strongly criticised 'the apparent unpreparedness in quite a few sections of our transport facilities for the rapid growth of traffic which the Common Market makes pretty well certain'. Something like a crash programme seems to be needed to improve Britain's transport services from the point of view of expediting exports to Europe.

Of course the biggest single improvement would be the construction of a Channel bridge or tunnel. Some sort of link is indeed a 'must' once Britain is in the Common Market—though it is worth while pointing out that it is no good having an efficient cross-Channel land route unless the transport system inside this country can handle the extra traffic. One does not want traffic jams stretching from Calais to Canterbury!

I am not concerned here to argue the relative claims of a Channel bridge or tunnel. That is partly a technical question (on which I am not qualified to pronounce), partly a matter of finance. The Channel tunnel is liable to cost upwards of £100 million, the bridge quite possibly more than £200 million. The bridge also involves complex questions of international law, over the freedom of navigation; if, say, the Russians objected, as they well might, on the grounds that the bridge was a violation of the freedom of the seas and a hazard to shipping in the Channel, there might have to be litigation before the International Court. This is a depressing prospect, which could involve a considerable loss of time. For this reason, and because of the relative costs, one's instinct is to plump for the tunnel, unless the technical advantages of the bridge prove overwhelming. The great danger is that the partisans of tunnel and bridge will each argue their case so stubbornly and convincingly that we shall be left, like Buridan's ass, unable to make up our minds and therefore getting nothing at all. The Oxford road controversy should have taught us how deadly an enemy the best can be to the good!

As has been pointed out in Part II, the Channel tunnel (or bridge) should be a strong candidate for investment aid from the European

Investment Bank in Brussels. Apart from its practical advantages, the 'abolition' of the English Channel would have an enormous symbolic importance in demonstrating the indissoluble links between Britain and the Continent—an epoch-making stage in the 'making of Europe', the reversal of a thousand years of history. For all good 'Europeans' it should be a high priority indeed.

It might well be argued that if transport bottlenecks hinder our exports, they also help to protect us from imports from the Continent. No doubt there is some truth in this, but less than appears at first sight. For the biggest consumer market in Britain happens to be situated close to the Continent. London and its environs, containing nearly a third of the population of these islands (and a rather larger proportion of the country's purchasing power), form a very accessible market to Continental exporters. There is a good distribution network, and a greater readiness to accept foreign goods than in other parts of Britain. London may therefore constitute an obvious target for European industrialists in the first stages of British accession to the Common Market.

The problem is that British industry is markedly less concentrated in south-east England than are British consumers. This raises some very awkward policy issues, which are going to give rise to many headaches in the next few years. For many years the natural drift of industry and population in Britain has been towards what planners describe as the 'coffin'—the London-Birmingham-Manchester axis—and particularly towards the south-eastern end of it, namely Greater London. The reasons for this drift have been partly economic—the desire to be near the London market, coupled with the declining importance of access to local raw materials; and partly social—the supposedly better amenities in the south.

The result of this trend has been increasing congestion and over-population in the south, and increasing structural unemployment and wastage of social capital in the declining areas of the north and west. For valid social, political and economic reasons, governments have set themselves to reverse these tendencies by trying to restrict new industrial development in the congested areas of central and southern England, and by providing incentives to industry to expand in the labour-surplus areas of Scotland, Wales, Northern Ireland and Northumbria.

Industry has tended to resist this policy of redistribution, even though it can be shown to have helped to keep down labour costs. (Shortage of labour in the Midlands and south-east forces up local wage rates, a process which trade union activity then proceeds to extend to the labour-surplus areas, where the 'market-price' of labour would be much lower. The best way of stopping this wage-drift is to have a more even distribution of labour throughout the country. This does not take into account other savings from a more even distribution of activity, namely the easing of traffic congestion, and a better utilisation of the fixed capital—roads, houses, shops, railways, etc.—locked up in the declining areas.) Industrialists argue that transport and other costs involved in operating away from the 'coffin', where the main market lies, can be considerable, and they often require a good deal of financial inducement to persuade them to do so.

These arguments are going to become a good deal more insistent, and a good deal more plausible, once Britain is in the Common Market. The pull on industry and population of south-east England—the gateway to the Continent—is going to become much stronger. Should the Government try to resist it? Is it fair to ask a motor manufacturer, say, to move to Scotland, and at the same time expect him to increase his exports to Europe? Will his movement to Scotland not threaten his hold on the market in London, let alone in Europe? On the other hand, the arguments against the excessive concentration of the country's life and activity in the south-east are as strong as ever.

The dilemma for policy-makers is such a difficult one that it is surprising that the anti-Europeans in Britain have not made more of it. Instead they have tended to concentrate on red herrings, arguing that under the Rome Treaty the Government will in any case not be *able* to provide assistance for declining areas or influence the location of industry. But this, as we saw in Part II, is quite false. It is true that the Rome Treaty provides for free movement of capital between countries. An industrialist refused permission to expand at Dagenham, shall we say, may decide to go to Milan or Cologne in preference to Glasgow or Belfast. But in fact this has been the situation for a number of years. It is a long time since the British Government exercised any effective check on British investment on the Continent, except for a brief period after the 1961 'Little Budget'. It is a moot point whether our membership of the Common Market will accelerate or slow down this investment. Hitherto getting inside the Common Market tariff wall provided an incentive; once we are in the Common Market this will cease to apply. On the other hand, of course, the Continent has not hitherto been a good base from which to try to service the British market; with

Britain in the Common Market, however, it will become a better one. Perhaps the crucial factor in deciding an industrialist where he is going to put up his plant in the European Economic Community of the future will be relative production costs. As we have seen, the last few years have seen a levelling-up to Britain's standard of one of the main elements of total cost—namely wages. If labour is as scarce on the Continent as it is here—which is now the case—the incentive to industry to locate its plants there rather than here will be to that extent diminished. The advantage of nearness to markets will, on the other hand, remain.

There is nothing in the Treaty which positively prevents governments from doing what they can to re-distribute their industry, provided that in so doing they are not overtly subsidising particular sections of industry at the expense of others. In fact most of the Six try to influence the distribution of their industries by the same sort of mixture of controls and incentives as Britain does. As we saw in Part II, the European Investment Bank and the Social Fund have a specific responsibility for helping under-developed areas within the Community, and both have considerable funds at their disposal. There is no reason why high-unemployment areas of the United Kingdom like Northern Ireland and Scotland should not qualify for special assistance from the institutions of the Community, just as Southern Italy and parts of France and Germany do now.

This leads on to another aspect of the Rome Treaty on which there is considerable misunderstanding and confusion in Britain—namely, the free movement of labour. There is a wide-spread fear among many British workers that as soon as Britain enters the Common Market Britain will be over-run by immigrant workers from the Continent, eager to take British jobs at lower wages than British trade unionists require. This picture hardly corresponds to reality. As we have seen, there is no longer any significant disparity between real wages on the Continent and here. The Continental worker may get slightly lower money wages, but he usually works somewhat shorter hours and gets longer holidays. He also tends to do rather better on 'fringe' benefits, to have greater job security—it is much harder for an employer to dismiss workers in most Continental countries than it is in Britain—and to get a number of benefits, such as family allowances, which British employers do not pay. It is hard to see what particular inducement there would be for a Continental worker to come to Britain for a job today, rather than—say—to France or Germany, where the labour shortage is more acute. In any case, as we have seen, the freedom of movement of labour in the Common Market is by no means complete, and its provisions prevent the immigrant from under-cutting the resident worker.

The British worker, in fact, will only suffer as a result of our joining the Common Market if British industry finds it cannot compete—or if there is a mass exodus of British firms to the Continent, which in view of the labour shortage there seems unlikely. On the other hand, labour stands to benefit in Britain in three ways. First, as we saw in Part II, the Rome Treaty contains a number of social provisions which are not embodied in present British legislation—for example, the commitment to equal payment for equal work. Second, the growing labour shortage on the Continent may lead Continental firms to establish themselves over here, thereby providing more jobs; at the worst, it will be much easier for unemployed British workers to find jobs elsewhere in the Common Market countries. Third—and this is potentially a very important factor, not only for the British worker but for Britain as a whole—Britain as a Common Market member is likely to attract a great deal of American industrial investment. In recent years there has been a growing tendency for U.S. manufacturers to establish plant on this side of the Atlantic, to benefit from the lower labour costs and mass markets of Europe. For reasons of language and customs, as well as access to the Commonwealth, Britain has up to now been the favourite location for U.S. industry. It has been clear for some time that if Britain were to remain outside the Common Market this would cease to be so, and U.S. firms might establish themselves instead on the Continent. While the question of Britain's relations with the Six hung fire, many U.S. industrialists hesitated. Once Britain is in, it is a reasonable bet that the inflow of U.S. capital will accelerate—and this will mean more jobs for British workers.

There is, however, one problem about the free movement of labour in the Common Market so far as Britain is concerned. This arises over the thorny question of Commonwealth immigration. *Pace* the Immigration Bill—and this can hardly be the last word on the subject—it would be a retrograde step if Britain were to close her doors to workers from Commonwealth countries, specially if this immigration is from countries which cannot provide jobs at home for their people. Circumstances could arise in which this inflow from the Commonwealth, coupled with an inflow from the Continent, threatened to upset the labour market in Britain. Alternatively, a situation could arise in which workers from the Commonwealth began to flood into Europe via

Britain to an extent which might embarrass one or more members of the Six. No action needs to be taken now on these hypothetical dangers, but it would be as well if both Britain and the Six reserved the right to restrict the free flow of labour between their countries in the event of difficulties arising through mass immigration from the Commonwealth.

The discussion so far may be summed up as follows: In the Common Market Britain faces the disadvantage of high transport costs. These may, however, be offset by the benefits of a slightly easier labour supply, which could well attract firms from the U.S. as well as the Continent. We are on balance more likely to attract new industry rather than foreign workers. The Government should do what it can—and under the Rome Treaty it can do quite a lot—to attract such firms. It should also continue its policy of trying to ensure a more even geographical distribution of British industry, but the fact must be faced that it will be more difficult to do this, and maintain our competitiveness, once we are in the Common Market. The best way to get round this problem is to take the lead in pressing for a Community-wide scheme of regional planning, backed by the resources of the European Investment Bank. (This is dealt with further below.) And, finally, there is an urgent need for Britain to improve her transport services—her ports, roads and railways—to help overcome her natural disadvantages.

So far as the transport policy requirements of the Rome Treaty are concerned, they are in most ways a good deal nearer to present British thinking than they are to current practice in most of the Six themselves. All of the Six, like Britain, have nationalised railway systems; none of them, except the Dutch, make a profit. All, including the Dutch, are subsidised. In nearly every case competition from road haulage is in some way or other restricted. In almost every case the rates charged by the railways are subject to some degree of State control, and railway rates are used as an element of internal subsidy, to help particular industries or regions.

The EEC Commission proposed to sweep all this away, and to introduce a complete free market in transport. This means that the railways must pay their way, and must face unrestricted competition from other forms of transport. Britain is already pursuing a policy which is aimed at making the railways financially viable. British Railways, unlike all the Six except the Dutch, already have full freedom in their pricing policy—outside London. And competition from road hauliers suffers from no restraints in Britain. It follows, therefore, that current British transport policy is already in line with the official thinking in Brussels. The question is rather whether the transport policy laid down in the Treaty of Rome will be fully practicable—whether railways can be allowed to compete on level terms with the innumerable small hauliers by road or waterway, who do not have to carry the social obligations of the railways. In short, the question which the Six will have to decide before long—the question with which the British are now wrestling—is how far the railways represent a profit-making enterprise and how far a social service. In view of the immense complexity of the problems, it may well be a long time before a common transport policy in fact emerges for Europe. But when it does, it should have few terrors for Britain.

'UNFINISHED BUSINESS': CARTELS AND MERGERS

British critics of the Common Market often refer to it as an association of cartels. This is a little unfair to an institution so dedicated to promoting the virtues of competition, but—as we are finding also in Britain—competition is often a lot easier to legislate for than to enforce! Industry in many of the Continental countries has a long history of cartellisation, and as we saw in Part II many firms have reacted to the increased competition from across national borders by reaching agreements with their competitors. Some of these agreements are harmless enough, such as those for co-operation in research or reciprocal use of distribution and sales networks. But the range of agreements concluded shades imperceptibly, through specialisation pacts, exchange of patents and so on, into straightforward cartel arrangements which have the effect of frustrating competition. It is extremely hard to tell at what stage the natural reaction to the opening of restricted markets has become in itself a distortion of the market.

The new anti-cartel regulations drawn up by the EEC Commission look effective enough on paper—indeed, they bear a close similarity to our own Restrictive Trade Practices legislation. It is to be hoped that each of the Six will eventually mould their own national legislation on the lines of the Commission's regulations, so that there will be a uniform policy on cartels whether they affect trade between member-States or not. With anti-cartel legislation, however, everything depends on how strictly the regulations are enforced.

British anti-cartel legislation, which has been enforced with remarkable strictness, has had one unfortunate by-product. It has tended to reinforce the trend towards mergers and take-overs in industry. This is inevitable. If it is made difficult to reach agreements with one's competitors, a natural reaction is to try to end their competition by merging with them or taking them over. A monopoly is an effective alternative to a cartel. Policy designed to enforce competition therefore requires strong legislation on monopolies to complement legislation on cartels.

Britain at present lacks effective monopoly legislation. The Monopolies Commission has no power to investigate potential—as opposed to actual—mergers or monopolies, and it is in any case under-staffed, with the result that its enquiries take a very long time; moreover, its reports are often ignored by Ministers. Britain does not try to ban mergers or monopolies as such, but only those that are found to be operating against the public interest. In other words, a cartel is guilty unless it can prove itself innocent; a monopoly is innocent unless it is proved guilty. The same applies in the Common Market, though there is the difference that the EEC can investigate monopolies independently of member-Governments or the Council of Ministers, whereas the British Monopolies Commission can only investigate cases referred to it by Government. Only in the ECSC do mergers or concentrations have to receive the prior approval of the authorities.

In the U.S. and Canada, on the other hand, mergers are regarded as inherently bad, and the authorities have powers—not always exercised—to stop take-overs and to break up monopolies. It seems clear that both Britain and the Six need to move some way towards transatlantic practice. Plainly it would be wrong to try to freeze the existing structure of industry in Europe. One of the main objects of the Common Market is to enable the benefits of large-scale production to be realised, and this can only be achieved if there is scope for competing firms to merge. The process of competition itself, as has been pointed out many times, kills competition; and technological trends increasingly favour large units. The authorities therefore need to exercise their powers with discretion. But the social and political dangers of monopoly are real enough. I would favour applying the rules of the ECSC to the EEC for mergers and concentrations above a certain size, or which would result in control of a dominant share of the market. But in any event the question of monopoly legislation is one which both Britain and the Six have to solve, and they can probably solve it more easily together than separately. As in energy and transport policy, the issues are essentially the same here as there; there is no basic conflict of national interest.

A related subject on which British industry has some anxieties is dumping from outside the Community. Here again, the question is one of application rather than of the nature of the legislation, which is on paper powerful enough. With increasing competition throughout the world, dumping could become an increasingly important problem during the sixties. It remains to be seen whether the machinery of the Common Market will be able to cope effectively.

COMMON MARKET AND THE COMMON MAN

We have now covered most of the immediate problems of British membership of the Common Market, and we can form a rough judgment on how it is likely to affect the man in the street, and indeed the British people as a whole. The initial impact will almost certainly be a lot less dramatic than many people expect. The fundamental institutions and way of life of the British will be little changed—at least in the short run. The housewife will have a greater range of products to choose from, but as we have seen the Common Market has made comparatively little difference to the consumer in the Six, and there is no reason to think things will be different here. Perhaps the most immediate effect will be a British decision to adopt the metric system for our currency, weights and measures, and temperatures. Certainly it is to be hoped that we will do these things; and even, perhaps, change to driving on the right! It is things like these which will, more than anything else, symbolise to the ordinary person the change in Britain's economic and political alignments.

In our schools, there should be a greater emphasis on the teaching of languages, and more instruction in Continental history and customs. Culturally, it is to be hoped that there will be greater inter-penetration between Britain and Europe. But none of these changes is a necessary consequence of signing the Treaty of Rome. In our daily life we can go on being just as insular as we choose!

Harmonisation of legislation is likely, over the long run, to involve some changes in our legal system. But none of these is likely to be fundamental. Our lawyers will have to learn to argue cases before the Court of Justice according to Continental law. But this again is hardly likely to prove a fundamental obstacle. Those who believe, as I do, that the English Common Law is the best legal system in the world, cannot but be convinced that it will in time influence the institutions and practices of the Six. (In any event, it is an illusion to think that our daily lives are dominated by the Common Law in Britain today. Our daily lives are regulated, here as on the Continent, primarily by Statute Law.) The same applies to the arrival of British officials among the 'Eurocrats' of Brussels and Luxembourg, and to the getting-to-gether of British businessmen, politicians and trade unionists with their opposite numbers among the Six. It is not true, as many people think, that the Six have acquired already a monolithic solidarity and unity, which renders them impervious to British influence, so that in our dealings with them we will always be one against six. If that were so, our prospects would be gloomy indeed; but it is not. It is precisely because the Six are not united, because they feel the need for the extra weight and stability which they think Britain can provide, that they are anxious to have us in. And so in all walks of life where British and Continentals meet, there is likely to be increasingly a two-way flow of influence and mutual adaptation. Perhaps *we* will learn to cook better, and *they* to play cricket! By joining the Common Market we are not selling our birthright, but entering into a marriage contract, in which each partner gives something to, and gets something from, the other.[1]

But for there to be influence, there must first be understanding. And there is no denying that historically and culturally the people of the Six share a heritage which is in many ways different from our own. In particular, the British must learn to live with the Continental passion for written constitutions. This may seem a trivial point, but it has been a source of continual misunderstanding for many years. The British businessman, with his motto 'My word is my bond', is sometimes shocked to find that his Continental counterpart may treat a verbal agreement more casually. Similarly, British politicians and civil servants tend to regard constitutional statements as arid formalism, and to look to common-sense for the answer to problems.

The visitor to Brussels soon finds that the approach there is rather different. The first reaction of a 'Eurocrat' on being presented with a problem is to reach for his copy of the Rome Treaty, and study the relevant passages with immense care to see what consequences for policy-making can be extracted from them. No doubt this is partly due

[1] Throughout this chapter I have been arguing on the assumption that Britain joins the Six in isolation. In fact, as I made clear at the beginning, this is a some-what unreal assumption. She will be joined almost certainly by Denmark and Norway, possibly also by Sweden and Switzerland (with Eire, Portugal and probably Austria and Finland in some sort of association). The Scandinavians, the Swiss and the Irish share many of the characteristics of the British, and will there-fore powerfully reinforce what might be called the 'Anglo-Saxon' as opposed to the 'Continental' element in an enlarged European Community. Much of what is said here about the British contribution to Europe applies equally to these countries.

to the fact that the Commission is the appointed guardian of the Treaty. The Treaty is, as it were, the Commission's weapon in its ceaseless struggle for power with recalcitrant member-governments. But, more than that, the Treaty is the symbol of the new Europe, an expression of the Continental love of written constitutions; it is akin to holy writ, and like holy writ admits of the most varied and elaborate exegesis.

At times, as in the lengthy dispute over whether a pipeline is a method of transport or an industrial process, this type of approach seems almost Scholastic in its pedantry. And yet on the answer depends whether the French, or the Italians, can run a pipeline into the heart of the Ruhr, and so threaten the German coal-mines with semi-bankruptcy! In fact, as the British visitor soon discovers, the Treaty is interpreted in a way which reflects the balance of political power and economic interest, the general good of the community, and so on—'common-sense' in fact. It is merely the process of arriving at the answer which sometimes seems doctrinaire. One suspects that it will not be long before the British officials who take posts in Brussels adopt the mental processes of their Continental colleagues on the Treaty and its applications. But the one thing which the British must *not* do is to regard the Treaty as a bit of 'flannel' and therefore irrelevant.

In many ways the Treaty is in fact a remarkably flexible instrument. Ideologically, it can admit of a very wide range of interpretations. It is quite untrue, for example, as many people in the British Labour Party seem to believe, that it is antagonistic to public ownership or national planning. It could indeed hardly be so, since all the Six practice public ownership in one form or another. Italy, whose public sector represents as big a share of the national economy as ours, is about to embark on a major programme of further nationalisation. France and the Netherlands both have national planning schemes, and France has done far more than Britain ever has to use her nationalised industries as a weapon in economic planning. Such planning has been found to be a very effective complement to the greater competition brought in by the Common Market. It is true that certain forms of economic controls practised by Britain in the past would be hard to reconcile with the Rome Treaty; and there are prohibitions, as we have seen, against State monopolies being so operated as to discriminate against competitors from other Common Market countries. But the field of manoeuvre left open to a Socialist government is in practice very wide.

One result of British membership will undoubtedly be closer liaison between British businessmen and trade unionists and their Continental colleagues. We saw in Part II that the establishment of the Common Market led to a great increase in co-operation and contacts between the industrialists of the different countries—some beneficial to the Community, some less so. There is no doubt that British membership will have the same effect—indeed, in many industries the process has already started.

The same thing is happening on the trade union side, and here the consequences could be even more significant. For, despite its internal weaknesses, the British trade union movement is still by far the strongest, and in many ways still the most respected, in Europe. The trade unions of the Six have tended in some ways to be by-passed in the development of the Common Market. It is true that they have been consulted at all stages, but sometimes the consultation has been fairly perfunctory, and their views have not always received very serious consideration. One result of British membership should be to strengthen the cohesion and influence of the trade unions in the Six, and to increase the effectiveness of the Economic and Social and Consultative Committees.

Another result will almost certainly be a gradual movement to co-ordinate trade union bargaining policies and objectives in the different countries. So far as Britain is concerned, we may well see an acceleration in the introduction of 'fringe' benefits, as part of a process of harmonising wages and social benefits throughout the Common Market. As we have seen, labour costs are now probably roughly equal in Britain, Germany, France and Benelux, and catching up fast in Italy. But the division between money wages and social benefits differs very markedly in the different countries. In 1959—and the situation has not changed significantly in this respect since then—social charges accounted for 43 per cent of the Italian wage-bill, compared to only 12 per cent of the British. The French figure came to 34 per cent, the German to 31 per cent, the Benelux countries' to 23-24 per cent.

The reason for this discrepancy is that social benefits on the Continent are predominantly paid by industry, rather than by the Government. These benefits include such things as social insurance, holiday pay, family allowances, recreation and health schemes, meals—and sometimes housing subsidies. Some of these benefits are fixed by law, others by collective agreement, while some are provided voluntarily by the employer. British workers have in many cases fallen behind their Continental colleagues in the range of fringe benefits they enjoy, and it seems reasonable to expect that there will be a process of 'levelling-up' in the various Common Market countries over the next few years. I feel personally that such a process would be entirely desirable; I believe that British unions' concentration on money wage claims and neglect of fringe benefits has been a serious mistake, and I think there is a great deal to be said for transferring part of the cost of financing the Welfare State from the Budget to industry—though the State must continue to provide a national minimum, as it does now.

There are certain other weaknesses in the Common Market as it is now constituted, which one hopes British membership may help to remedy. Some people in Britain have criticised the Treaty of Rome on the grounds that it does not provide as explicit a commitment to full employment as the 1944 White Paper to which both the main British political parties are committed. In fact this hardly seems an important line of criticism, as things stand now. None of the Six can fairly be accused of pursuing a low-employment policy, and it is probably not being unduly cynical to argue that the main guarantee of full employment in Britain is not the 1944 White Paper but the knowledge that no government which allowed unemployment to grow on a large scale could expect to be returned to office. And the same political pressures to full employment exist on the Continent as they do here. In any case the terms of the Treaty, though they may not contain an overt commitment to full employment, quite plainly imply it.

However, it would do no harm, and it might help to add social content to the Community, if the member-States were to accept a specific pledge to maintain full employment, suitably defined (for example, to take account of the special problem of Southern Italy). This could be particularly important if, as is possible, the pace of expansion slackens in the later sixties, and the pace of technological change —'automation and all that'—quickens. In that case Europe might find itself with the same sort of structural problem of technological unemployment as the U.S. In particular, the problem of regional pockets of unemployment in peripheral areas—the Ulsters and Sicilies of the Community—could become more serious. There is a case now for stepping up the pace of regional planning to cope with this sort of eventuality, and since some of the potentially vulnerable peripheral areas are in the U.K., this is an issue of particular significance for us.

As it happens, the European Parliament carried a resolution in February 1962 calling for 'the preparation of a co-ordinated and prompt reaction to special economic situations' and 'the development of a long-term economic policy guaranteeing a steady economic growth of the Community'. The new Italian Government, predominantly Catholic but with Socialist support, is making one of its first objectives the acceleration of economic development in the backward South, using for this purpose the weapons of State planning and public enterprise. This is the sort of initiative which Britain's representatives in the Community should seek to support and encourage.

However, the most important contribution Britain can make to Europe is to strengthen and broaden the forces of democracy within the Community, and give it greater stability. As everybody knows, democracy is still a tender plant on the Continent of Europe. Britain, with her traditions of personal freedom, of Habeas Corpus and respect for the individual and the rule of law—Britain above all can give European democracy the roots and the strength it needs. With this we come to the heart of the problem of Europe. But to discuss it involves a look into the future of the Community, an investigation of the outlines of the emerging, but still wraith-like, United States of Europe. That is the subject of the next chapter.

2

Towards a United States of Europe

CLOSER UNION: FINANCE

THE FURTHER integration of Europe has three main aspects: finance, defence, and politics. In the financial field it is becoming increasingly clear, as was shown in Part II, that the policies and problems of individual countries cannot fail to impinge on others, and so on the stability of the EEC as a whole—and pressures to harmonise policy within the Community are therefore growing, and are likely to grow still further as time goes on. Britain, the country with the most complex international financial relationships—and at present Europe's shakiest major economy—is peculiarly involved in these pressures.

First, there are increasing pressures to harmonise fiscal policy, to prevent distortions of trade. These pressures on the Continent happen to coincide with a growing feeling in this country—in my view entirely justified—that our whole system of taxation needs to be overhauled, and readjusted on something like Continental lines: not simply to bring us into line with the Six, but because their fiscal policy is on the whole more appropriate to our present needs than ours is.

I have already said that I approve of the European fashion of using industry to finance extensions of the Welfare State, and I hope the trend catches on here. A second major characteristic of the tax structures of all the Six is their reliance, in some form or other, on a general turnover tax; this is in contrast to the British system of purchase tax, which because it falls on a much more limited range of goods is inevitably more discriminatory, and has to be levied at much higher rates. By specifically exempting exports from the general turnover tax, the Continental countries are able to give their export industries a useful incentive without falling foul of any of the international prohibitions against export subsidies. I think it is not entirely coincidental that the export trade of the Six has been noticeably more buoyant than our own in recent years.

There are other aspects of the tax structure of the Six which I think Britain could usefully copy—for example, the separate company tax (all capital gains by companies are treated as taxable income), and the faster rate of depreciation allowed for tax purposes, which encourages capital investment. Again, the Six operate a system of inheritance taxes in place of our estate duty; the liability to this tax varies according to the degree of relationship to the deceased.

It seems highly desirable that Britain should try to bring her tax structure more closely into line with the Six forthwith, concentrating particularly on the replacement of purchase tax by an 'added-value' turnover tax from which exports are excluded. That having been done, it seems only common sense to press ahead as fast as possible with a general harmonisation of tax structures within the European Community.

Fiscal policy is one of the four main ways in which a country regulates its economy. The second—controls—we have already briefly glanced at; we have seen that while there is no ban on controls in the EEC as such, controls which would distort competition within the Common Market—for example, if a member-country imposed import or exchange controls unilaterally—would certainly be frowned on.

The third main weapon in a State's economic armoury is monetary policy, or manipulation of the rate of interest. Here again, there are increasing pressures within the EEC for a harmonised interest rate policy throughout the area. We have been finding in Britain that changes in monetary policy can have highly embarrassing international implications. If one country tries to cover an adverse balance of payments by raising its interest rate higher than its neighbours, it at once attracts an inflow of speculative short-term capital or 'hot money'. This 'hot money' adds no real strength to the country's economy, because as soon as the interest rate premium goes it will go too. But it upsets the payments position of those countries from which it has flown, who are naturally annoyed. Because of the internationally unsettling nature of 'hot money' flows, it looks as if monetary policy changes as a major weapon of economic adjustment may be on their way out, and that the nations of the world may seek from now on to harmonise their interest rates more closely than in the past. Certainly this looks like being the case in Europe.

This leaves us with only one major weapon of economic adjustment —namely, fluctuations in the exchange rate: devaluation or revaluation. Once again, this is a weapon with grave international implications, in that it upsets the whole delicate equilibrium of international currency relationships, and weakens confidence in the international payments mechanism. It is a far more drastic step, obviously, than short-term changes in interest rates. On the other hand, if a country's currency is plainly over-valued or under-valued, there is obviously no point in maintaining permanently a 'phoney' rate of exchange just to avoid unpleasantness.

These, then, are the four main economic weapons at the disposal of national governments. Use of any one of them may cause difficulties to other States. Let us now take the argument a little nearer home, and consider the likely position of Britain on joining the Common Market.

Until a short while ago it was generally thought on the Continent that sterling was over-valued, and that the shock of entering the Common Market might force a devaluation of the pound. Now this looks less likely, but economic difficulties for sterling at some stage in the next few years clearly cannot be ruled out. The strength of sterling is therefore one of the factors that the negotiators at Brussels must take into account when considering the conditions of British entry. Europe, in other words, must assume some degree of responsibility for sterling, because of the effects which a change in the value of the pound would have on the rest of Europe. In the same way, in weighing up the pros and cons of devaluation, the British authorities have to take into account the effect of any action on the Six, if only because their reaction may affect our future position within the European Community. The problem of sterling is therefore not only a national one; it is an international problem, and particularly a European one.

It follows that there must be close and intimate contact between the British Government and the EEC Monetary Committee. Britain must consult the Committee before taking any action which would adversely affect her partners, and must take their advice if she possibly can when framing her economic policies. On the other hand, she cannot renounce the right to take action in a crisis. If the Six want to minimise the risk of embarrassing unilateral action by Britain[1]—of which sterling devaluation is only one, though the most dramatic, possibility—then they must plainly be prepared, if necessary, to put up an alternative. And the obvious method is a stand-by credit or similar accommodation.

Of course, there is nothing very new in this. The interdependence of currencies is not a new phenomenon; the closer integration of economies through the EEC merely dramatises and accentuates it, and —more important—provides a means of doing something constructive

[1] They cannot hope to avoid it altogether—see below, p. 222.

about it. The 'Basle agreement' of 1961, under which the European central bankers agreed unofficially to support each other's currencies, was an excellent example of *ad hoc* co-operation to ensure international stability. On more than one occasion since the war, Britain—among other countries—has had recourse to loan or standby facilities from the International Monetary Fund. The summer of 1961 was the most recent example. And to those who protest that in entering the Common Market Britain is putting her economic policy at the mercy of a clique of deflation-minded capitalist bankers, it is fair to point out that that is exactly the situation that obtains now—and will go on doing so until the British economy becomes strong. Creditors will always call the tune. When the 'little Budget' was introduced on July 25, 1961, the voice was the voice of Selwyn Lloyd but the hand looked remarkably like that of Dr. Per Jacobsson.

Ultimate control over national financial policies must, it would seem, increasingly pass out of national hands into those of international committees. The power of the EEC Monetary Committee seems bound to grow—and should grow; and, because of the growing interdependence of the North Atlantic currencies and economies, the role of the OECD also seems bound to become more important. This does not mean that a country cannot follow its own bent in such things as planning for growth, social welfare, distribution of industry, and a thousand other things. It merely means that it cannot do these things at the expense of its neighbours, and that it must pay its way. If it earns a surplus, what it does with that surplus is—within the broad limits of the Rome Treaty, and provided it contributes its fair share to the common task of international aid and investment—its own affair.

I do not mean to suggest that fiscal, monetary and exchange rate policy at national level should all be frozen into immobility from henceforth, just because any changes are likely to upset one's partners. Obviously if a country has a persistent deficit, it is in everybody's interest that something should be done to cure it. Harmonisation of the basic tax structure throughout the Community obviously does not mean that in all countries the same tax should be applied at the same rate. That would be unnecessarily rigid. It means only that the different countries should use the same broad fiscal weapons, and raise taxes from the same broad sources. Again, if one country's exchange rate is out of line, it is obviously better that the adjustment should be carried out as a single isolated operation, instead of setting off—as these things tend to today—a chain reaction which defeats the object of the exercise.

And this can best be achieved inside the Common Market by prior (though necessarily secret) consultation with the Monetary Committee.

Has the time now come to consider a new 'great leap forward', by institutionalising this trend towards interdependence and supra-national control of national financial policies in Europe? Does not the logic of events point towards a common reserve bank for the whole EEC, on the lines of the Federal Reserve Bank system in the U.S.? This, as we have seen, was proposed in 1961 by Jean Monnet's Action Committee, and in April 1962 the Economic and Financial Committee of the European Parliament passed a draft resolution to the same effect. What is proposed is that the central banks of the member-countries should hand over a fixed proportion of their reserves to a central reserve fund. This proportion should be steadily increased, until eventually all the reserves of the Common Market countries are held by a central bank under supra-national control. The individual countries would of course have accounts with the central bank, their initial drawing rights corresponding to what they had paid in. But of course, if the central bank agreed, there would be nothing to stop one country running a temporary overdraft at another's expense. The system would work in fact like the sterling area system, except that there would be a greater degree of central control to keep it solvent. Also—unlike the sterling area—the central banker would not start off his life with more liabilities than assets!

Plainly, the progressive unification of Common Market reserves would of itself impose greater integration of national financial policies. Eventually, the separate national currencies would be merged in a single European currency, and the central monetary authority would levy its own taxation. This is looking rather far ahead, but the creation of a common reserve fund is a necessary first step. It would institution-alise the process of economic co-operation which, as we have seen, is increasingly taking the place of 'beggar-my-neighbour' autarky on the European financial scene.

There is however one awkward feature. Central bankers the world over tend to be cautious and rather rigidly orthodox in their financial views. And the Europeans, despite the expansionist philosophies of their countries in recent years, are certainly no exception. Despite the spread of economic enlightenment in recent years, their attitude to a country in balance-of-payments difficulties might still tend to be an unnecessarily deflationist one. It would be a bad thing for the European

Community if bankers acquired too great a control over its destinie
—and it would perhaps be particularly disastrous for Britain, whose
great need is for more expansion but whose payments position may be
weak, for a variety of reasons, for some time to come.

There are, I think, two answers to this. First, as Professor Meade has
suggested in his Hobart Paper, *U.K., Commonwealth and Common
Market*, Britain should refuse to accept any commitment not to devalue
during the interim phase of adjustment to the conditions of Common
Market membership—though she should, as I have suggested above
consult very closely with the Monetary Committee before taking any
action; and one would hope that enough assistance would be available
from the Six to make it unnecessary. But the right must be reserved
until a stage is reached at which Europe can begin thinking in terms of
a common currency (which would of course make exchange rate
adjustments in individual countries impossible).

Second, an explicit EEC commitment to a policy of full employment
—discussed in the previous chapter—might help to offset any defla-
tionary bias which the creation of a common reserve fund might have.
That is why the time may now be appropriate for the Community to
take such a pledge—apart from the political and psychological advantages it would have in reconciling British Labour to Common Market
membership.

How would Britain be affected by these developments? Clearly, the
position of sterling would be transformed. In the first place, as a member of the Common Market Britain will be expected to offer citizens
of the Six the same freedom of capital movement as members of the
overseas sterling area now have. We will be expected to dismantle our
remaining restrictions on the movement of foreign funds into and out
of British securities. If we abolish these restrictions for Europeans, can
we go on applying them discriminatorily to Americans and other
foreigners? It seems unlikely. And this means a further extension of
sterling convertibility, with consequently greater vulnerability in times
of economic crisis.

This would put another nail in the coffin of independent sterling
viability. We saw in Part I how Britain's heavy weight of indebtedness
has hampered her effectiveness as a world banker, by making her
terribly vulnerable to speculation when foreigners lose confidence in
her currency. Her industrial weakness in relation to her commitments
has meant that confidence is always in fact somewhat precarious. In
order to maintain confidence Britain has had to adopt a slower rate of

growth, putting a stable pound before a faster rate of expansion. This in turn has kept our economy weaker than it would otherwise have been. Britain, in other words, has been caught in a vicious circle, from which she has never been able really to break free.

This weakness has affected the rest of the sterling area too. The other sterling countries hold their central reserves in a system which has a bad exchange risk, and which because of its weakness is unable to provide adequate lending facilities. Britain is in the position of a banker who cannot afford to give an overdraft, and who can afford comparatively little in the way of long-term loans. This is merely another way of saying that we lack the strength to carry out the international financial responsibilities we have assumed, with the result that the sterling area is a basically unstable financial and economic bloc.

The creation of a common European reserve fund offers Britain a unique way out of this dilemma, and one which would help the other sterling area countries too. One obvious approach would be for the reserve fund to start off by acquiring the sterling reserves of the member-countries, together with a proportion of their gold and dollar reserves. Britain would not only contribute a proportion of her gold and dollar reserves, but would also hand over to the central reserve her sterling balances—that is, the reserves of the sterling area countries. In other words, Britain's liabilities to her sterling area partners would be taken over by the new European central bank. Britain, in place of these liabilities, would acquire a long-term debt to the central reserve.[1]

Of course, such a solution could not be imposed on our sterling area partners against their will. They would have to be given the choice of adopting this procedure or making alternative arrangements. But the sterling area system as such would be wound up as a separate entity, being merged in a new European currency area. The new bloc should have much more cohesion than the old, for the central banker would have many more resources and a greater base of industrial strength at his disposal. The new system should prove an excellent mechanism for channelling European investment and aid to needy Commonwealth

[1] This scheme, as Robert Neild points out in an interesting article in *Time and Tide* (February 1st, 1962), really represents an application of the Triffin Plan on a regional scale. Neild suggests that in exchange for their surrendered reserves, the national banks should be given deposits in a new unit to be called a 'Europa'. The central fund should have the power to create more reserves as and when necessary. It should in fact act like an embryo international central bank.

countries, and there would be a very much smaller risk of exchange depreciation than there is for sterling holders today. The liabilities of sterling would become a European responsibility, rather than just a British one. Britain would acquire a greater freedom of economic manoeuvre, and the world as a whole a greater degree of international monetary stability.

Between them, the pound and the dollar have up to now shared the responsibility of financing world trade. The dollar has had strong enough shoulders to bear this burden—just. The pound has not. It has continually staggered beneath it. The two industrial and economic poles of the free world are the U.S. and a United Europe—poles of roughly equal strength. It is fitting that the monetary organisation of the western world should be readjusted to reflect its basic economic and industrial structure. Britain's entry into the Common Market offers a unique opportunity to do this.

Although it has been plain for some time that the sterling area system has become a source of weakness rather than of strength to Britain,[1] such a radical change will not be universally welcomed here. Like the Commonwealth, the sterling area has become an international status symbol for Britain. Moreover, it has provided the City of London with a good deal of useful income. The City has always been orientated towards the Commonwealth and sterling area, rather than towards Europe. This will need to change rapidly once Britain is in the Common Market, if London is to become—as it should—the Community's financial centre. Fortunately most of the necessary changes are now beginning to be made. British merchant banks are forging links with Continental syndicates. As *The Times* put it ('London's Role in Europe', July 27th, 1961)— 'London has the skill, the experience and an array of financial institutions unrivalled anywhere in the world. But there is a shortage of capital and trade finance continues to be exceptionally dear. Continental centres, on the other hand, while lacking the institutional framework, can supply cheaper trade credit and, increasingly, a growing volume of capital. The question is whether the two can be merged in a way that is profitable to both'. If this can be done, the City of London should gain business from the merger of the sterling area system with the Common Market, rather than lose it.

To sum up, the prospect of a common financial reserve for the

[1] See for example Andrew Shonfield's *British Economic Policy Since the War* (Penguin, 1958).

European Community, leading eventually to a common European currency and an integrated financial policy, offers a unique opportunity to Britain and to her sterling area partners to put their financial structure on a more solid basis. In March 1961 the Six held $16,000 million of reserves against short-term liabilities of $2,000 million—a net reserve of $14,000 million. Britain's reserves stood at $3,000 million, against which she had short-term liabilities (representing, *inter alia*, the reserves of the rest of the sterling area) of $10,900 million—a net reserve of *minus* $7,900 million. These figures speak for themselves. The liquidation of the sterling area system in its present form represents one of the biggest potential benefits Britain could gain from Common Market membership, and one for which it is worth making sacrifices. In the financial sphere, therefore, Britain's interest emphatically lies in pressing forward to the United States of Europe as fast as possible.

CLOSER UNION: DEFENCE

The question of Europe's defence has been inextricably intertwined with the question of European integration ever since 1945. Europe's vulnerability to Soviet power was one of the motivating forces behind the original urge for unity, and one of the reasons why it has consistently attracted such support from the U.S. The failure of the EDC, however, has left the Six without any common organisation for defence other than NATO, where they are in a minority and where the U.S. is emphatically the senior partner. French jealousy of American domination has caused a great deal of friction in NATO, and the lack of any supra-national powers to force member-countries to co-ordinate their policies, or even to honour their commitments, has weakened its effectiveness. Has the time come to try to revive the idea of a European Defence Community?

Britain, as we have seen, has for most of the postwar period sought to avoid supra-national integration of her armed forces. She refused to join the EDC, made the minimum commitments needed for the WEU, and at great expense made herself into the world's third independent nuclear power. Since 1959, however, it has become increasingly apparent that the costs of Great Power military status are beyond us. The decision to abandon the Blue Streak rocket programme in 1960 left us with no effective independent means of delivering our H-bombs, other than the V-bombers. We thus became dependent on U.S. goodwill for rocket delivery of our own 'independent' deterrent. Similarly, cutbacks have had to be made in other sectors of Britain's defence programme—notably in aircraft manufacture—because of the prohibitive cost of modern weapons.

Recognition of these facts played a big part in turning Britain's attention to the possibility of closer integration with the Six in 1960 and 1961. Together with the collapse of the Paris Summit meeting in 1960, they revealed more clearly than ever before the limits of British power and influence in the modern world. Second, they set British minds working on the possibility of spreading the costs of defence by more co-operation and integration with Europe. The costs of effective defence, it had been found, were beyond the capacity of any single nation outside the U.S. and Russia. 'Interdependence' and 'integration' thus became the key words in military planning.

Unfortunately, at the time when Britain was turning hopefully to the Continent with ideas of 'Europeanising' the defence programme, France had already set out on the same nationalistic path which Britain had been treading since 1945. At enormous cost, France is duplicating the efforts of the U.S. and Britain in seeking to become the world's fourth independent nuclear power. This effort adds nothing to the strength of the West. Apart from its wastefulness, it increases the risks of world war—the more nations develop their own H-bombs, the harder it is to achieve effective agreement on the control of nuclear weapons—and the hazards to health through radiation. The French atomic bomb is an unmitigated disaster, for which no good thing can be said. But in developing her own H-bomb, France is simply following the example set by Britain; and others will follow after if she succeeds. Already Western Germany is beginning to agitate for her own nuclear weapons.

The best way of stopping this dance of death is for Britain to take the lead in offering to 'Europeanise' her own nuclear capacity. Such an offer should form part and parcel of a detailed programme of military integration among the European countries, designed to re-create the abortive European army. In the field of military equipment, as in the field of trade, far more specialisation and standardisation is needed to secure economies of production and efficiency of operation. Obviously Europe cannot support three or four major aircraft industries; one is enough. And the same goes for other items of defence equipment, if Europe is to free herself from her present dependence on America. This requires a central supra-national procurement organisation working to a centrally-agreed plan.

Supra-national control is also required to ensure that the burden of common defence is equitably shared among the member-nations, both in terms of their financial contribution and their conditions of military service.

NATO is not an effective instrument for this purpose. It lacks both the political unity which would induce members to make the sacrifices of sovereignty required, and the powers of discipline to enforce them. Congress would certainly not be prepared to concede to a NATO political organisation power over the deployment of American forces or over the U.S. nuclear armoury. And NATO is rent by the internal feuding of the French, who are not prepared to integrate their forces more than is absolutely necessary into a supra-national organisation dominated by Anglo-Saxons. For these reasons, proposals to turn NATO as such into a nuclear power seem quite unrealistic.

At present the Six are in a minority in NATO. But if Britain were to throw in her lot decisively with Europe, the picture would change dramatically. It would then become possible to build up a new European Defence Organisation, with its own Anglo-French nuclear capacity, no longer overwhelmingly dependent on the U.S. That should appeal to General de Gaulle, whatever his emotional antipathy towards international armies. It should be possible, therefore, to re-constitute NATO eventually on a healthier basis as a joint alliance between two equals—America and Europe—in place of the present unsatisfactory relationship of rather mutinous dependence. (This leaves out of account the position of Canada as an independent NATO member, but in view of her close relations with both Britain and the U.S. this is not likely to give rise to any special difficulties.)

Such an arrangement would give Europe an insurance policy against the danger that at some future time, in an age of inter-continental ballistic missiles, the U.S. might conceivably pull out of Europe and retreat into a 'Fortress America'. It would enable Europe to re-arm efficiently and economically. It would help to stop the dangerous spread of independent national nuclear forces. And it would end the present tensions which limit the effectiveness of NATO.

This does not mean that a European Defence Organisation could afford to dispense with the American alliance, or that it should try to duplicate U.S. military resources. Europe will never, by reason of geography, be as viable an atomic-age unit as either Russia or America. Her vulnerability to nuclear war will always, one imagines, be greater. In any event, for Europe to try to build up a fully integrated defence force with nuclear capability in complete independence of the U.S.

would be grotesquely wasteful. Europe and America must continue to co-ordinate their military effort as closely as possible. One reason for advocating a European Defence Organisation is that this might make such co-ordination more politically acceptable to at least some of the Europeans than it is today. One would like to see Europe in fact dispensing with nuclear armaments of her own altogether; but this, unfortunately, does not seem to be a practical possibility as yet.

A European Defence Organisation can hardly be created overnight. Indeed, closer union on defence really implies and requires closer political union as a prior condition. (This was one of the mistakes made by the original advocates of EDC, to put defence before political unity rather than the other way round.) For many of the potential members of the new EDC would have important military commitments outside Europe. This applies obviously both to Britain and to France, and—though probably not for much longer—to the Netherlands in Irian. Worst of all, what about Portugal? If the nations of Western Europe are to pool their armed forces and defence organisations, there must plainly be some central political direction which can determine in what conditions the forces of Europe can be used. Otherwise we might find ourselves committed, say, to defending Portuguese interests in Angola, or—even worse—conceivably being asked to support a Portuguese attempt to re-take Goa. The needs of defence, like the needs of finance and economics, bring us back inexorably to the central question of European integration—namely, the nature and extent of her future political unity.

CLOSER UNITY: POLITICS

As we saw in Part II, the political future of the European Community is now in dispute between the 'Europeans' and the French partisans of *L'Europe des patries*.[1] Outside France, the Benelux countries are heavily committed to a 'European' solution, while Italy too leans in this direction. Western Germany also tends to favour this form of solution, but Dr. Adenauer is—as always—ready to go further than most of his fellow-countrymen to appease France. Given the importance of the issue, and the strength of views on both sides—and given also the veto powers enjoyed by individual countries—it seems likely that the issue will still be in dispute by the time Britain signs the Rome Treaty. It is therefore important for the British to decide what their attitude should be.

[1] On this subject, see Dr. Roy Pryce's *The Political Future of the European Community* (Marshbank, 1962).

There is no doubt that the predilection of Mr. Macmillan and his colleagues is towards the Gaullist *L'Europe des patries*—ironically, since on the whole it is the 'Europeans' who are most anxious to get us into the Community, and the Gaullists who hitherto have been readiest to keep us out. But to British minds there is something cosy and familiar about de Gaulle's ideas for Europe. It is all comfortingly reminiscent of the Commonwealth—a friendly club whose members are well-disposed towards one another, even go out of their way to help each other, and always take care to consult other members before taking any drastic action; but where, in the last resort, each member is free to go his own way, and where no awkward sacrifices of sovereignty have to be made or contemplated. It is the sort of organisation in which a British statesman naturally feels at home.

But the Commonwealth analogy in fact applies only very imperfectly to Europe. In the Commonwealth there is a common language, a common institutional legacy and common political traditions. There is also a natural focus and leader—Britain, the 'mother country'. The Commonwealth is an international extension of the British personality, its unity based on past history. None of this applies to Europe. There is no single language, no common body of institutions and traditions, no natural leader. Most important of all, the unity of Europe is based not on the past—the past is something from which Europe is trying to escape—but on the future; and the future still has to be won. Therefore the political institutions of Europe have to be much stronger than those of the Commonwealth. They have to be strong enough to bind together nations whose whole history pulls them apart. Can *L'Europe des patries* do this?

In this book we have surveyed the immense labour which has been involved in the 'making of Europe', and the enormously powerful sectional and national interests which have had, and still have, to be overcome for the good of the whole. We have seen how powerful the individual countries still are, with what circumspection the Commission has had to go about its work. We have seen how much remains to be done, and what sort of opposition is likely to be encountered. In the last few pages we have been discussing how much Europe as a whole will benefit from an even closer degree of unity, going beyond the Rome Treaty. But there is no use in blinking the fact that the greater the inroads made on national sovereignty, the stronger will be the opposition. If we accept that the path of unity is the right one—and this is the assumption on which the whole experiment of integration has been based—then we have to ensure that the political institutions of Europe are strong enough to carry her along that road, as far and as fast as she can go. Her institutions must be radical and not conservative; they must serve as an accelerator and not a brake. And we have to ask ourselves whether the institutions envisaged by the French Government are likely even to begin to perform these tasks.

Again, we have to remember that the integration of Europe is not taking place in a vacuum. The unity of the Six is in many ways still precarious. Can anybody be confident that the German people have forever renounced the dangerous dreams on which Hitler fed? Can this restless, passionate, divided people in the heartlands of Europe be relied on to stay faithful to the West, or will the urge to unite and to dominate revive? Are neutralism and imperialism dead in Germany—or only dormant? And what about France? The future of French politics remains as enigmatic as the character of the great intransigent who now directs them. In France, in Italy, indeed in all the countries of the Community, a stable social structure is being transformed by a process of headlong economic growth; the wind of change in fact is blowing throughout the Continent. Everywhere a new middle class is being thrown up, with new tastes, new dreams, new desires. The political systems have yet to adapt themselves to this transformation of society. '*L'Europe de papa*' is dead, and those who do not understand this will die with her!

This political turmoil and uncertainty is frequently cited by politicians in Britain—particularly in the Labour Party—as a reason for staying out of Continental entanglements. It is, on the contrary, one of the main reasons why we must go in. Two world wars have shown that Britain cannot escape the consequences of unrest in Europe. It would be fatal to try once again, as we did after 1918, to isolate ourselves from the Continent and pretend that its troubles need not concern us. The best contribution we can make to our children's safety is to go into Europe, and try to take the lead in steering the new, dynamic forces there in the direction of unity and democracy. And for this purpose we need to ally ourselves with the 'Europeans', and not with the partisans of *L'Europe des patries*. We have to set our sights firmly on the ultimate objective of a true United States of Europe, with federal institutions—its own army, its own executive and parliament, its own judiciary, constitution, currency and fiscal policy. This does not mean that the independent national States with their institutions will disappear. It means that they will voluntarily subordinate their interests to, and combine in operating, a higher central (federal or confederal, the word is unimportant) authority. This is the target towards which we should deliberately aim. For the process of integration cannot, as Europe is already discovering, be a halfway house. It must be a continuous process, and it must therefore have central institutions which are sufficiently powerful to maintain the momentum against the forces of sectional interest and inertia.

The first priority, if this is to be achieved, is to democratise the European institutions, by building up the European parliament. Ultimately, the United States of Europe cannot be built by autonomous technocrats, however able and dedicated. Still less can it be made by a committee of foreign ministers whose first care is to protect national interests. An effective, representative European parliament could provide the motive-force of unification, and an outlet for the 'European' enthusiasms of so many of the younger generation in Europe—and, even more important, ensure that the process of unification takes place in a democratic fashion and subject to democratic control. This is something that the British, with their unique parliamentary traditions, are peculiarly fitted to contribute to the 'making of Europe'[1]. For there is little point in creating a United States of Europe which is not at the same time a democracy. And there is no reason why the future political complexion of Europe should not be a good deal more progressive than it is today. The Europe of Adenauer and de Gaulle will not last. One result of the movement for unification and the economic revolution in Europe may well be the establishment of a new, moderate Left, playing the same sort of role as the Labour Party in Britain or the Scandinavian Socialists, and driving the Continental Communist Parties into the limbo where they belong. One would like to see the British Labour Party take the lead in building up this new Left in Europe, harnessing the scattered progressive forces and challenging the present dominance of the Right.

British influence should, therefore, be directed towards making Europe safer for democracy—and at the same time hastening her along the road to unity. So far from being incompatible, these two objectives are, as we have seen, closely interlocked. Britain could, in short, become the 'Anchor-man' of Europe, countering the fissiparous tendencies of France or Germany, welding the nations closer together in an everstronger democratic unity. But Britain should have a third objective in the European Community—to keep its eyes fixed on the broad

[1] The Scandinavians and the Swiss would also help here.

231

horizons of the outside world, away from exclusive introspective concern with its own problems and achievements. Just as Britain can no longer isolate herself from Europe, so Europe can no longer isolate herself from the world. The responsibilities of a united Europe will not stop at the Elbe or the Pyrenees. They will extend across the oceans to the remotest corners of the globe. That is a lesson which the British at least should be able to understand.

3

Europe and the Outside World

RULES OF ADMISSION

THE EUROPEAN Community has already demonstrated its powers of attraction. Applicants for membership or association are queueing up outside its gates. What rules are members of the club to apply when deciding whom to admit? If the conditions of membership are made too loose, the club will lose its cohesion—and with it much of its value. But if on the other hand the Community becomes an exclusive club for a handful of rich nations in Western Europe, from which no one else is allowed to benefit, it will have betrayed its mission.

In dealing with applications from European states, it is reasonable to ask prospective members to accept the full political implications of the Community. This implies loyalty to democratic systems of government, and a willingness to accept supra-national control in the fields of financial and economic policy, defence and political institutions. Nations that will not accept these conditions cannot complain if they are excluded from the economic benefits of the Common Market. Two classes of states would seem to qualify for association rather than full membership—those who cannot accept the political conditions for reasons beyond their control (Finland, Austria), and those whose economies are not strong enough to meet the full competition of the Common Market (Greece, Eire, possibly Israel). In this second class, associate status will presumably be temporary; in the course of time, it is to be hoped that the economies of the associates will be strong enough to stand the pressures of full membership. Sweden and Switzerland, as we saw at the beginning of Part III, present a more difficult case. The best solution would be to allow them some form of probationary association for a fixed period, while they made up their minds on whether or not they were prepared to play their full part in a future political United States of Europe.

Turkey and Portugal would seem to be border-line cases; Portugal's case politically seems much weaker than Turkey's, though her membership of 'Efta' gives her a certain moral claim on Britain which her own merits hardly justify. Spain's application would seem to be ruled out on political grounds unless and until she changes her régime—though it can again be argued that if Spain were given some form of temporary associate status it might facilitate a change of régime as well as greater prosperity, while exclusion might simply serve to perpetuate autocracy along with poverty.

There is of course nothing to stop a European Community negotiating trade agreements with individual countries outside its orbit. There is a good case, for example, for negotiating such treaties with the Communist countries of Eastern Europe—in particular with Jugoslavia, to whom reasonably favourable terms should be offered. It would be a sad day for the West if European integration threw Jugoslavia back into economic dependence on the Soviet bloc.

But the Community should also seek good relations with the countries of the bloc. It must not be allowed to degenerate into an anti-Communist *entente*. It must strive, rather, to break down the economic and political barriers of the Iron Curtain, and to revive the frozen arteries of trade and commerce in the centre of Europe. In particular, no opportunity should be lost of trying to secure by peaceful means the reunification of Germany. I must confess that I do not rate the chances of reunification at all highly for the foreseeable future. Western Germany would be foolish in the extreme to sacrifice the substance of integration with Western Europe for the shadow of reunification with the East in a neutralised German State. Indeed, if Germany is ever to be reunited it must be inside the framework of a Western European Community. At the same time, the statesmen of Europe must never lose sight of the need for a solution of the German problem and an easing in the intolerable tensions to which it gives rise. And it is in the field of trade agreements that a first, modest start can perhaps best be made.

AN ATLANTIC COMMUNITY?

Perhaps the most dramatic tribute to the growing power of the European Community on the world scene is the changing attitude towards it in Washington. The Eisenhower administration viewed the Community with a somewhat remote benevolence. Its emergence was treated almost entirely as a political phenomenon, to be welcomed as a contribution to the strength and cohesion of the free world, without serious economic implications for America. The Kennedy administration has had to adopt a rather more sophisticated approach. The State Department's support for the idea of a United States of Europe is as strong as ever. Indeed, Washington looks to Europe to help shoulder more of the U.S. burden of defence spending and of aid and investment in under-developed countries. At the same time, President Kennedy's distrust of German and French views on foreign policy have made him much more anxious than his predecessor to see Britain inside the Community.

But the biggest change is America's realisation that her export trade is vulnerable to the Community's tariffs. Ideas for an Atlantic Community, or an Atlantic free trade area, are circulating in a way which reminds the British observer of the state of mind in Whitehall in 1956 when it was realised that the Six really were going to have a Common Market. One wonders cynically whether the Americans are going to play their hand any better than we did!

The chances are of course that they will. Clearly America's bargaining power *vis-à-vis* Europe is much greater than Britain's ever was, provided that Congress gives the White House enough room in which to manoeuvre. Continental statesmen realise well enough that the stability of the West demands the friendship and co-operation of its two great constituents—America and Europe. The idea that Europe can be built up into a 'Third Force', holding the balance of power between Russia and America, poised neutrally between the two, is an illusion which today commands little support. Whatever else she may be, Europe is and must remain irrevocably of the West.

Certainly, Britain as a member of the European Community can be expected to do everything possible to promote the realisation of an Atlantic Community—to bring the U.S. into closer and closer conjunction with Europe. From inside the Community, Britain can and should continue to exercise her old role of America's closest ally and friend—more effectively, in fact, than she could outside it, where her value to America is much smaller.

The form which an Atlantic Community might take is far from clear. Politically, it is plain, the U.S. is not prepared to merge her sovereignty with Europe for as far ahead as one can see; nor is there any necessary reason why she should. The Community should rather be based on the foundations of an industrial free trade area, a military alliance to replace NATO, and close economic co-operation both to preserve international stability and to promote the wealth and welfare of the under-developed countries. It would in fact be a Partnership rather than a Community.

An Atlantic free trade area would account for 90 per cent of the industrial production and 90 per cent of the trade in industrial goods in the non-Communist world. It would therefore be an extremely powerful instrument for expanding world trade. The U.S. President has already asked Congress for authority to negotiate with an enlarged EEC for the complete abolition of tariffs on all products of which the U.S. and Europe are the main suppliers, and where they account between them for 80 per cent or more of world trade in the goods concerned. This is a dramatic proposal. Not only would it in fact take the U.S. and Europe—assuming Europe agreed—a very long way along the road to a free trade area; it would also help other industrial countries like Japan. For the proposal is that both the U.S. and Europe should abolish these tariffs irrespective of the country of supply. Japanese motor cars, for example, would have free entry into the markets of Europe and America equally with U.S. and European cars.

What the President is proposing, in fact, is a programme of mutual tariff cutting by the highly industralised countries of the West, with the results of the tariff cuts generalised to the other countries of the world whether they reciprocate the cuts or not.

The American proposals do not stop there. President Kennedy wants authority from Congress to negotiate a halving of tariffs in conjunction with the Europeans for all other goods, again on a non-discriminatory basis. He wants the U.S. and the EEC to agree to the total elimination of tariffs on all tropical products which do not compete with home-produced goods. And there are plans in the air for a series of international price agreements covering the main 'temperate foodstuffs'—starting with wheat. Such schemes would have to include the main producing countries—Canada, Australia, Argentina—as well as the U.S. Finally, despite its obvious limitations, the U.S. initiative on cotton textiles—the Kennedy conference to induce the industrial countries of the West to open their markets on a mutually equitable basis to the low-cost exports of Asia—looks like setting a precedent for other Asian manufactures. It is to be hoped that future agreements of this sort will go beyond the rather limited provisions of the cotton pact, but at least it represents a beginning.

The exact form of the 'package deal' which the U.S. will at some stage propose to an enlarged EEC is not yet clear. But the general drift of what President Kennedy wants to do is obvious enough. It is also obvious that Congressional opposition to U.S. tariff cuts will be very strong—*vide* the 1962 increase in U.S. tariffs on glass and carpets. It is essential that Europe should do all it can to help President Kennedy to win his battle with the protectionists in Congress, for on his success may depend the future of the West.

It would be easy for Europe to stay sitting tight behind the wall of the common external tariff, the tariff which has been the symbol of her unity so far. But to do this would be to condemn the Common Market for the introverted, selfish 'rich man's club' which its enemies accuse it of being. The common external tariff should not be made into a shibboleth. It has served its purpose in helping to create a united Europe. But by the time that the negotiations between Europe and the U.S. come to fruition, the European nations should have taken further strides towards unity, and built up closer and more positive links than the common tariff. It should no longer then be true, as it may have been during the free trade area negotiations, that the common external tariff is the one thing holding the Europeans together.

It is essential, therefore, that Europe should be prepared to negotiate on tariffs, and to reduce them where possible, even if this means that some European farmers and some European industrialists will go out of business. It is essential that the European Community should adopt a liberal, outward-looking stance to the world, rather than the inward-looking and protectionist attitude it has sometimes seemed to in the past. British membership should greatly help here, and not only because Britain has on the whole been good at recognising her obligations to the less developed and poorer peoples of the world. The very fact that in negotiating Britain's entry the Six have had to concern themselves intimately with solutions to the problems of the Commonwealth has forced them to look outwards. And, as we have seen, in almost every case the solutions to these problems have been seen, ultimately, to involve agreements on a world scale rather than a regional one.

In fact the record of the Six in recent years has been more generous and outward-looking than their critics give them credit for. The Six today provide one-third of the free world's aid to under-developed countries, while Britain provides only one-ninth. But some of them have a distinctly less attractive record when it comes to trade. At GATT the Common Market has too often presented the appearance of a protectionist group of rich countries which is too ready to keep out the products of poorer countries that do not happen to be in its sphere of influence. This impression persists in many parts of the non-European world, in spite of the increasing flow of aid and investment and in spite of the 20 per cent cut in the common external tariff. As a result, there is a good deal of suspicion in many of the under-developed countries—

particularly in Africa and Latin America—of the EEC and of British association with it. The support given to President Nkrumah's castigation of associated overseas territory status as a form of neo-colonialist exploitation of Africans illustrates the force of these suspicions.

It would be disastrous if the European Community came to be seen as an instrument of racialism, when in fact it offers one of the world's best hopes for ending the appalling division between rich and poor which disfigures the international landscape of our age. The EEC must not only be liberal, it must be seen to be so. And it is not hard to see how this can be done.

First, action is needed on the lines of President Kennedy's mutual tariff-cutting proposal—free trade in all industrial goods where the U.S. and Europe account between them for four-fifths of trade and production, and a halving of tariffs on all other industrial goods. These tariff cuts should apply to imports into the U.S. and Europe from all sources.

Second, further measures are needed for those industries dominated by Asian producers, where imports into the U.S. and Europe are currently limited by quotas. What is needed here is an international agreement for the progressive lifting of these quotas by the U.S. and the EEC—and preferably by other nations as well—on a parity basis, so that each country liberalises its trade in step with the others.

Third, the special trade privileges attaching to the African and other associated overseas territories in the European market should be progressively generalised, so that eventually there should be world-wide free trade in tropical agricultural products. Once again, liberalisation in Europe should proceed in parallel with liberalisation in the U.S., and if possible elsewhere.

Fourth, international commodity agreements should be negotiated for the main temperate zone foodstuffs of the world—wheat, meat and dairy products. These agreements should progressively take over from the special interim measures which Britain and the Six are, as I write, discussing in Brussels to ease the problems of British accession to the Common Market for Canada, Australia and New Zealand. The U.S. and Europe should take the lead in working out such agreements, and both should be prepared to accept a lower degree of protection for their own farmers as part and parcel of the agreements.

Obviously all this will not be achieved overnight. The technical as well as the political problems involved are formidable. But there is everything to be said for drawing up an international plan of campaign now, for it is on its relations with the outside world—and particularly with the under-developed countries—that the European Community will from now on increasingly be judged. It must show that when it talks about tackling world poverty and extending to other peoples the benefits the Europeans have won for themselves through integration, it is not just mouthing platitudes. And time is not necessarily on its side.

NEW PATTERNS OF AID

In the field of trade, therefore, there should be a progressive withering-away of the special preferences now enjoyed by those overseas countries hitherto associated with Britain or France or other European countries. There should be no more favouritism among the under-developed countries.

Does this mean that the special relations built up in Eurafrica, in the Commonwealth and the sterling area will simply disappear? If they did, this would be a tragedy, not only for the countries concerned but for the world as a whole. The multi-racial links provided by the Commonwealth and by Eurafrica are of immense benefit in a world where race is becoming the great international irritant.

But in fact, outside the field of trade, these links should not be affected. The loose alliance and system of friendly consultation which holds the Commonwealth together need not be adversely affected by British membership of the EEC. In fact Britain can play a useful role as the advocate and spokesman for Commonwealth interests in Europe. In the same way, France's relationship with the former French Union —which is increasingly developing along Commonwealth lines—is manifestly not suffering from her membership of the Common Market. In fact, here again France has been able to further the economic interests of her African partners very considerably through influence with the Six. Peace in Algeria, it is to be hoped, will round off the structure by enabling Morocco, Tunisia and Libya to join in close association with the EEC. The closer Britain and France come together in the European Community, the closer too should come their respective former colonies and dependencies.

But one should beware of trying to fit the emerging African countries into political straitjackets of European fashioning. The African countries will find their own natural political groupings. Europe can only offer them her friendship and help, and economic assistance. She cannot dictate their allegiances, nor should she try to do so.

But, in the field of economics, what is to take the place of the trade preferences which Europe's associates will be losing if and when the proposals outlined in the previous section take effect? The answer is in fact fairly obvious. If Europe can no longer have favourites in the field of trade, there is no reason why she cannot go on doing so in the field of aid and investment. And indeed it is natural that she should. It is right and reasonable that in the campaign to help the under-developed countries and raise world living standards the U.S. and Europe should each concentrate on the parts of the world where they have traditional interests and responsibilities, the U.S. concentrating primarily on Latin America (through the Alliance for Progress) and the countries bordering on the Pacific—and the Europeans concentrating on Africa, the Middle East and the overseas Commonwealth countries. These divisions would not of course be rigid and exclusive, but they would indicate different national priorities in a common enterprise.

The three things which the under-developed countries want from Europe and America are, essentially, markets, capital and 'know-how'. The progressive liberalisation of world trade discussed in the previous section should help to provide these countries as a whole with better markets for their produce than they enjoy today. At the same time, the European nations should step up their export of capital and 'know-how' to the countries in their sphere of influence, starting with the associated overseas territories of the Common Market and the overseas Commonwealth countries. It is worth remembering that if the Bank of England's responsibilities for the sterling area are transferred to a new European reserve bank, this bank will be ultimately responsible for the economic viability of the individual members of the sterling area, and they will enjoy the same rights of free access to the capital market in Europe as a whole as they now do in Britain. It follows, therefore, that there will be automatically an intimate connection between the economic policies and progress of the different sterling area countries and the central directorate of the European Community, just as there is now between the sterling countries and Britain. Inevitably there will be conferences between leading statesmen and bankers, attempts to co-ordinate economic policy, and so on. To this extent the sterling area countries, so far from being thrown out into the cold by Britain's marriage with the Six, are liable to be drawn increasingly into Europe's orbit so far as economic policy-making is concerned. And this close connection, paralleled as it is in the French Union, will facilitate the flow of aid and investment from Europe to the countries that need it.

The chances are in fact that the climate for overseas investment will become more propitious in the sixties than it was in the fifties, if only because the competing attractions of investment in Europe itself may become less overwhelming as the European boom levels off. There is a good deal of evidence to suggest that the pace of growth in Europe will be somewhat slower in the next few years than it has been in the last few—though by comparison with much of the rest of the world Europe will continue to present a picture of dynamic expansion. If the pace of growth slackens, the rate of return on investment will fall, and profit margins will narrow. This is indeed already happening to some extent, and the process looks like going further in the next few years. In this case investment outside Europe, in the under-developed countries, will begin to look much more attractive.

Similarly, if it becomes harder to sell goods in Europe there will be a greater interest in expanding the market overseas. It will therefore be in Europe's immediate interest to increase the flow of aid to the under-developed countries so that they can buy more European goods. Altruism and self-interest will tend to move closer together.

Institutionally, the establishment of a central European bank or reserve fund can help considerably to channel and co-ordinate the flow of investment capital to the needy countries. The fund could be given powers to lend to the under-developed countries, either directly or through the medium of the World Bank—or perhaps through the European Investment Bank in Brussels. There is a lot to be said for co-ordinating the various institutions for European overseas investment— the Development Fund for Eurafrica, the European Investment Bank, the activities of the individual governments (including the various British organisations, such as the Colonial Development Corporation and so on)—under a single central organisation.[1] This could well become one of the main functions of the European reserve fund or bank when it is in operation.

* * *

The challenges facing Europe in the years ahead, both internally and externally, are formidable in the extreme. Nobody can be confident that she will meet them successfully, though on the record so far it is reasonable to be optimistic. In joining Europe, Britain will not be

---

[1] At present the Investment Bank is limited in its activities to Europe, but there are suggestions that the Development Fund for Eurafrica should become part of the Bank's responsibilities. This seems a sensible measure of integration.

taking the easy way out, or jumping on a band wagon to effortless prosperity. Still less will she be opting out of the conflicts of the world, by losing her identity in a European collective.

On the contrary, she will be acquiring both the opportunity and the obligation to play a bigger and more constructive role than her diminished power has allowed her to play as a separate nation since 1945. At the beginning of this book we saw how Britain's reach since the war has consistently exceeded her grasp. We have seen also how, for all its promising beginning, the 'making of Europe' is still a long way from completion. Hazards and obstacles block the way ahead. If Britain stands aside, and the European experiment comes to grief, the world will be a poorer and a more dangerous place. If Europe goes forward to union, and Britain stands aloof, the quality of public life in Europe will amost certainly be the poorer for Britain's absence, and Europe's role in the world less valuable. But for Britain herself, shunted on to the sidelines of world politics, the consequences could ultimately be disastrous. Those who want Britain to play her part in the building of a United States of Europe do so, not because it is a soft option for Britain, but because they believe that Britain has a unique and vital role to play on the world stage, and that it is in and with Europe that this role can and must be played today. As a member we can influence the course of the European Community decisively; and I am patriot enough to believe that this influence will be immeasurably for good. On the other side I see only the twilight of a faded empire, an empire on which the sun is indeed setting, a people shuffling into the shadows to grow old and die—alone. History is not kind to those who make wrong choices.

A Glossary of Initials

AOT	Associated Overseas Territory (of the Common Market)
ECSC	European Coal-Steel Community
EDC	European Defence Community
EEC	European Economic Community (Common Market)
EFTA (Efta)	European Free Trade Association (Outer Seven)
EPC	European Political Community
GATT	General Agreement on Trade and Tariffs
IMF	International Monetary Fund
NATO	North Atlantic Treaty Organisation
OECD	Organisation for Economic Co-operation and Development
OEEC	Organisation for European Economic Co-operation
WEU	Western European Union

A Short Bibliography

A GOOD deal has been written on the Common Market in Britain recently. Among other organisations, PEP (Political and Economic Planning), the Fabian Society, The Economist Intelligence Unit, *The Times* and *The Daily Telegraph* have published useful books or pamphlets on various aspects of the subject. So has H.M. Treasury, with its pamphlet *Britain and the European Communities*.

Books on the general question of the Common Market and British association with it include:—

The Challenge of the Common Market, by U. W. Kitzinger (Blackwell)

Britain and the Common Market, by John Pinder (Cresset Press)

The Common Market, by J. F. Deniau (Barrie and Rockliff with Pall Mall Press)

Europe Will Not Wait, by Anthony Nutting (Hollis & Carter)

The Political Future of the European Community, by Roy Pryce (Marshbank, for Federal Trust).

INDEX

45 81TF   BR **4815** GBC
03/94 24-950-00